Global Witness Through Weakness

Global Witness Through Weakness

Insights into Missionary Life and Ministry from Paul's Second Epistle to the Corinthians

JOSEPH M. LEAR SR.

WIPF & STOCK · Eugene, Oregon

GLOBAL WITNESS THROUGH WEAKNESS
Insights into Missionary Life and Ministry from Paul's Second Epistle to the Corinthians

Copyright © 2025 Joseph M. Lear Sr. All rights reserved. Except for brief quotations in critical publications or reviews, no part of this book may be reproduced in any manner without prior written permission from the publisher. Write: Permissions, Wipf and Stock Publishers, 199 W. 8th Ave., Suite 3, Eugene, OR 97401.

Wipf & Stock
An Imprint of Wipf and Stock Publishers
199 W. 8th Ave., Suite 3
Eugene, OR 97401

www.wipfandstock.com

PAPERBACK ISBN: 979-8-3852-4566-6
HARDCOVER ISBN: 979-8-3852-4567-3
EBOOK ISBN: 979-8-3852-4568-0

04/16/25

Scriptures taken from the Holy Bible, New International Version®, NIV®. Copyright © 1973, 1978, 1984, 2011 by Biblica, Inc.™ Used by permission of Zondervan.

Scripture taken from the New King James Version®. Copyright © 1982 by Thomas Nelson. Used by permission. All rights reserved.

Scripture quotations taken from the (NASB®) New American Standard Bible®, Copyright © 1960, 1971, 1977, 1995, 2020 by The Lockman Foundation. Used by permission. All rights reserved. lockman.org

Scripture quotations marked NLT are taken from the Holy Bible, New Living Translation, copyright © 1996, 2004, 2015 by Tyndale House Foundation. Used by permission of Tyndale House Publishers, Inc., Carol Stream, Illinois 60188. All rights reserved.

The ESV® Bible (The Holy Bible, English Standard Version®). ESV® Text Edition: 2016. Copyright © 2001 by Crossway, a publishing ministry of Good News Publishers. The ESV® text has been reproduced in cooperation with and by permission of Good News Publishers. Unauthorized reproduction of this publication is prohibited. All rights reserved.

The New Testament in Modern English by J.B Phillips copyright © 1960, 1972 J. B. Phillips. Administered by The Archbishops' Council of the Church of England. Used by Permission.

I dedicate this book to my wife Alice who has faithfully served at my side for forty-three years as both a home and foreign missionary. Her courage, commitment, and willingness to participate in the sufferings of Christ has made our labor together a fruitful endeavor for the glory of Christ.

Contents

Introduction | ix

1	Suffering Invokes Comfort	1
2	Integrity	19
3	Emotional Engagement	43
4	Identification with Christ	64
5	Incarnating Christ	83
6	Glorious Gospel	103
7	Reconciliation	127
8	Commitment to the Cause	144
9	Spiritual Warfare	162
10	Perseverance	185

Appendix A: Missionary Vow of Simplicity | 209

Bibliography | 213

Introduction

This is a study that explores life and ministry of the apostle Paul as delineated in the second Epistle of Paul to the Corinthians, where Paul is presented as *the mastery missionary*.¹ The book's author presents 2 Corinthians as an insightful and essential treatise of what it means to live a life in conformity to the gospel as a messenger sent by God in obeying Christ's command to make disciples of every nation (Matt 28:18–20).

In defining 2 Corinthians's purpose and value to the church Martin writes, "In this apostolic *vade mecum*, a directory of apostle's trials and triumphs, we see the kind of service that God's chosen messengers are called to, what they may expect to experience, and above all, how they may gain comfort from seeing how Paul acted and reacted in regard to his destiny."² As a description of the apostle's own missionary ministry, 2 Corinthians can be of great value when exploited as a missionary guide for the church in the selection, preparation, and sending of missionaries to the four corners of the earth. This is Paul's apostolic *vade mecum* and can be applied today by missionary training institutes and missionary sending agencies as their *vade mecum* on how to properly release those called of God to bring the gospel of life to the ends of the earth.

THE "WEAK" APOSTLE

We shall see that for Paul missionary life is a life of service that is demonstrated in "weakness"—a person whose total identity is that of being "in Christ," one who daily participates in the death and sufferings of the cross. David Allen Black explains the importance of Paul's use of "weakness" as

---

1. Keener, *IVP Bible Background*, 505.
2. Martin, *2 Corinthians*, 188.

found in the Greek word "*astheneia* and its cognates."³ He writes, "Paul has made the word-group the vehicle of a profoundly important element in his teaching and parenesis. Indeed, one may even speak of Paul as the 'Apostle of Weakness' . . . we may with some justification regard him as the creator of the 'doctrine' of weakness."⁴

Paul's apostolic life and ministry is a paradox of a person who found that divine strength only comes through weakness (2 Cor 12:10). Martin concludes: "Christ's messengers are consigned to a life of humiliation and risk."⁵

For Paul it is this paradoxical ministry that releases God's resurrection power into the world for the salvation of mankind. "Paul's ministry is a paradox, but it is the kind of ministry God accepts."⁶ We will demonstrate that as the missionary daily takes up the cross of Christ (Matt 16:24) that resurrection grace is released—opening of blind eyes (2 Cor 3:14)—freeing from the god of this world (2 Cor 4:4)—entering souls into new creation (2 Cor 5:17).

THE SUPER-APOSTLES

In 2 Corinthians are recorded Paul's struggles with the false teachers (super-apostles, 2 Cor 11:5; 12:11) that have infiltrated the church and have gained a foothold. Using persuasive words of deception they have gained control of the minds of a segment of the church and have turned them against the apostle. They have brought into question Paul's apostolic authority and ministry, boasting of their superiority as being true apostles.

Black writes,

> That they were Jewish Christians is clear from 2 Cor 11:22–23. . . . It is evident they were intruders from without. They arrived preaching a different gospel . . . (11:4) and attacking the person

---

3. Black writes, "In these two letters alone the words appear twenty-nine times, or 66 percent of the total, in Paul, while the largest single convergence of weakness language in the NT is in 2 Corinthians 10–13, where the words occur a total of fourteen times. Along with Romans (8 occurrences), these documents embody the most fertile soil of knowledge concerning the apostle's unique understanding of weakness and its implications for Christian living" (*Paul,* 53).

4. Black, *Paul,* xv.

5. Martin, *2 Corinthians,* 94.

6. Martin, *2 Corinthians,* 187.

of Paul directly (10:1, 10; 11:6), as well as his teaching (10:12–18; 11:7–12; 2:17), and honesty (1:15–18; 10:9–11; 12:16–19). Priding themselves in their Jewish distinctiveness . . . (11:22), spiritual ecstasies (5:13; 12:1, 7), and special relationship to Christ (5:16; 10:7; 11:23), they claim the apostolic authority they deny to Paul, who only at a distance is bold (10:1, 10) and whose behavior and message are weak and offensive (5:11–13; 6:3–10; 10:2). In bold opposition to Paul's gospel, they exalt their own philosophy of knowledge against the knowledge of God (10:5). Glorifying in fleshly wisdom . . . (1:12), boasting in their assumed superiority to Moses (3:4–11) and in worldly things . . . (11:18), and encouraging indiscriminate behavior (6:14—7:1), they have nearly succeeded in bringing the community to open revolt against Paul.[7]

PAUL'S BOASTING

With the purpose of maintaining his converts in the truth of the gospel Paul defends his apostolic calling and ministry. Martin explains, "In regard to this letter we suggest that it came out of a distressful period in the writer's life when he knew himself to be bereft of human support and saw the prospect of his life's mission evaporating before his eyes as his congregations at Ephesus and Corinth were in danger of sliding away from him as their apostolic 'father in God.'"[8]

The super-apostles use personal boasting—a culturally "acceptable" means of introducing and promoting oneself—to further their own cause. Paul therefore finds it necessary to boast, which he knows is not the manner of Christ (2 Cor 11:17), to resist and correct the deception of his opponents.

Paul chooses his own pattern of boasting. While the false teachers boast of their eloquence and accomplishments, Paul chooses to boast of his weaknesses. "In 2 Corinthians weakness is not only a sign of Paul's humanity but of his apostleship."[9]

It is in Paul's paradoxical boasting that Paul's theology of suffering is laid bare. Throughout the letter Paul refers to his trials and hardships as proof that he is indeed a true apostle who brought the true gospel of reconciliation to Corinth. His converts' own lives are a living testimony

7. Black, *Paul*, 54–55.
8. Martin, *2 Corinthians*, 94.
9. Black, *Paul*, 110.

to his apostleship and to the power of the message he proclaimed unto them (2 Cor 3:2).

PAUL'S CONFIDENCE

Martin lists four pillars on which Paul builds his apostolic ministry that gives him confidence before God and man. These four confidences are applicable to present-day missionaries as they proclaim the eternal gospel to the world.

First, Martin tells us that Paul is confident in his own sincerity which is open for all to see (2 Cor 4:2). There must be a sincerity in ministry that is plainly seen by the missionaries' manner of living—their truthfulness, purity, and lack of greed. Missionaries must demonstrate a deep conviction and commitment to the truth of the gospel that is preached not for personal benefit but purely for the benefit of the those still in darkness. Missionaries must work with singleness of purpose to please God in everything, living in such a way that their behavior will never be an obstacle to others' acceptance of the gospel.

Secondly, Martin tells us the gospel message of Paul was reinforced by the character of Paul and his co-laborers. Missionaries must be people of the highest character, demonstrating a godly life that clearly reinforces the gospel message. They must demonstrate that the gospel frees from sin's slavery and transforms by living free from sin's bondage (Rom 6:18), being daily renewed (2 Cor 3:18). If ambassadors of Christ proclaim a holy God who calls sinners unto repentance, then they must be holy as he is holy (1 Pet 1:16). They must learn to live in the sanctifying grace of God, allowing that transforming grace to daily flow into their lives so that it can in turn flow out to others (2 Cor 9:8).

Thirdly, Martin emphasizes that Paul was constantly aware of the spiritual battle that he daily faced. It was Satan who was blinding the minds of those who do not believe (2 Cor 4:4). Missionaries who are sent today to the many dark places of the earth must be prepared for the spiritual struggle they will face. Many places are entrenched in spiritual darkness—places where evil forces have ruled for centuries. Satan will not give up territory easily. His sent servants must be deeply committed to prayer and thereby daily put on the whole armor of God (Eph 6:11). They must be filled with the Spirit, walking daily under his guidance (Eph 5:18).

INTRODUCTION

To be prepared for the battle missionaries must saturate their minds and souls with God's powerful word (Heb 4:12). They must be wise to their enemy's schemes and daily resist him in faith (2 Cor 2:11). They must not let his attacks become distractions that keep them from proclaiming the word of life. In the powerful name of Jesus, they must refuse his lies, putting him under their feet (Rom 16:20).

Finally, Martin tells us that when Paul had success in ministry, he gave all the glory to the God of infinite grace. Paul had no personal ambitions and did not seek to be important in the eyes of men. Like Paul, God's sent servants must not preach themselves but preach Jesus Christ as Lord and themselves as his obedient servants (2 Cor 4:5). They must live for the glory of God (Col 3:17).[10]

PAUL'S EXAMPLE

Paul calls the gospel message a treasure (2 Cor 4:5–7) whose eternal "value is in no way diminished by the cheap and disposable pots that carry it. This is how Paul saw himself—having no inherent worth save as a messenger and transmitter."[11] He was a privileged messenger sent under the authority of God. "His favorite self-designation is 'servant' (v 5) or 'honored vessel,' useful for allowing the Lord of glory to shine forth through his feeble and often threatened life (v 7)."[12]

In 2 Corinthians, through Paul laying open his heart and life, there is placed before the reader a totally committed life to the cause of Christ. This is demonstrated by the things that he endured as one called to plant the church of Jesus Christ on earth. Presented are his endless labors, deep trials, many afflictions and persecutions—of one who finds his identity as a participant in the sufferings of the cross (2 Cor 4:7–12; 6:4–10; 11:23–29).

As the truth of 2 Corinthians is uncovered and contemplated, it will be shown that there are compelling applicable parallels between Paul's apostolic ministry and present-day missionary life and ministry. These truths can illuminate his servants' paths as they strive to be faithful to the call to make disciples of every nation.

---

10. Martin, *2 Corinthians*, 93–94.
11. Martin, *2 Corinthians*, 94.
12. Martin, *2 Corinthians*, 94.

THE CALL OF GOD

"Paul, an apostle of Christ Jesus by the will of God, and Timothy our brother" (2 Cor 1:1). The bedrock of Paul's apostolic ministry was the unwavering assurance of God's call upon his life.

A deep conviction of a calling is essential for a commitment to lifetime missionary service. There must be an inner conviction before God that leads to an unwavering determination to carry out the will of God.

"Paul, an apostle—sent not from men nor by a man, but by Jesus Christ and God the Father, who raised him from the dead" (Gal 1:1). Missionaries must have a deep inner conviction that has laid hold of their hearts that they can do nothing else but go where God is sending them. It is a calling that is demonstrated by an outward, visible testimony of a life dedicated to and engagement in the task of bringing the gospel to the ends of the earth. It is this commitment that will sustain the missionary during the intense riggers of missionary life and ministry.

"Therefore, since through God's mercy we have this ministry, we do not lose heart" (2 Cor 4:4). Missionaries must know that the ministry they have is a ministry given by God. In the deepest times of trial and discouragement, when the devil raises his ugly head, and things seem to be going backward rather than forward, it is the assurance of a heavenly calling that will keep his messengers and enable them to endure unto the end. It is the call of God that will sustain them, allowing them to see the light of God at the end of a dark tunnel. It is the call of God as the foundation of their lives that empowers them to go from one kingdom victory to another.

THE HARVEST BEFORE US

"For such a time as this" (see Esth 4:14). Since a great harvest still lies before the church, God is revitalizing and reorganizing his missionary sending churches, calling them back to their roots of world evangelism. They are again being gripped by the desperate need of the millions who are perishing. They are enabling men and women who are called and committed and fully prepared, to go in the power of the Spirit to the ends of the earth, making disciples of all nations, baptizing them in the name of the Father and of the Son and of the Holy Spirit, and establishing local vibrant churches in every community on the earth.

1

Suffering Invokes Comfort

> "Out of suffering have emerged the strongest souls; the most massive characters are seared with scars."
>
> KAHLIL GIBRAN

> "An experience of collective pain does not deliver us from grief or sadness; it is a ministry of presence. These moments remind us that we are not alone in our darkness and that our broken heart is connected to every heart that has known pain since the beginning of time."
>
> BRENÉ BROWN

> "How long, Lord? Will you forget me forever?
> How long will you hide your face from me?
> How long must I wrestle with my thoughts
> and day after day have sorrow in my heart?
> How long will my enemy triumph over me?"
>
> KING DAVID (PS 13:1,2)[1]

SUFFERING FOR THE GOSPEL

"Adoniram Judson (1788–1850) and his first wife were among the first commissioned foreign missionaries in American history."[2] Adoniram

---

1. All scriptural citations are taken from the NIV unless otherwise indicated.
2. Finn, "Missionaries You Should Know," para. 1.

and Ann arrived first in India where they met missionary William Carry but soon found India to be a close door for them and sailed to Burma, "which had been Adoniram's first choice of mission work—until he heard frightening reports of brutal treatment of foreigners."[3] "They painfully separated from Carey and other missionaries and sailed to Burma. There they would spend the rest of their lives under extreme hardship and privation in an effort to bring the gospel to the people of that closed and uninviting land."[4]

Things became very difficult for Adoniram and Ann when war broke out between Burma and England, "and all foreigners were suspected of being spies."[5] Adoniram and his coworker Dr. Jonathan Price were imprisoned, "confined in a death prison, where they awaited execution."[6]

> Life in prison was appalling. The missionaries were incarcerated with common criminals in a filthy, vermin-infested, dank prison house, with fetters binding their ankles. At night the Spotted Faced (prison guards whose face and chest were branded for being one-time criminals themselves) hoisted the ankle fetters to a pole suspended from the ceiling, until only their heads and shoulders rested on the ground. By morning the weary prisoners were numb and stiff, but the daytime offered them little relief. Each day executions were carried out and prisoners never knew who would be next.
>
> Adoniram's suffering was difficult for Ann. Daily she sought out officials, explaining that, as an American citizen, Adoniram had no connection with the British government. Sometimes her pleas and bribes allowed her a brief visit and gained Adoniram temporary relief; but all the while he continued to languish in prison.[7]

After nearly a year and a half Adoniram was finally released "with the stipulation that he would help interpret peace negotiations with the British.[8]

Adoniram reached the Burmese people with the gospel through the concept of *zayat*. Tucker writes,

3. Tucker, *From Jerusalem to Irian Jaya*, 132–33.
4. Tucker, *From Jerusalem to Irian Jaya*, 130.
5. Tucker, *From Jerusalem to Irian Jaya*, 135.
6. Tucker, *From Jerusalem to Irian Jaya*, 135
7. Tucker, *From Jerusalem to Irian Jaya*, 135–36
8. Tucker, *From Jerusalem to Irian Jaya*, 137.

A *zayat* was a shelter open to anyone who wanted to rest or discuss the day's events or listen to Buddhist lay teachers who often stopped by....

Almost immediately visitors who would never have come to the mission house began stopping by, and the Judsons entered a new phase of ministry. The following month Maug Nau made a profession at a Sunday service in the *zayat* packed with Burmese people. This was the beginning of the Burmese church in Rangoon, and by summer 1820 there were ten baptized members.[9]

Paul, in 2 Corinthians, limited his self-commendation to his life of suffering:

> Paul openly embraces a certain type of self-commendation: "In every way we commend ourselves as ministers of God" (6:4). The hardship list that follows shows that Paul's self-commendation is grounded in his difficulties and distress, an ironic testimony to the power of God working through and sustaining him in whatever circumstances he encounters. In 6:4–10 irony functions as did a fool's mantle and thus places Paul's self-commendation in perspective.[10]

Missionaries are often faced with the wearing of a fool's mantle. The missionary's life with its many sacrifices is seen as outside the realm of reason—people who have lost their minds. "Why would you ever take your family to such a place" is the response of the incredulous encountered in the churches where the missionary seeks financial and prayer support to go to their place of calling. Paul himself was accused of being out of his mind (2 Cor 5:13).

Martin explains that Paul's words "'in all our trials' (1:4) has the idea that this is the lot of the followers of Christ living in a fallen, rebellious world so often opposed (hostile) to the gospel."[11] Hardship was part and parcel of the calling of the messengers of God.

> We do not want you to be uninformed, brothers and sisters, about the troubles we experienced in the province of Asia. We were under great pressure, far beyond our ability to endure, so that we despaired of life itself. Indeed, we felt we had received the sentence of death. But this happened that we might not rely on ourselves but on God, who raises the dead. He has delivered

---

9. Tucker, *From Jerusalem to Irian Jaya*, 137.
10. Sampley, "Second Letter to the Corinthians," 31.
11. Martin, *2 Corinthians*, 9.

us from such a deadly peril, and he will deliver us again. On him we have set our hope that he will continue to deliver us, as you help us by your prayers. Then many will give thanks on our behalf for the gracious favor granted us in answer to the prayers of many. (2 Cor 1:8–11)

THE SUFFERINGS OF CHRIST

Paul writes of "Christ's sufferings" (1:5). These are the sufferings that Christ himself experienced for us that are extended to his followers as they share in his sufferings. His messengers share in "the afflictions of messiah [a Jewish doctrine] implying not the sufferings endured by the messiah but rather sufferings associated with him in the messianic age as a prelude to the coming of the age of bliss. . . . Paul has in view Christ's ongoing sufferings that are endured in the church under the trial and specifically the apostolic ministry in his (Paul's) own person."[12]

The sufferings of Christ's messengers are based upon the suffering that God himself suffered at the cross. "God suffers to redeem out of the changeless perfection of divine love."[13] Paul is emphasizing that what they are suffering is not in vain, rather it comes to Paul and to the Corinthians because of God's divine purpose.[14]

For missionaries on the missionary field of their calling, their sufferings show that they too are fulfilling divine purpose. This is the way of the cross. Jesus endured the ultimate suffering in bleeding and dying on the cross, taking on himself the sins of humanity. So, his servants also must be willing to suffer if they are to be faithful messengers of the gospel to the lost and dying.

Paul emphasizes throughout 2 Corinthians that life comes only through death. Only dead men (dead with the crucified Christ and dead to self) can bring life to the spiritually dead. It is the suffering of the cross and our participation in the same suffering that brings resurrection, delivering life to lost humanity.

---

12. Martin, *2 Corinthians*, 9–10.
13. Macchia, *Tongues of Fire*, 193.
14. Martin, *2 Corinthians*, 10.

THE CALL TO SUFFER

Many followers of Christ today, in many corners of this world, are suffering persecution—some severe persecution—losing their livelihood and some losing their lives. Human nature teaches us to avoid suffering. But the gospel calls the ambassadors of Christ to endure hardship as a soldier of Christ (2 Tim 2:3).

"For we who are alive are always being given over to death for Jesus' sake, so that his life may also be revealed in our mortal body" (2 Cor 4:11). Martin clarifies: "'Always' refers to Paul's life as a constant struggle: 'all our days' we as living persons are 'being delivered up to death.'"[15] Martin also explains that the "technical verb" translated "'to hand over' [is] used regularly of Jesus' destiny as a suffering figure who is fulfilling his life in God's plan as one required . . . to suffer."[16]

Martin continues,

> This is Paul's fate decreed by God. Popkes speaks of Paul's destiny to suffer as a "core" element in his thought. He did not choose to live a risky life, as if he were a foolhardy person . . . or one who emulated the stoic ideal of a person challenged to bravery by life's vicissitudes. . . . Rather, he suffered in line with his apostolic vocation, and that is proof that such a calling is God's purpose for his life and that he is a "true" apostle (12:12 RSV).[17]

Biblical suffering is not masochistic—rather it is a reality that must be accepted as his sent one's lot as they join in the Messiah's suffering and bring the gospel to a dark, demon-infested world. They don't desire persecution, but they know it will come.

Martin further comments on 2 Cor 4:11, "'For Jesus' sake,' lit., "because of Jesus' . . . on account of loyalty to the Gospel of his death and resurrection, gives the rationale for Paul's sufferings and exposure to death."[18] Missionaries must live with a loyalty to the Gospel, being willing to pay a price for that commitment.

"It is written: 'I believed; therefore I have spoken.' Since we have that same spirit of faith, we also believe and therefore speak" (2 Cor 4:13). "Paul's conscious desire to identify with the psalmist (Ps 116) for whom

---

15. Martin, *2 Corinthians*, 88.
16. Martin, *2 Corinthians*, 88.
17. Martin, *2 Corinthians*, 88.
18. Martin, *2 Corinthians*, 88.

the issue was one of life and death."[19] The psalmist spoke out of his suffering, so Paul boldly speaks out of the conviction of his sharing in like suffering. Suffering leads to a boldness in proclamation. God's messengers speak with conviction because they are "sold out" to the cause of Christ.

In 2 Cor 1:6–7 we see Paul setting an example of how to live for Christ in the midst of suffering. He is reminding his readers that suffering is a normal, inevitable, God-ordained part of following and serving the Savior. What has come upon Paul and is also coming upon them is to be expected. He is pointing them to the way of living an overcoming life during times of great trial and difficulties as one embodies the gospel. God does not give his messengers more than they can endure, but rather gives them interventions of his consolation at their most difficult moments, allowing them to grow in grace and in trust in a faithful God, and thereby making their lives fruitful.

THE SENTENCE OF DEATH

Second Corinthians 1:8–11 is an illustration of the suffering of Paul and his co-laborers—a time when they needed the comfort of his heavenly Father. He does not tell the details of the experience. He does emphasize that it was a life-threatening occurrence. Paul says that they were afflicted beyond measure, surpassing their strength, to the point that they despaired of life. He says it was like they had been given a sentence of death.

The pressure had become too much to bear. The threats on their life too real. Paul's own strength had been tapped; his vitality bled out. He relinquished his soul to God, feeling life's energy was being hopelessly drained out of his body.

Was this a particular trial, or was it an accumulation of overwhelming pressures? Whatever the circumstance, the hardship proved too much for him and his companions. The attacks were too frequent. The pressure of human resistance and demonic oppression was far too great for them to endure. They were facing assured death. All hope of escape seemed to have left them.

They now realize that the trial had fallen upon them so that they would not trust in themselves but in God who raises the dead. Paul saw God's providential purpose. This extreme hardship came upon them so

---

19. Martin, *2 Corinthians*, 89.

that they would be stripped of self-trust and put their full confidence in God who resurrects the dead.

Even if life was taken from them, they had the hope of everlasting life—God would raise them from the dead as he had raised his own son from the dead. Paul and his companions had learned that God delivers the helpless. They served a God who intervenes in time of severe crisis to rescue.

Keener commenting on 2 Cor 5:6–9 writes, "Jewish accounts of the righteous dead in heaven portrayed them as experiencing a measure of future glory now, while awaiting the resurrection. Although this state was inferior to the resurrection (5:4) it meant an end to the present toils—and Paul's continual experience of gradual martyrdom (4:8–10)."[20]

Missionary suffering is a "gradual martyrdom" as they daily take up their cross of death and follow after him. They die daily as they identify with the shame of the cross and join in the pain of the rejection of this world (see John 1:11).

Missionaries experience "gradual martyrdom" through the many sacrifices and trials that they daily face, often in harsh environments, among some who hate them because of the message they proclaim and the person they follow. They die daily as they live under the pressures (sometimes extreme pressures) of the struggles of the existence of life—of holding body and soul together as they testify of the gospel message through a Christlike humble life.

Paul accepted that his life could very well be cut short. Paul was afflicted to the point of despair, having lost hope of his own survival. Martin says he was "burdened" like an overburdened ship. It was extreme, beyond his own strength. It was an intense affliction that is still very vivid in Paul's mind: "we felt we had received the sentence of death" (2 Cor 1:9a).[21]

Paul's life was often in danger. In Acts 23 we read how his own people the Jews had plotted to kill him. They pledged not to eat or drink until he was dead (v. 12). But God delivered him, and he knows that presently God is still protecting him, and he also has the full assurance that he will deliver him in the future (2 Cor 1:10).

---

20. Keener, *IVP Bible Background*, 507.
21. Martin, *2 Corinthians*, 14.

HEROES OF THE FAITH

The heroes of the faith are the African pastors living out in remote villages, who sacrifice and suffer to bringing the gospel to those yet in spiritual darkness. They labor both in their fields (for food for their families) during the day and in their churches (small mud-walled buildings with tin roofs) at night far from modern medicine or conveniences. They are resisted by those who practice traditional, demonic, animistic religions—by religious practitioners (witch doctors and shamans) who do not want to lose their influence and income.

Some of these pastors suffer physical harm (beaten and abused) and some lose their lives. They willingly join into the sufferings of Christ so others might hear the message and be saved. Only eternity will reveal the full measure of the sacrifices paid by these forgotten soldiers of the cross who labor faithfully in some of the most remote and forgotten places on earth.

THE SUFFERING OF DEATH

"We always carry around in our body the death of Jesus, so that the life of Jesus may also be revealed in our body" (2 Cor 4:10). Martin points out that the Greek Word "nekrosis" (death, dying) "strictly refers to a process or state of dying rather than the act when death supervenes . . . as speaking of the extended process of his life regarded as a continual dying."[22]

Paul is saying that the only way for the life of Jesus to be manifested in his servants' lives is for them to participate in his death. They must die with Christ on the cross in order to experience the power of grace flowing through them to a lost and dying world.

The suffering and death of the Messiah brought life to a dead world. In like manner, his sent ones' participation in redemption's story requires daily death so that his life might be manifest through them. This is God's eternal plan. This is God's means of the liberating a lost world from sin and death.

Living missionaries can only bring themselves. Dying missionaries can bring the glorious gospel of life. His servants must give up the desire to live so that as dying men and women they can bring hope and see the spiritually dead raised to life.

---

22. Martin, *2 Corinthians*, 87

The pressures upon today's missionaries can be overwhelming. There are revolutions and unstable governments. Laws are made and not enforced—or randomly enforced. Water and electricity are cut off. Police are corrupt and demand bribes. Roads deteriorate and are never repaired. Thieves multiply and turn violent. Gas prices skyrocket and gas is rationed. Termites eat your clothes and medical help is limited. Missionaries must learn to doctor themselves and their families. Governments are deceitful and dysfunctional. There are revolutions, violence, and burning.

There is no answer to the many "why" questions concerning daily burdens endured. His sent servants must learn to accept and learn to live with things as they are—without specific answers to nagging questions. There is the constant pressure of the enemy that resists the spread of the gospel. Stones are thrown, threats are given. Bullets fly—corpses lie on the streets. Missionaries live in the midst of pervasive poverty and untreated brokenness and diseases—cripples and lepers. Stress weakens the body leading to unwanted, often repeated sicknesses.

Attacks come from what Paul the apostle calls false brethren (11:26 KJV)—those whose manner of life is contrary to the gospel. They are people who have "politically maneuvered" and found places of authority in the church—people who vex the soul of God's sent ones.

Missionaries are rejected and despised by those from whom they should be receiving support. Draught and famine strike the land, and his messengers suffer as those around them suffer. Missionaries do all they can to relieve pain, but it never seems enough.

Churches are attacked and burned, and pastors martyred. Condemning jealousy is felt from those who should be an encouragement. Those who work for you steal from you. A vehicle is fixed but immediately breaks. Many vehicles are being stolen and each missionary fear theirs could be next. Missionaries taste the suffering of death. God's comfort is so very real.

INCREASED DANGER

> I have been constantly on the move. I have been in danger from rivers, in danger from bandits, in danger from my fellow Jews, in danger from Gentiles; in danger in the city, in danger in the country, in danger at sea; and in danger from false believers. (2 Cor 11:26)

Missionaries are often on the move, bringing the gospel to those who have yet not heard. Danger increases with every movement. They must daily accept that they live in a fallen dangerous world. In following the Great Commission, they go to those who have not heard, and their movement often brings them into hostile environments, inviting physical danger—the loss of limb and life.

Missionaries take on the challenge of an increased reality of bodily harm so that others will hear the words of life and be saved. Food poisoning, tropical diseases, harsh climates, and hostile encounters become a common occurrence as they take up their cross and follow him.

Missionaries are faced with lies and deception—often from those who should be telling the truth. They help others in their time of need but when they are in need those they have helped are nowhere to be found.

No one seems to empathize with what God's sent ones are suffering. They are surrounded by troubled, broken people who need God's help but often refuse the help offered. Flights are canceled and baggage is lost. Sleep is depleted and burdens of the soul multiply out of concern for the perishing and the churches that are struggling.

All of this drives the missionaries to their knees seeking help from heaven for the earthly cares that have become too much to bear. Prayer—the missionary's own prayers and the prayers of the sending saints become their source of hope and strength. They draw closer to God and God in his mercy draws close to them (Jas 4:8). Heavenly consolation descends—refreshing the soul.

SUSTAINING GRACE

It is his hand upon their life that sustains them. Missionaries listen to songs of praise and worship and their spirits are lifted. They sense in their sufferings that they are abiding in Jesus and by his grace they are being made more like him. Their eyes are open, and they see life more clearly as they perceive the faithfulness of God. Scriptural promises become more precious. They cling by faith to every promise of the word of God as the only unmovable foundation of life.

They pray in the Spirit and are self-edified, being fortified within (1 Cor 14:4). They learn deepening dependance on God. They find that he is an ever-present help in their time of need (Ps. 46:1). They hold on to the promise that he will never leave them or forsake them (see Heb 13:5; Deut 31:6).

The oppression lifts for a season and their souls finds relief—they breathe more easily. Their faith is strengthened as they ponder all that God has done in their behalf. They daily drink living water (see John 4:10) and they eat heavenly manna (see John 6:35). They walk in the Spirit as God empowers them by his presence. The Spirit breathes upon their lives, and they have strength to go on.

They know that if all men forsake, God will never forsake them (see Heb 13:5). They understand that if all the foundations of this life are removed, they have an eternal home in heaven that God has prepared for them (2 Cor 5:1).

The gospel is ever advancing as the eternal grace of God has its powerful effect. Lives are being changed—the Spirit is revealing the truth, and the truth is setting free (see John 8:32). By these miracles of mercy they are satisfied. They are ever earning to live by what is not seen rather than by what is seen (2 Cor 4:18).

Though all seems to be shifting they find their feet planted on a solid foundation. Their hearts are being purified and their desire grows to please God (2 Cor 5:9). They find in having Jesus that it is more than enough (see John 17:8). He is their soul's treasure—the love of their life. He daily speaks peace to their soul as they face the chaos of life. They learn to cling to the gospel of grace as the only hope for the lost and the only hope for their own soul.

As they pray, grace saturates their souls—heavenly grace comes down and enters them—they then go out to share this heavenly grace with others. They are crucified with Christ but still alive as Jesus lives his life through them (Gal 2:20). They daily labor in the mission God has given them because they know that it is not in vain (Gal 6:9)—as it is done in love it will last for eternity (1 Cor 13:13).

By the grace of God and the sanctifying Spirit, they are being changed to be more like the one they serve (2 Cor 8:13). The suffering of the cross is accomplishing God's redemptive plan.

To share abundantly in the sufferings of Christ is the normal experience of missionary life. It is a daily experience that drives his servants to their Heavenly Father, seeking daily comfort from the God of compassion (2 Cor 1:3). Sufferings followed by loving comfort is their way of life as ambassadors of Christ (2 Cor 5:20).

GOD'S COMFORT

> Praise be to the God and Father of our Lord Jesus Christ, the Father of compassion and the God of all comfort, who comforts us in all our troubles, so that we can comfort those in any trouble with the comfort we ourselves receive from God. For just as we share abundantly in the sufferings of Christ, so also our comfort abounds through Christ. If we are distressed, it is for your comfort and salvation; if we are comforted, it is for your comfort, which produces in you patient endurance of the same sufferings we suffer. And our hope for you is firm, because we know that just as you share in our sufferings, so also you share in our comfort. (2 Cor 1:3–7)

Paul writes of the first person of the Trinity, who is the God and Father of our Lord Jesus Christ. Paul writes of the closeness of the Father to his children in their time of need. He is "the Father of mercies and God of all comfort" (NKJV). He is a loving God who is always within reach in our time of need. His embrace is always merciful, bringing comfort to his servants' souls in times of affliction. It is always comfort received with purpose. God uses those who have received comfort to impart comfort to suffering companions in the faith (2 Cor 1:4).

"'The Father of mercies' is obviously a semitic expression, patterned on the prayer of the synagogue . . . and it is more than 'merciful Father'; it characterizes what God is in himself, the fountain of mercy . . . 'the creator and original source of mercy.' . . . He is the Father 'from whom mercy comes.'"[23] God shows his mercy by meeting his messengers in their affliction with consolation.

The Old Testament promised comfort to the people of God with the coming of the Messiah (Isa 40:1). Paul is saying because the Messiah has come both he and the Corinthians can experience messianic comfort in all their trials.[24]

A Servant of Comfort

Dominique was hired by missionaries living in West Africa to help with household chores (something expected as a sign of generosity). He was a

---

23. Martin, *2 Corinthians*, 8.
24. Martin, *2 Corinthians*, 9.

frail-looking man—kind and soft spoken. He was a person with a heart filled with faith—a person who communed with God in prayer.

Harmattan daily blew in from the desert, continuously laying a thin layer of dust on the floors and furniture and requiring repeated cleaning. Dominique diligently kept everything dust free, also helping with other household chores, freeing the missionaries for gospel ministry.

Living in remote Africa, out of necessity, the missionaries had sent their children to a missionary boarding school in a neighboring African nation. Every six weeks, as scheduled, they would cross country borders and go see their children. As time progressed, these trips became more and more difficult and dangerous. In the neighboring country cars were being stolen and lives were being threatened.

An appointed time arrived for the missionaries to visit their children at the boarding school. Preparation was made for the trip. Dominique, having heard that missionaries' cars were being stolen in the neighboring country, said with great conviction of faith to the traveling missionary couple, "You can know that when you travel *your car* will never be stolen."

Dominique's declaration brought great encouragement and consolation to the missionaries, knowing that as they traveled, they had someone standing with them in faith and prayer, calling down God's protective angels to surround their lives and vehicle. Dominique held them up in prayer and by the mercy of God their car was never stolen.

Bonds of Comfort

Paul uses "we" and "us" in these verses (1:3–7) to emphasize the solidarity of all of God's children before the God of all comfort who was meeting them all in the fiery trials they were now facing. "Paul ties together the sufferings of Christ, which abound to 'our' benefit, with our consolation, which abounds on account of Christ. The two are directly linked for Paul. Paul's eschatological frame of reference and his confidence upon which it is based lead to affirm that as surely as 'we' share Christ's suffering, 'we' are assured that our consolation/comfort abounds because of Christ (v.5)."[25]

Central to Paul's thought is his belief that God does not abandon his people during their time of trial and suffering. Rather God comes with abundant and "overflowing comfort." What keeps his sent ones from

---

25. Sampley, "Second Letter to the Corinthians," 41.

failing is the abundant, endless, descent of comfort upon their lives from the God of all comfort.

It is suffering for the gospel that brings down to earth heavenly comfort. As the heavenly Father stood with his son in his times of greatest suffering in the wilderness and in the garden, sending his angels to strengthen and comfort (see Mark 1:13; Luke 22:43), so his messengers who go to distant lands can have the assurance that the same heavenly Father will be with them. He will be very near in their time of need—to console his servants who are suffering as Jesus suffered. If he so chooses, he can send his angels to comfort them (see Heb 13:2).

Paul depicts the Father as a never-changing, merciful, and compassionate God who comes to his people in their time of need and brings comfort and consolation. "God is continually and faithfully merciful. God's mercy and compassion are attributes that consistently characterize God."[26]

For Paul his servants receive comfort from God in their affliction with purpose. They receive from God so that they can be a channel of the comfort received to someone else who is now afflicted. The experience of affliction and the receiving comfort is to transform his messengers into vessels of comfort and consolation to others.

It is the experience of suffering and finding God's faithful help that empowers them to be vessels of comfort giving. It is the blessed experience of receiving heavenly consolation that enables his sent ones to bring uplifting help to those who suffer.

Martin explains, "There is a divine purpose in human suffering that is borne for the Gospel's sake. Thereby the cause of Christ is advanced (see Acts 14:22; Col 1:24 ff.). But one special reason is given in our passage. Those who receive encouragement from God are qualified to enter sympathetically into the experience of others whose pathway leads them through a vale of tears (vv 4, 6, 7)."[27]

Paul rejoices that though he has faced many harsh trials because of his missionary calling he has been given personal encouragement by God. It was his own sufferings and the sufferings of those in the churches he planted that formed a "bond of fellow sufferers." They were suffering together for the same faith and Paul and his converts could be assured of an abundance of consolation from a God who cares. Martin explains

---

26. Sampley, "Second Epistle to the Corinthians," 41.
27. Martin, 2 *Corinthians*, 11.

Paul's ministry of comfort, "And he joins together his vocation with that of his people who in passing through troubled times learn with him to receive divine encouragement and to minister that encouragement to others"[28]

Common suffering binds together missionaries (often from different missionary sending agencies) as shared difficulties (deceases, torturous weather, meningitis in the air, stoning, civil unrest, floods, insults, governmental interference, electricity and water cut-offs, violent coups, etc.) lead to the generous sharing of mutual comfort.

Consolation is bestowed from fellow missionaries who themselves in the past received much needed comfort. They transfer merciful comfort, lightening burdens and inspiring new hope to those downtrodden. These loving interventions of comfort strengthen bonds of friendship and testify to the power of the gospel of grace and love.

Paul writes, "So our comfort abounds through Christ (2 Cor 1:5b)." It is in the time of enduring hardship that missionaries find God to be near, knowing the abundance of his merciful comfort. God places his hand upon his servants, giving them divine strength to continue in the struggle. They are brought into an intimacy with God, knowing him more fully as their loving Heavenly Father. In a far-off land, they find that the Father of compassion and God of all comfort is very near.

"The principle that suffering teaches one how to treat others is rooted in the Old Testament."[29] "Also you shall not oppress a stranger, for you know the heart of a stranger, because you were strangers in the land of Egypt" (see Exod 23:9).

The missionary treats their fellow missionary with kindness, transmitting comfort and consolation because they know the heart of a stranger (what it is like to suffer in a foreign land, often far from family and friends). From their hearts, they want to give relief to the one suffering as they remember how they themselves were relieved by others.

It is hard to overstate the blessing of mutual support and comfort given to an afflicted fellow missionary. This is a gift of God—a gift that is desperately needed and readily received. It brings a thankful heart and a renewed trust in the faithfulness of the Father of mercies.

A missionary couple whose entire family had gone through severe trauma on the missionary field during a time of civil war was later visited

---

28. Martin, *2 Corinthians*, 8.
29. Keener, *IVP Bible Background*, 500.

by a single missionary who had participated in the same traumatic event. She brought tender, sympathetic words of comfort. She listened and understood the pain and brought encouraging relief to the missionary couple as each understood each other's suffering—each imparting consolation to the other.

Comforting Presence

Paul writes of his intimate concern for his Corinthian converts. In spirit, he is with them with heart-felt love (2 Cor 2:4, 3:2, 6:11, 7:3). Such comforting love needs to be the mark of every messenger of God. Often comfort comes from just being present (at the side of the sufferer) in a time of pain and loss.

On being a "comforting presence" of God's consoling grace to others Frank Macchia writes,

> There are times while bearing one another's burdens when silence is better than words. There is an important place for theological discussion, but not always. One must be wise. In the midst of lamentation, the best course of action may be to weep with those who weep and be a silent presence of inner groaning and strength. We may on occasion be an instrument of God in bearing with them as they work through their pain. Sometimes, those who suffer withdraw into themselves. We can be a presence that helps them to stay connected to community support, prayer, and witness. We all need to lean on one another as we lean on Jesus, or, better put, to lean on Jesus in part through leaning on one another. Hope can burst into flame at any moment. In fact, we should expect it. "And hope does not put us to shame, because God's love has been poured out into our hearts through the Holy Spirit" (Rom 5:5).[30]

It is the reception of comfort from others that prepares us to impart comfort to those God has given us to encourage. It is the receiving of comfort that opens our spiritual eyes and widens our hearts to have compassion on the hurting.

Missionaries must be fellow sufferers and fellow comforters, together looking for grace and love from above as they form a missionary community of compassion and care. The missionary community then

---

30. Macchia, *Tongues of Fire*, 143.

becomes a model of the gospel of mercy as they lead their disciples into maturity in Christ.

Paul teaches the Corinthians that the imparting of mutual comfort is a way of life in the community of believers. The followers of Christ will always be called upon to join in the sufferings of Christ. God's comfort leads to patient endurance of suffering, not the alleviation of suffering. Therefore the impartation of compassionate comfort will also be a necessity. The suffering of the cross continues so that comfort might continue to flow into us and out of us to others.

Missionary gospel ministry brings distress and suffering. We are called upon to minister in the weakness of the cross. This calls for the humble receiving and giving of comfort that leads to endurance in suffering. As suffering multiplies, so the giving and receiving of comfort must also multiply as we minister to each other through the mercies of our heavenly Father. This brings great hope as we see the faithfulness of God and the endurance of his laborers.

God's sent servants would not know the comfort of their heavenly Father if they did not know the sufferings of Christ. To know the blessing of the comfort of God not only makes suffering bearable but it makes our suffering precious.

God draws near in our times of weakness and reveals his closeness bringing eternal comfort. His consolation strengthens his sent ones to endure and to shine forth the glory of a faithful God who is very near in the moment of temptation. We come to know him more truly as a gracious and loving God who is our heavenly Father. He sustains us and transforms us by his comforting presence.

SHARED JOY

"Seeing Titus again would be a reason for Paul to rejoice. Another reason for him to have joy was that he saw the joy of Titus."[31] "As always with Paul, his joy was enhanced at the joy of another."[32]

In missionary ministry, as in all ministry, there must be an intimacy of fellowship in the sharing of burdens and trials faced. It is as we enter with compassion into each other's sufferings that we find a shared joy in recounting God's victories.

---

31. Martin, *2 Corinthians*, 225.
32. Martin, *2 Corinthians*, 228.

In our fellowship, joy endears joy, as we find mutual edification to remain steadfast in faith in doing good. There must be an understanding of grace that allows his sent ones to stop hiding their weaknesses and failures so that there can be open mutual trust to express the reality of sufferings and the need for comfort.

This is an important goal of missionary involvement. His messengers must look for mutual joyful edification that leads to unity and spiritual maturity, striving in all things to see the kingdom of God advanced on earth. There must be a steadfastness and determination to show that they are indeed there for each other—allowing each affliction to become a shared affliction—every joy a shared joy.

THE CLOSENESS OF GOD

Paul was dependent on the closeness of God that brought to him heavenly comfort. For Paul, the source of his comfort was God himself. He was very thankful for the comfort he received from Titus, but he knew that if there was a lack of human comfort there was always an abiding divine presence to comfort him.

In times when he was all alone (abandoned in the open sea, 11:25), he was not alone because the God of all comfort was very near consoling his soul. It is the closeness of God that sustains missionaries today. When all seem to abandon them, and the battle rages, it is the comforting presence of the almighty that sustains his servants, bringing rest and encouragement to their souls.

2

Integrity

"Integrity lies in doing what one speaks; speaking what one does."
M. K. Soni

"Integrity is telling myself the truth.
And honesty is telling the truth to other people."
Spencer Johnson

"When Jesus saw Nathanael approaching, he said of him,
'Here truly is an Israelite in whom there is no deceit.'"
John 1:47

Now this is our boast: Our conscience testifies that we have conducted ourselves in the world, and especially in our relations with you, with integrity and godly sincerity. We have done so, relying not on worldly wisdom but on God's grace. For we do not write you anything you cannot read or understand. And I hope that, as you have understood us in part, you will come to understand fully that you can boast of us just as we will boast of you in the day of the Lord Jesus. Because I was confident of this, I wanted to visit you first so that you might benefit twice. I wanted to visit you on my way to Macedonia and to come back to you from Macedonia, and then to have you send me on my way to Judea. Was I fickle when I intended to do this? Or do I make my plans in a worldly manner so that in the same breath I say both "Yes, yes" and "No, no"? But as surely as God is faithful, our message to you is not "Yes" and "No." For the Son of God, Jesus Christ, who was preached among you by us—by me and

Silas and Timothy—was not "Yes" and "No," but in him it has always been "Yes." For no matter how many promises God has made, they are "Yes" in Christ. And so through him the "Amen" is spoken by us to the glory of God. Now it is God who makes both us and you stand firm in Christ. He anointed us, set his seal of ownership on us, and put his Spirit in our hearts as a deposit, guaranteeing what is to come. I call God as my witness—and I stake my life on it—that it was in order to spare you that I did not return to Corinth. Not that we lord it over your faith, but we work with you for your joy, because it is by faith you stand firm. (2 Cor 1:12–24)

INTEGRITY DEFINED

A definition of missionary integrity: No secrets, no plotting, no hidden agendas—a simple sincerity—no fear of exposure (an open book)—everything explained—everything agreed upon is put into practice—wanting to please God in everything—desiring to maintain unity through understanding and trust—striving for total clarity—giving no opportunity to the devil to divide—no seeking of personal importance—pursuing a Christlike, God-honoring life.

One of the principal foundations that missionary life and ministry must be built upon is integrity. Paul has been accused by his enemies, the false apostles that have infiltrated the Corinthian church, of being a person who lacks integrity. They accused him of saying one thing and doing another.

In response, Paul says that he has a clear conscience before God as being a person of integrity and godly sincerity. He is a person of his word—what he says he will do, he does. It has been often noted that Paul is not primarily defending himself, rather he is defending his apostleship that has come into question because of the accusations of the false teachers now in Corinth.

Paul ties together his own personal integrity with the integrity of the message of the gospel that he has brought to them. Paul knows that you cannot separate the message from the messenger.

Paul grounds his integrity in the person of the gospel, the Lord Jesus Christ. Paul sees his life hidden in the Savior. The life he lives is "in Christ" and the Savior who engulfs his life is the Savior-God who is always faithful and true. All the promises of God find their "yes" in him (2 Cor 1:20).

INSPIRATIONAL LEADER

J. Philip Hogan throughout his missionary career was known as an inspirational leader of the highest integrity. He and his wife Virginia first pastored a church in River Rouge, Michigan. While ministering in that church Hogan invited Leonard Bolton, a missionary to China, "to speak at his church for a special mission's emphasis."[1] After those services and having gathered all the information he could from Leonard Bolton, Klaus and Peterson explain "that since the greater need for missionaries seemed to be in China, Phil decided that was where he and Virginia would go."[2]

The Hogans boarded a ship for Shanghai in February 1947. Their primary task upon their arrival in China was Bible school training in the city of Ningpo. But because of unrest, their time in China was cut short.

"Within months, the political unrest that had been simmering beneath the surface in China would explode into a violent and bloody conflict. The armed struggle between the ever-expanding communist movement and the local provincial governments had extended to threaten the lives of foreigners."[3] They were evacuated to Shanghai and then to Taipei to escape the violence.

Hogan began to preach and teach "at every opportunity, just as he had in Ningpo." But by November 1949 the communists were threatening to invade the island. Virginia and the children were evacuated first and then "with the communist invasion imminent," Philip evacuated to Hong Kong. "The Hogan's ministry to China was over."[4]

When Hogan assumed the leadership of the Assemblies of God missions' program then called the Division of Foreign Missions (DFM) he demonstrated himself to be a person of integrity. To be intellectually honest he first asked himself the question, "Can the world be evangelized?"[5] And he rhetorically asked, "Who decides when a man or city or locality

---

1. Klaus and Peterson, *Essential J. Philip Hogan*, 11.
2. Klaus and Peterson, *Essential J. Philip Hogan*, 11.
3. Klaus and Peterson, *Essential J. Philip Hogan*, 11.
4. Klaus and Peterson, *Essential J. Philip Hogan*, 14.
5. Klaus and Peterson, *Essential J. Philip Hogan*, 14.

or a nation or a generation is witnessed to?"[6] "His answer was honest and straight forward. 'I'll be frank to tell you I do not know,' he said. 'I do not know with what minimum God will be satisfied.'"[7]

Hogan was unsure if world evangelism was possible. "In any case, Hogan concluded, the task was so overwhelming that he would need to leave his questions with the Lord."[8]

Hogan was not swayed by every idea that came his way concerning the best and quickest way to evangelize the world. He had a clear missiological commitment. "'The Great Commission' meant winning converts who would form indigenous local churches."[9] The chief emphasis of DFM, therefore, would be to cooperate with the Holy Spirit in "the establishment of the indigenous church and the training of national workers."[10]

Klaus and Peterson describe Hogan's life as being a "resonance leader":

> Resonance is a reservoir of equity that frees the best in people, drives their performance, and enables individuals and organizations to achieve common goals and objectives. Resonance fuels the cultural climate of the organization. It inspires, arouses passion and enthusiasm, and keeps people committed and motivated. Leaders who generate resonance enable the organization to thrive amidst chaos and turbulent change. These leaders have the inner strength to be honest in the midst of painful truths. They inspire colleagues to stay loyal and committed when other opportunities beckon. They encourage innovation, foster warm and lasting relationships and empower all-out performance. Resonance leaders inspire success![11]

Klaus and Peterson explain how Hogan was a person of integrity by showing himself to be a resonance leader. "Time and again, during crisis or change, Hogan would draw upon an inner reserve of resources enabling him to thrive during times of turmoil. He encouraged creative and

---

6. Klaus and Peterson, *Essential J. Philip Hogan*, 14.
7. Klaus and Peterson, *Essential J. Philip Hogan*, 14.
8. Klaus and Peterson, *Essential J. Philip Hogan*, 14.
9. Klaus and Peterson, *Essential J. Philip Hogan*, 13.
10. Klaus and Peterson, *Essential J. Philip Hogan*, 13.
11. Klaus and Peterson, *Essential J. Philip Hogan*, 18.

entrepreneurial people, embraced their ideas, and rewarded outstanding performance."[12]

Every sending mission agency and every mission field need such leaders of integrity (every missionary is at some level functioning as a leader) that by their lives and leadership they "create resonance."[13] Men and women are needed who are full of the Spirit and who act out of the wisdom received from the word and the Spirit. Men and women who continuously call fellow missionaries to the task of carrying out the "Great Commission" are essential.

Missionaries of the essence are those who lead by example, men and women who are totally committed to the cause of Christ. Missionaries must be selected who lead in humility, wanting only for the work of God to advance, not looking for personal gratification. Missionary leaders must be sent who join themselves to the commitment of the Savior himself who "for the joy set before him he endured the cross, scorning its shame, and sat down at the right hand of the throne of God" (Heb 12:2b).

PURE HEARTS

Missionaries must ask God to give them pure hearts, knowing that it is the pure in heart that will see God (Matt 6:8). They must pray for the self-control of the Spirit (Gal 5:23), always "slowing down," speaking and acting with God-fearing purpose, asking God to help them see their real motives—asking in prayer for their hearts to be changed. They must ask God to flood their hearts with his humble self-sacrificing love so they can act out of the integrity of his love. It is only with a pure heart that God's ambassadors will be able to build God's kingdom in a God-honoring manner.

It is missionaries full of humble grace who will truly impact the world for Christ. When the Spirit of grace (Heb 10:29) is flowing through them, the name of Jesus is exalted, and the kingdom of God marches forward for the glory of God.

In a far-off land, if God's servants do not guard their hearts and minds, they can forget the example of Christ and their constant need for his helping grace and begin to seek for the accolades of men. They can choose the route of least resistance, seeking to accomplish their

---

12. Klaus and Peterson, *Essential J. Philip Hogan*, 18.
13. Klaus and Peterson, *Essential J. Philip Hogan*, 17.

self-serving goals and depart from God's will as revealed in the word of God.

Missionaries must often ask God in prayer to give them a pure life that is driven by pure motives. Though a missionary's motives in this life will never be completely pure, there can be an ongoing progression as God's sanctifying grace purges their souls and humbles them deep within, giving them the desire to please him in everything.

The missionary must speak from the heart—a heart that has been touched by God—a heart that is experiencing daily sanctification, leading to integrity of life before God and man. Missionaries must be engaged in putting off the old self and putting on the new (Eph 4:22, 23). God looks at the heart (see 1 Sam 16:7) and he works through those that are pure in heart (Matt 5:8).

As ambassadors sent by God, his sent ones seek to persuade men (2 Cor 5:11). But their persuasion must come from a heart that has been given over to the Holy Spirit. It is eternal truth that is lived out and then proclaimed that the Spirit takes to penetrate sin filled hearts, delivering from the slavery to sin. It is in holiness of life that his messengers appeal to the conscience of men, calling them to leave the path of death and destruction and find life and freedom in the Savior (2 Cor 5:20).

CHRISTLIKENESS

"Now this is our boast: Our conscience testifies that we have conducted ourselves in the world, and especially in our relations with you, with integrity and godly sincerity. We have done so, relying not on worldly wisdom but on God's grace" (2 Cor 1:12). "The Greek word translated 'sincerity' connotes the idea of testing to prove the genuineness of an article or a person. Paul claims to have consented to such evaluation—by God."[14] Paul emphasizes to the believers in Corinth his sincerity because he knows that a relationship can only be built on trust. A messenger of God must be known as a person of character that is demonstrated in Christ-honoring words and actions.

The ambassador of God must set aside the wisdom of this world, demonstrating his commitment to internalizing the gospel so that it becomes the compass of his life. He must purpose to bring every thought captive to Christ (2 Cor 10:5).

---

14. Martin, *2 Corinthians*, 20.

Transforming grace must be all-pervasive, affecting body, mind, and spirit. Every area of the missionaries' lives must be touched by grace through the sanctifying work of the Spirit. They must live in the atmosphere of grace, fixing their minds on the cross—the place from which the river of grace flows.

Paul boasted in his manner of living—his Christlike behavior. He did not boast about his number of converts or the miracles he performed. He boasted in the grace of God that empowered him to live a holy life (2 Cor 10:17). Holy, Christlike behavior must be the priority of every missionary.

PLEASING GOD

"Therefore we also have as our ambition, whether at home or absent, to be pleasing to him" (2 Cor 5:9 NASB). "Therefore" indicates that "the apostle is ready to present a logical conclusion.... Paul writes that it is the Christian's ambition ... to please the Lord."[15] "The Greek word translated 'ambition' means 'to aspire' (BGD, 861) or 'to devote oneself zealously to a cause' (Hughes, 178, p. 54)."[16]

This must be the missionary motto: "my ambition'" "I aspire to," "I devote myself zealously to the purpose of," pleasing the Lord in everything. Only a humble heart can see this brought to fruition. The proud and boastful find themselves excluded. It is only in following the example of the humble Savior that God's sent ones can please their master.

Paul calls upon God as "a witness upon his soul."[17] As missionaries minister in the field of their calling, they must daily humble themselves and present their souls to God. They must learn to "self-counsel," asking God to give them lives of integrity, knowing that God evaluates every action and all the words that proceed from their lives (see Matt 12:36). Therefore, missionaries must daily humble themselves and submit to God's sanctifying will. They must take up the towel of Christ and wash the feet of others, knowing that the first will be last and the last first (see Matt 20:16). Pleasing their Lord in everything must be their ambition—that to which they devote their God-given energies. This places the focus

---

15. Martin, *2 Corinthians*, 113.

16. Martin, *2 Corinthians*, 113, citing Bauer, *Greek-English Lexicon* (BGD), and Hughes, *Second Epistle*.

17. Sampley, "Second Epistle to the Corinthians," 49.

rightly on motivation—wanting Christ to be the treasure of their hearts (see Matt 6:21).

A CAREFUL LIFE

Integrity is a recognition of accountability. A servant is to live to please their master. Missionaries must live as those who are accountable to their master. Pleasing their Lord must be their joy—that which brings their deepest soul satisfaction. The longing of their hearts must be to please the one who gave his all for them. They must pray for a fixed heart—zealously devoted in mind and soul—on pleasing him in everything (see Ps 57:7).

Integrity calls for a careful life. It demands contemplation and reflection. His servants must pause and reflect about not only what they are doing, but what is their motivation. They must often stop and pray, imploring God by his Holy Spirit to search their hearts and to purge their hearts of any desire that is not pleasing him (see Ps 139:23, 24).

What can keep his servants from a heart devoted to God's pleasure is selfish ambition (2 Cor 12:20; Gal 5:20; Phil 1:17, 2:3; Jas 3:14, 3:16). Like the "super-apostles" in Corinth (2 Cor 11:5), some set aside the ambition to please their Lord and Savior and find themselves controlled by other ambitions. A longing to be important in the eyes of men leads to personal boasting, wanting to be seen as the first among many. Such desires are blinding desires—cravings that are often hidden from one's own recognition. Sinful boasting derives from underlying, controlling ambitions. It is a life of judging by outward appearances (2 Cor 10:7a) and the comparing oneself with others (2 Cor 10:12).

The desire for integrity for Paul is all-encompassing—all-consuming. It is an integral life of loving God with all our heart, soul, and strength and your neighbor as yourself (see Mark 12:30, 31). Those who seek integrity are people whose lives are offered up as living sacrifices, holy and acceptable to God (Rom 12:1). As messengers of the gospel, missionaries are to give their total self over to this life commitment, not leaving any room for any other desire in their hearts but to honor him in every detail of their lives.

The world needs missionaries with such a singleness of devotion. It is such men and women who will turn the world upside down for Christ (Acts 17:6), seeing his kingdom advanced to the ends of the earth.

Christ's messengers find encouragement when men are pleased with their lives and message. But gospel ministry can quickly change into times of resistance and persecution. It is in these times of trial that his servants can rest in peace, knowing that they are living with singleness of heart, doing the will of the one they love.

"We put no stumbling block in anyone's path, so that our ministry will not be discredited" (2 Cor 6:3). Jesus said, "If someone causes one of these little ones to stumble, it would be better to tie a millstone around his neck and be cast into the sea" (Matt 18:6). Great care must be given to avoid anything that would cause another to stumble.

Missionaries must give care to every word spoken and every action taken. Vigilance must be their way of life. There must be a continuous surrender to the enabling grace of our Lord Jesus Christ and a daily cleansing of his sent messengers' lives "from everything that can defile body or spirit," working toward complete holiness because they fear God (2 Cor 7:1 NLT). Such watchfulness is essential for missionary life and ministry. Missionaries must model the message that they preach.

The missionary must demonstrate a life that is filled with the Spirit (Eph 5:18) and possessing self-control. There must be a daily yielding to the Spirit, producing the fruit of the Spirit (Gal 5:22, 23). The missionary must receive wisdom from God in an ever-growing measure (Jas 1:5) to carry out the will of God in making disciples in all the nations of the earth.

"Trust is built one brick at a time. The structure we build by our day-in-and-day-out dependability is the house where we live and into which we invite our friends."[18] The daily life of godly dependability is an essential foundation for missionary ministry. It is through the dependability of missionaries' unchanging character that trusting relationships are built on their field of service. It is these God-honoring trusting relationships that become the foundation for the kingdom of God to advance.

CONTEMPLATIVE LIFE

While ministering the gospel in Corinth, Paul was very careful with his life. He lived to be an example, of the Savior who redeemed him, and the power of the gospel to transform a life.

---

18. Sampley, "Second Epistle to the Corinthians," 46.

On the mission field of one's calling, one must live a contemplative life. Words must be chosen with care—words that edify the hearers and honor the one who is worthy of all our praise. They must be words that match one's actions (Eph 4:29).

The word of God must be our constant guide. Missionaries must daily saturate his mind and soul with biblical truth (see Josh 1:8). They must continually ask themselves consciously and unconsciously, "What does the Bible say?" "What biblical truth or principle can give me guidance concerning the issues of life I face at this moment?" They must prayerfully allow the Holy Spirit and the word of God to work together in their hearts and lives producing Jesus-like behavior as shining lights of the world (see Matt 5:14).

In so many cultures of the world building and sustaining relationships are seen as the central foundation of life. As missionaries go into these relational societies, they must give heed to their lives, living in a manner that portrays honesty and sincerity.

As missionaries, they must be an "open book," making clear that they have nothing to hide. In humility they are to invite others to observe their lives and see the active power of the grace of God within them. Missionaries must daily demonstrate that they live a life of integrity in all of their interactive encounters. God sent messengers claim no sinless perfection, but by the grace of God they daily take steps in the right direction, seeking to please their master in everything.

Missionary ministry is more than words spoken. Missionaries will impart who they are. Who they are will "speak" much louder than what they say. What they say and do will reveal what is in their hearts (Luke 6:45). They must therefore live a thoughtful life, contemplating—choosing words and actions that honor Christ and that testify of his saving grace.

SINCERITY

"Since Paul must stand before God and since he has been sincere before men and women, there is no need to offer any further 'credentials' as to the soundness of his call."[19] An insincere life is a barrier to lasting God-honoring influence over others and a hindrance to the work of God.

---

19. Martin, *2 Corinthians*, 123.

Whereas sincerity opens the door for long-lasting missionary ministry that advances the kingdom of God.

In most cultures of the world, sincerity is of utmost importance and people are keen to observe if a messenger sent to their country has a sincere manner of life—if the person can be trusted as a person who truly seeks the very best for others. Sincerity is vital trait in fulfilling God's command to make disciples of every nation.

People want to sense missionaries' sincere love and their unwavering commitment to Christ. Theologically sound teachings and powerful preaching (as vital as these are) will fall on deaf ears if the person behind the teaching and preaching fails to display a life of humble sincerity through a true love for the Savior and a true love of his people.

Sincere missionaries will gain the confidence of the people they are reaching with the gospel. This confidence will open a door of lasting influence upon many lives and see the kingdom of God advanced on earth in a manner that brings glory and praise unto the Savior.

The yoke of the Savior is light (Matt 11:30), and the demands of discipleship are great (Matt 10:37)—both can be more easily accepted from a sincere ambassador. Sincere messengers of Christ will have a great impact for the cause of Christ. Missionaries who portray sincerity lay a foundation for an authentic church. Through their modeling of humble sincerity they will make honest, maturing disciples, who will themselves go and make other sincere, Christlike disciples.

ONLY FOR THE TRUTH

"For we cannot do anything against the truth, but only for the truth" (2 Cor 13:8). Paul was unequivocally, in all sincerity, committed to the truth. God's sent servants must pray that God will give them the same uncompromising commitment to the truth.

Such a commitment grows out of an intimate walk with Christ— the truth incarnate. Though many trials come, and evil arises against his servants, missionaries stand fast as they stand upon the truth. They will move forward, producing eternal fruit that sees the work of God's kingdom grow and flourish as they build their lives and ministry solidly on the foundation of the truth of the gospel. In making disciples, missionaries must accurately handle the word of truth (2 Tim 2:15 NASB), giving their disciples a firm foundation of faith that will keep them in the storms of life.

It is not just the truth that is important, but also the one who bears the truth. The gospel that is proclaimed must be lived. Converts must be conformed not only to the truth proclaimed but also be conformed to the truth lived out by the messenger in the daily difficulties of life. Missionaries who, like Paul, do everything for the truth will produce followers of Christ who are committed to the truth.

For missionaries to rightfully proclaim the truth of the gospel, first the truth must find deep lodging in their own hearts. Their own lives must be transformed by the gospel before they proclaim the transforming message to others. The truth of the gospel must be alive within them; a living reality that calls others to know the same liberating, life-changing truth.

COMING JUDGEMENT

"For we must all appear before the judgment seat of Christ, so that each of us may receive what is due us for the things done while in the body, whether good or bad" (2 Corinthians 5:10). In 2 Corinthians Paul is careful to emphasize the importance of God-honoring behavior. The Christian is warned that they will face judgment, appearing before Christ in the last day, being held accountable for acts done while in the body (5:10). God will judge not only our acts but also our motives (Rom. 2:16, 1 Cor 4:5).

Most commentaries believe that when Paul speaks of the judgment of the believer, he is referring to a pattern of life rather than individual acts. Missionaries will not be excluded from the judgment. They too will give an account on the day of judgment for their use or misuse of the grace that they have received.

All will be exposed on that day when all will stand before the omniscient one. A title or position or the apparent "success" of ministry will not impress God on the day of judgment. God knows the deepest motives of every heart and the true state of each person's character. All will be exposed in the brilliant light of God and judged justly, each receiving their due.

At the judgment seat of Christ, the eyes of men will be nonexistent. Each missionary will stand completely exposed before the eyes of the all-knowing Christ. It is then they will receive their reward not only for their works but for the motivation behind the works performed.

Missionaries must live in the reality of Christ's imminent return. It is then that they stand before the righteous judge who will bring every motivating desire and their daily manner of living to light and reward them according to their deeds done while in the body.

Paul's example of prioritizing integrity in gospel ministry calls Christ's sent servants to complete transparency in the work of God's kingdom. They must live as people that have nothing to hide. They must be perceived as servants who live their lives before God in the light of eternity.

In the place of their service assigned by God, in all their dealings with men, they must do what is right out of the simplicity of an upright heart. Though corruption often surrounds them, missionaries must be a shining light of integrity for all to see.

Missionaries must be people devoted to communing with God in prayer. They must daily baptize their souls in the living, sanctifying word of God (Heb 4:12).

God's servants must submit to the power of Calvary's grace, being progressively set free from their remaining brokenness and sins. They must daily open their minds and hearts to the Holy Spirit's work of transformation daily taking on Christlikeness.

"Whether good or bad" (2 Cor 5:10). "Though each individual is judged on the basis of his or her behavior, the person's habitual action, and not his individual acts, are the basis for judgment. . . . Thus God's judgment is also impartial, for what is due to a person is what is given that person."[20] On that day everything will be exposed. Our religious self-deceptions will all be laid bare. Daily contradictory words and actions will be brought out into the light.

The seeking after position, personal recognition, and all boasting will come under the blinding light of the judgment of God. His sent servants will be held accountable for what they did with the call that God placed upon their lives.

The question of what his messengers have done with God's great salvation will be answered. "Paul is suggesting that those who do well will receive good. This is consistent with his picture in 1 Corinthians 3:10–15.

---

20. Martin, *2 Corinthians*, 115.

The Christians whose work turns out to be gold, silver, and costly stones, will receive their reward."[21]

> The condition of the believer at the Parousia is immaterial for the saving event.... Whether asleep or alive, the Christian will receive the resurrection of the body at the Parousia. The point is that ... at all times the person should seek to please the Lord. ... What he adds is the exhortation to make efficient use of the time left to one.... Thus, Paul is saying in 5:9 that regardless of how the 'end' comes about—through death or the Parousia—the Christian is not relieved of his or her responsibilities to please the Lord. Until the end happens, Christians are responsible to account for their conduct, if it should fall below the standard of good behavior.... It is only by a life of goodness in the concrete situations of bodily existence ... that a person's claim to be representing God is shown to be authentic.[22]

What we did "in the concrete situations of bodily existence" will be brought out into plain view. Were we authentic (not perfect but authentic) in our Christian walk with God? Did we live in the light as God himself is in the light? Did we live in humility and repentance and dependency on God? Were we a shining light in the darkness or barely a flickering of light? Were we known to be authentic, letting the Savior live his life through our lives? Were we noticeably different than unbelievers? Did we live in love, showing love in tangible ways? Were we quick to repent of our failures, asking God for divine help for God-honoring change? Did we make great outward religious sacrifices but fail to love others—our lives being a "resounding gong or a clanging cymbal"—gaining nothing (1 Cor 13:1–3)?

Paul sets "before the Corinthians the stimulus for behavior that is pleasing to the Lord. Though the Christian's future is secure no matter what his state at the Parousia, Paul writes against false security."[23] In 1 Cor 9:27, Paul already had warned them of the possibility of being "disqualified" on the basis of conduct. Missionaries must not live in the false security of their calling. God knows all and everything will be brought to light on that day.

It is easy for missionaries to become deluded into thinking that because they have left home and friends and traveled to far of country that

---

21. Martin, *2 Corinthians*, 115.
22. Martin, *2 Corinthians*, 113–14.
23. Martin, *2 Corinthians*, 114.

somehow, they will be excluded from the divine judgment. Missionaries should not be deluded into thinking that their judgment will be less because they have sacrificed more—or that because they are "devoted" to the cause of Christ they can be careless with their lives.

> The tribunal of Christ for the Christian is needed to complete God's justice, both in terms of holiness and impartiality . . . the life of faith does not free the Christian from the life of obedience. . . . That God's judgment is universal is seen in that no one escapes, not even Christians . . . "each one" must stand before the judgment seat of Christ. . . . Judgment is not rendered en masse, but in each case, one by one. . . . The reason that all Christians (Bruce, 206) stand before Christ and are addressed individually . . . "in order to receive recompense" . . . "receive back or receive what is one's own."[24]

Paul lived with the understanding that he too would be judged and that he too needed grace-empowered careful living to ensure his entrance into God's eternal kingdom and to ensure he would stand before God unashamed on that day. Missionaries must live sober lives, with a consciousness that they are always under the watchful eye of God—in humility always living a disciplined life (2 Cor 7:1).

"'For all of us' denotes the sum total of Christians . . . Paul considers all Christians liable to judgment . . . to appear . . . not in the sense of 'showing up' but in the sense of being laid bare, for all the world to see the true nature of one's character. . . . The possibility of not pleasing God while here in the body is put before the Corinthians as something to be avoided. The inference is that Paul's desire is to please God, even if it means displeasing men"[25]

HARDSHIP AND INTEGRITY

"We put no stumbling block in anyone's path, so that our ministry will not be discredited. Rather, as servants of God we commend ourselves in every way: in great endurance; in troubles, hardships and distresses" (2 Cor 6:3–4). "The point is not merely that Paul has endured, but that he has endured and has kept his integrity intact, which shows his character. His virtues show how he handled hardships. The hardships and virtues

---

24. Martin, *2 Corinthians*, 114–15, citing Bruce, *1 and 2 Corinthians*.
25. Martin, *2 Corinthians*, 114.

together are meant to demonstrate that Paul has pure motives and authenticity as an ἀπόστολος."[26]

On the mission field missionaries face many challenges, including many hardships, often in a hostile environment. It is the heat of spiritual battle that brings to the surface what is really in the heart of his sent servants. Their character is exposed as the pressure increases. Under stress, others see if they are spiritually mature people who have grown in grace by the Spirit's help or if they are spiritually immature, being selfish, lacking the character of Christ.

The motives of missionaries' hearts are exposed in how missionaries react to times of trial and suffering. Are his sent servants seeking self-glory or are they seeking only to glorify God? Are they seeking importance in the eyes of men through self-promotion? Or are they boasting in God alone (2 Cor 10:17)? If the inner motives of God's messengers' character are not aligned with the gospel of Christ, they will fail to honor Christ in the moment of trial and temptation. Missionaries must daily pray the prayer of the Psalmist, "Create in me a pure heart, O God, and renew a steadfast spirit within me" (Ps 51:10).

"To the Corinthians Paul presents himself as one who has been honest and above board as he has sought to love them. He has done nothing out of motives of selfish ambition but has served them with their best interests always in mind. . . . His credentials consist not of external 'honors,' but of a life marked by dedication to God and to the people to whom he sent Paul."[27]

Ambassadors of God can learn from Paul's example concerning the motive for serving others. It must begin with an honest life. Lying and the telling of half-truths must never be the pattern of a missionary's life. Dishonesty leads to the loss of credibility and to the loss of godly influence in ministry. Christlike character is demonstrated in a life that is totally committed to "truth-living" and "truth-speaking."

The people missionaries serve must know that they can be trusted. The truth of the gospel must be matched with a truthful life. Everything must be out in the open, aboveboard, being unquestionably honest in all things. Once a missionary is perceived as dishonest and self-seeking, his influence ceases, whether he realizes it or not. Dishonestly leads to

---

26. Witherington, *Conflict and Community*, 399.
27. Martin, *2 Corinthians*, 120–21.

distrust. Once the missionary is labeled dishonest, his every act is brought into question.

Rather than dishonesty, the missionary must be known as a person who serves out of a heart that always seeks the best interests of others. He must be seen as a person who lives out of a heart of kindness and gentleness in times of difficulty. The missionary must be a person who seeks to be an instrument of blessing and edification, always wanting the very best for each person God has brought into his life.

Missionaries' lives must speak of dedication to the cause of the gospel and to the people God has sent them to reach. A dedicated life that endures hardship will give birth to more dedicated lives that also will endure hardship. They must show the way of full commitment to the one who gave his all for lost humanity and to the "Great Commission" he has placed into his messengers' hands.

CLEAR CONSCIENCE

"If Paul could stand before God in clear conscience, then what does he have to hide or cover up (or overcome) in the eyes of the Corinthians?"[28] All the ministry that a missionary does must be based on a solid foundation of a clear conscience before God. It is this cornerstone that enables missionaries to be unmovable in the trials of life and ministry. A clear conscience before God is the anchor of life that enables his ambassadors to endure and rejoice when all around them seems to be sinking sand.

When Satan raises his ugly head, missionaries with a clear conscience can look up and know that God their heavenly Father is there, willing to work in their behalf. A clear conscience comes by living in God's grace, quickly applying the shed blood of Christ to their every sin and failure (see 1 John 1:9). It comes by daily walking in the Spirit, depending on the Spirit's power (Gal 5:16).

Missionaries have assurance before God by applying the gospel to their lives every day (moment by moment), fixing their minds and hearts on the cross and the finished work of Christ for all their brokenness and sins. Missionaries live with a clear conscience as they set aside pride, walking in the humility of the Savior. It is the "weak" missionary that has the confidence of a clear conscience before a holy God as he stands in the shadow of Calvary's redeeming, transforming cross.

---

28. Martin, *2 Corinthians*, 122.

"Such people should realize that what we are in our letters when we are absent, we will be in our actions when we are present" (2 Cor 10:11). Missionaries must have a clear conscience through a consistency of the life. They must display the same character in every circumstance. They must be people who live humbly lives through the grace and love of Christ. They must be people who are quick to forgive, as they have been forgiven. They must show forth the fruit of the Spirit as a person who is growing in maturity in Christ.

"Make room for us in your hearts. We have wronged no one, we have corrupted no one, we have exploited no one" (2 Cor 7:2). "In Paul's mind there was not a single instance in which he harmed anyone."[29]

There is a peace in missionaries' souls as ministers of the gospel in knowing that their conscience is clear, empowering them to reject every false condemning accusation. In calm reliance on God, with a pure and humble heart, they can place every past, present, and future life and ministry experience into the hands of almighty God, allowing him to work for the honor of his own name, knowing that he can never fail and that he will bring about his eternal purposes. "Not a single instance" of intentional harm to others must be the testimony of his sent servants as they seek to bring the gospel of light to every dark place on earth.

MATERIAL WEALTH

"You see, we are not like the many hucksters who preach for personal profit. We preach the word of God with sincerity and with Christ's authority, knowing that God is watching us" (2 Cor 2:7 NLT). "Professional speakers had long been accused of changing truth into error for gain (like a merchant providing impure products to save money). . . . The public often perceived wandering teachers and holy men as charlatans, no doubt because many of them were (in Scripture, cf. Jer. 6:13–14; 8:10–11; Micah 3:5, 11). . . . Thus many philosophers and moralists felt the need to repudiate the charge, as Paul does here."[30]

The Bible clearly warns us against the evil of lusting after money. Jesus said that a person cannot serve both God and money (Matt 6:24). Paul writes that money is the root cause of many evils in the world (1 Tim

---

29. Martin, *2 Corinthians*, 217.
30. Keener, *IVP Bible Background*, 503.

6:10). Missionaries must live in such a manner that the love of money has no place in their hearts or control over their lives.

Along with all the sinful cravings of the fallen heart, the love of money (material wealth) has bought great harm in this world. Families have been destroyed and lives have been enslaved through the untamed love of riches.

Unfortunately, this unholy love is found on the mission field. Big egos joined with the love of material wealth have infected the work of preaching the gospel to the nations. Sending churches with financial means to gain influence, and in attempting to build their own kingdoms on earth, have used money to influence and control the work of the gospel in foreign lands. Unscrupulous pastors and church leaders on various mission fields have been more than willing to open their churches to the ministries of wealthy churches in other countries, wanting to enrich themselves.

On the mission field, the longing for the reception of foreign wealth often pits one pastor against another, breeding jealousy and discontent (as some receive more than others). Faith is extinguished as church leaders place more faith in incoming foreign funds than in God himself. Evangelism becomes a thing of the past. Hearts are polluted and bound with a continuous lust of material gain.

As the love of money finds its roots, the devil finds an open door to move into the church and the Holy Spirit is forced out. Prayer becomes an empty act and worship a farce—all for the sake of mammon (see Matt 6:24 KJV). The church becomes self-deceived into thinking that the devil and the Holy Spirit can work together under the same roof—not realizing that Ichabod has already been written on the doors of the church. All hope of building an indigenous God-honoring church is dashed. The church becomes the Laodicean church (see Rev 3:14–22).

Witherington explains the nature of the false teachers in Corinth: "The false ones, Paul suggests, boast in matters of form or outward appearance and not matters of substance or matters of the heart that really count. This was in fact a typical complaint against Sophists—they were all show and no substance. They paid special attention to their clothing, appearance, and delivery and to the sound of their voices."[31]

Missionaries can be infected with this materialistic disease. Pretending to be sacrificing for the gospel, on the field they move into large,

---

31. Witherington, *Conflict and Community*, 6.

plush homes and eat the best of foods. With large missionary accounts they often spend more time traveling back to the States than being on the field. They order the most comfortable vehicles, making sure that no other missionary has one better than their own. Their hearts become cold, and they lose touch with the voice of the Spirit. They claim to be called of God but labor in the flesh because of the idolatrous desire for material wealth and prestige that have taken up residence in their hearts.

"For our boasting is this: the testimony of our conscience that we conducted ourselves in the world in simplicity and godly sincerity, not with fleshly wisdom but by the grace of God, and more abundantly toward you" (2 Cor 1:12 NKJV). "Simplicity" can be a powerful truth for every servant of God.[32] Missionaries must live with simple heart, shown in a simple lifestyle, that demonstrates that they serve a Savior who was born in a manger; had no place to lay his head; had zero material wealth; ate and drank with sinners (those considered spiritually contaminated); suffered under Pontius Pilate; as a condemned criminal, bore the world's sins in his own body; died and was buried in a borrowed tomb.

Missionaries must live with a heart and life that is detached from material lust as a means to honor and glorify the Savior they serve. They must demonstrate that they are not "double minded" (2 Cor 1:17–20) but rather they live with only one desire to know him in the power of his resurrection and in the fellowship of his suffering (Phil 3:10).

With so many charlatans around, Paul could boast that God had called him to be an example of sincere, holy living as a servant who was laying up a treasure in heaven rather than on earth (see Matt 6:20). Paul rightly boasted that he was free from the lust for the material. He lived in poverty (2 Cor 6:10) doing all to honor his Savior and see God's kingdom advanced on earth. Paul had been crucified with Christ and therefore boasted as a man dead to the lusts of the world, pointing others to the source of all goodness and satisfaction.

"And now, brothers and sisters, we want you to know about the grace that God has given the Macedonian churches" (2 Cor 8:1). Paul writes of the gift of grace that came to the Macedonians that transformed

---

32. Every missionary applicant should be asked to sign a commitment form to live a life of simplicity. This commitment would be a personal commitment before God that every missionary would then live out from their own conscience in humble obedience to God.

The form that calls for simplicity should not be given as a legalistic obligation but rather as a call to personal commitment out of a love for Christ and a desire to please him in everything. See example in appendix A.

them into a generous people. Paul calls it an incredible gift. "Thanks be to God for his incredible gift" (2 Cor 9:22). Receiving the grace of giving leads to gratitude and thanksgiving.

Rather than missionaries loving money they are to allow the grace of God to make them into generous servants. Grace comes into God's messengers' lives so that it can then flow out in generous giving to others. And as generous grace flows out to others, Christ's servants open their lives for more generous grace to flow in. This produces among God's people an ever-increasing flow of generosity, all for the honor and glory of God.

Missionaries in this manner model the truth that "God loves a cheerful giver" (2 Cor 9:7) as God himself is a cheerful giver. As grace flows through his sent ones in abundance, they become more and more like their generous God. They abound in every good work, experiencing God's grace of giving knows no limit. By his grace, missionaries join their lives to the abundant, never ending, grace of the giving of God—an incredible gift from heaven.

THE LEVEL GROUND AT THE CROSS

In 2 Cor 7:2, "the idea of 'overreaching' or 'exploiting' (NIV) someone else carries with it the larger meaning of using that person to one's own advantage, financially or otherwise."[33] There is always the temptation to exploit on the missionary field. In arrogance, messengers of God can look down on those of lower education and means as inferior and use them for their own advantage. Such behavior displays a lack of the love of Christ in their hearts, and a failure to appreciate the value of the image of God imbedded in every soul. Such behavior also demonstrates a total lack of understanding of the desperate need of every soul for the grace of the cross.

Those sent by God cause misunderstandings and divisions by making prideful comparisons for the purpose of exalting themselves (what Paul calls "judging by appearances," 2 Cor 10:7a). Nothing can be farther from the love and humility of the cross than self-exalting comparisons (2 Cor 10:12). This behavior is a failure to internalize the truth that every man is a sinner and every man needs forgiving, healing grace for his own brokenness.

33. Martin, *2 Corinthians*, 218.

All over the world, cultures are formed by fallen sinners who are joined together by common language and common customs. Every culture and those that inhabit that culture are broken and flawed by sin and rebellion against God. All that varies is the way the sinful brokenness is manifested.

Missionaries go simply as people from one sinfully broken and flawed culture to another, proclaiming the Savior that both missionaries and nationals so desperately need for reconciliation and wholeness. Missionaries are to love from a heart that is filled with a realization of the equality of "soul sickness" that has affected all men, leaving all humanity wounded, confused, and desperate for God's redemption to lift them out of their rebellious darkness and sinful blindness. Every man needs healing through God's forgiveness, being transforming into something beautiful and glorious as the enter into new creation (2 Cor 5:17).

Missionaries are to love people as they are—just as God in Christ has loved them in their fallenness and continues to love them in their many failures. Missionaries look in faith to what someone else can become in the same manner that others have invested the gospel in their lives to become the person others believed they could become. What is needed for each person in each culture is saving grace that leads to an ever-growing transformation into the likeness of Christ (2 Cor 3:18). This understanding of level ground at the cross must be God's sent ones' mindset and the focus of their labor of love.

"For Christ's love compels us, because we are convinced that one died for all, and therefore all died" (2 Cor 5:14). Some missionaries in the past have been accused of exploitation. Unfortunately, at times it has been true. If messengers sent by a compassionate God do not love as Christ loved, they will inevitably exploit those for whom the Savior died.

Missionaries must be constrained and motivated by the love of Calvary in all their dealings on the field of our calling, being God's instrument of compassion to lost humanity. They must ask God to rid their hearts of the seeking of importance in the eyes of men that inevitably leads to the exploitation of others. They must ask God to fill them with the self-giving grace and love of the cross that seeks always to serve as their Lord served (Mark 10:45).

UNITY AMONG MISSIONARIES

When the power of certain personalities and giftings are use in a selfish manner the fellowship of missionaries can be robbed of the joy of working together. A missionary can, because of his power of influence, become an instrument of the devil by pulling certain national workers in places of church leadership into his "camp," gaining a position of power and influence at the expense of the other missionaries. This leads to the other missionaries finding themselves in a position of having "lost influence," seeing their lives and ministry diminished in the eyes of church leaders, giving an opportunity to the devil to divide, causing hurt and misunderstanding.

This is why it is critical that every effort be made to keep the unity of the Spirit in the bond of peace (Eph 4:3). Self-interests must be crucified, and the humility and love of the Savior magnified. To maintain integrity and loving cooperation, the national church should always be approached with one united voice of the entire missionary fellowship. No missionary should seek personal gain and influence. All support given to the national church, whether financial or material, should be given in the name of the mission and never in the name of an individual missionary.

The unity of the missionary team on any field must be of the highest priority. Decisions and policies that are made by the missionary fellowship must be followed by every missionary. Failure of a missionary to implement decisions made by the missionary fellowship must be addressed and corrected. Failure to submit to the team's decision because of self-centered pride and rebellion must be corrected and, if necessary, the rebellious one disciplined.

Discipline is to be always given with the hope and with a plan of restoration (2 Cor 2:6, 7). Acts of discipline for the rebellious and unruly are a necessity for the missionary fellowship to keep its purity and its kingdom focus so that the work of reaching the lost and making disciples continues moving forward without interruption.

Conflict intervention that seeks restoration and forgiveness must be backed up with the real possibility of removal from the field for those being divisive or those who are trapped in serious sin. In following the example of the apostle Paul, every effort, with great loving patience, must be used in bringing a straying missionary or national brother back to their spiritual senses, leading to true godly sorrow and repentance (2 Cor 7:9).

The missionary must teach and model this repentant fear of God. Blatant sin and rebellion must be dealt with to protect the mission, the church, and for the sake of the offender. Not having the courage to discipline—making excuses for what is destructive—will weaken the mission's and the church's testimony and diminish their influence.

Those who refuse repentance must be rebuked—at times openly (1 Tim 5:20). Missionaries must do everything to establish a strong foundation for the national church and part of the that process is teaching and modeling church discipline (Matt 18:15–19).

Some fields have never developed, being greatly retarded, by letting destructive carnal attitudes and practices continue without correction. Missionaries must strive to live a pure and disciplined life as an example of what is the biblical standard for leadership within the church.

TRAINING LEADERS OF INTEGRITY

The most spiritually mature individuals must be trained for leadership roles—people of deep prayer and dedication—humble servants. Self-seeking individuals placed in leadership will poison the work and greatly retard its advancement. Personal abilities are not enough. The person must be a servant—someone with the character to become a true shepherd of the flock of God.

When "religious politicians" come into leadership, the mission and the church lose their purity and become a place of disgrace rather than a place where people can find a holy God. Missionaries must build a kind of church for which Jesus bled and died. The Bible tells us that Jesus poured out his life "to make her holy, cleansing her by the washing with water through the word, and to present her to himself as a radiant church, without stain or wrinkle or any other blemish, but holy and blameless" (Eph 5:26–27).

Integrity must be one of the vital foundation stones on which the work of God's kingdom is built on every mission field in the world. It is a firm foundation that will guarantee the endurance of the church and flourishing of the making of disciples of every nation.

3

Emotional Engagement

"My emotions are invisible, untouchable—invincible even—and their power far outweighs my own. And so it seems unfair that for all the little I can do to them, they can do so much to me."

Kelseyleigh Reber, "If I Resist"

"I used to give too much importance to reason until I discovered the world was shaped not by reason but by emotion."

Bangambiki Habyarimana, "The Great Pearl of Wisdom"

"Arise, cry out in the night: in the beginning of the watches pour out thine heart like water before the face of the Lord: lift up thy hands toward him for the life of thy young children, that faint for hunger in the top of every street."

Lamentations 2:19 KJV

EMOTIONS LAID BARE

A missionary and his wife with their two small children who have recently arrived in the country of their calling on the continent of Africa now find themselves in the middle of a coup d'état. In the capital city gun fire is heard around their home, many buildings are being burned, and they have been advised that they should not leave their home. They remain hunkered down, emotionally distraught, not knowing the full scope of their danger. They anxiously wait for the trouble to pass, praying for peace and stability to return, not knowing how long they will be confined in their home. Their house worker brings them sustenance bought at the market and pieces of news from the outside.

These kinds of dangerous upheavals and political instability will be their lot in life in the years to come as injustice often arises to the boiling point followed with mob violence and more burning. Peace must be found outside themselves—the peace of God that transcends all understanding (Phil 4:7). They learn to trust in the one who said that he would never leave them or forsake them (see Heb 13:5).

In missionary life and ministry, these messengers of God find that the Lord truly is the prince of peace (see Isa 9:6). As troubles increase and hardships multiply, they can find peace in the Lord himself. It is the Scripture's promises of eternal peace that sustains them:

> You will keep in perfect peace
> all who trust in you,
> all whose thoughts are fixed on you! (Isa 26:3 NLT)

Often in times of crisis, in a far-off land, God brings to his servants' remembrance a hymn or chorus that brings comforting words of encouragement, calming the emotions with hope. In times of great upheaval (revolution, civil war) missionaries learn to use the spiritual weapon of worship to bring to their souls the peaceful assurance that God is near.

It is in songs of praise and worship that the missionary is reminded and reassured that the Lord is in control—that he is a strong tower of protection (see Prov 18:10). Through worship the missionary draws near to God and God to the missionary, calming the emotions and giving strength to the missionary's soul.

PAUL'S EMOTIONAL LIFE

Second Corinthians is a very emotionally "messy" letter. Paul experiences many emotional ups and downs as he received news concerning the church in Corinth. In this epistle we read more than any other Pauline writings of the apostle's emotions. This is helpful in understanding his human frailty and his dependance on God. Paul knows he is in a spiritual battle for the souls of his converts (2 Cor 2:11). The devil is using the false teachers who have infiltrated the church to bring division, working to overthrow the faith of some.

His greatest concern is the spiritual welfare of the church, which he fears is being damaged by inside and outside influences. He agonizes for them, fearing that they will be deceived by the devil (2 Cor 11:3). He pleads with them and reasons with them to be reconciled to God and to renew their love for him as the father of their faith.

Paul is deeply affected by what is happening in the church in Corinth. He has a profound concern for their spiritual condition.

"For I wrote you out of great distress and anguish of heart and with many tears, not to grieve you but to let you know the depth of my love for you" (2 Cor 2:4). This verse "speaks of Paul's physical and mental state when he wrote the sorrowful letter. He was anxious in heart, undergoing suffering, and weeping while writing."[1]

One cannot read Paul's writings without recognizing that Paul was a man full of passion. He displayed "a wide range of emotions."[2] He has times of anger and distress because of his opponents and because of the news he has received of the struggles and apparent drifting of his converts "under outside influences."[3]

What causes Paul emotional stress is the fact that his apostolic ministry is being brought into question as well as his loving authority over the church. "The major issue is the legitimacy of Paul's ministry. It is this above all else that is in question in Corinth and therefore also in this letter."[4]

False "super-apostles" (2 Cor 11:5) for their personal benefit had come into the Corinthian church and were working to undermine Paul's authority as an apostle and bringing into question his ministry. Paul suffers much emotional pain and labors in this letter to call the Corinthians back to the gospel he had brought them and to return to a mutual loving, trusting relationship.

Martin describes Paul's emotional life as seen in 2 Corinthians: "A sensitive person such as Paul here mirrors the frailty of the human person under the stresses and pressures of daily living."[5] No other writing of Paul so exposes his human frailty and his fluctuations of emotions. One sees the pressures of apostolic ministry that expose his emotions—his personal hurt and his many apprehensions out of his concern for the spiritual state of the church he founded.

---

1. Witherington, *Conflict and Community*, 65.
2. Sampley, "Second Epistle to the Corinthians," 20.
3. Sampley, "Second Epistle to the Corinthians," 20.
4. Witherington, *Conflict and Community*, 360.
5. Martin, *2 Corinthians*, 223.

Paul was dishonored and unrecognized as a person of importance. The Corinthian church wavered in their support for him and were made to question his authority. Paul did not take these attacks lightly. He suffered emotionally because of their rejection—fearing that their rejection of him was also the rejection of the message he had brought them. Paul also knew great moments of joy as he received good reports from Corinth and heard of the spiritual progress of his converts.

Paul's life is an encouragement to missionaries now on the field as they too face the trials of life and ministry and the accompanying emotional fluctuations of pain and joy. Paul's life as seen in 2 Corinthians informs Christ's servants that it is normal for a missionary to experience deep emotional pain and the enjoining moments of joy inexpressible (see 1 Pet 1:8).

Paul daily faced not only physical suffering but also the adjoining emotional affliction. He endured for the sake of the gospel. His sole concern was that his converts in Corinth continue in the faith until the end. He longed for them to grow in grace and to move on into maturity in Christ.

He fears that his past correction may have been too strong (2 Cor 7:8) and that those in the Corinthian church may be discouraged. He weeps from his heart, longing to see the completion of the work that God has begun in their hearts.

Witherington writes about Paul's desired heartfelt response from the Corinthians (2 Cor 6:11–13):

> Paul has "opened his mouth wide" and has shared everything concerning his feelings, attitudes, desires, exhortations, and circumstances (v. 11). What he wants is for the Corinthians not to be reserved about him, but to open their hearts fully to him again. The verb in v. 12 means "cramped." The Corinthians had not been assigned to a small corner in Paul's heart, and Paul wants reciprocity. They are to act like his children and show themselves expansive toward him (v. 13).[6]

Missionary life and ministry are not a "cramped" life and ministry. It is a ministry that comes from an open heart that longs for an open-heart response. The missionary desires that his emotional feeling motivated by the love of God will engender the same like-felt emotional response in his

---

6. Witherington, *Conflict and Community*, 400.

converts. There is a longing for the joining of hearts in love because of a like precious faith.

Spending ourselves emotionally for others brings a longing for a like heartfelt emotional response. The experience of redemption—the freeing from sin and darkness—calls out for a heartfelt response and a bonding of those of like faith. We are to be bound together by the tender love of the Savior poured out in our hearts by the Holy Spirit (Rom 5:5).

Throughout 2 Corinthians we see Paul exposing his heart and expressing his emotions out of his concern for his converts. The false apostles that have entered the church are doing damage and he fears the long-term effect of their deceptive teachings. This touches Paul deeply, wanting to intervene but not sure what path to take.

He attempts to reason with them, he warns them, at times he uses strong language to try to awaken them out of their spiritual waywardness. He fears that he may lose some of them to the devil's cunning (2 Cor 11:3) and calls them back to the simplicity of the gospel from which some of them have apparently fallen.

He is forced to defend himself against the accusations of the false teachers. This all brings inner turmoil, emotional uncertainty, as he lives with a deep care and concern for his converts, fearing for their spiritual condition.

Missionary life is not a detached life. To love as Christ loves is to expose one's heart to the possibility of emotional pain and rejection. Paul's life encourages God's ministers of reconciliation, knowing that God in his faithfulness will join his enabling grace to our times of emotional uncertainties.

Ministers of the gospel need, through the help of the Holy Spirit, a determination to endure many spiritual attacks that deeply affect them emotionally. They must learn to rest on the knowledge that God will not test them beyond what they can endure as he comes in their greatest times of need to make a way of escape (1 Cor 10:13). They will "escape" as God meets them with the inner enablement of the Holy Spirit, calming the soul by reminding them of their eternal hope (2 Cor 5:1).

EMOTIONAL STABILITY

"I still had no peace of mind, because I did not find my brother Titus there. So I said goodbye to them and went on to Macedonia" (2 Cor 2:13).

"No peace of mind." The messenger of God often must carry burdens that press on the mind and affect his emotions throughout the day. Mental turmoil from adversity afflicts the mind and soul—false teachings, strained relationships, personal accusations, insults, material and financial needs, falsehoods, sicknesses, satanic attacks.

Like Paul's experience with the Corinthians, missionaries' open hearts are often met by closed hearts. This brings emotional pain, feeling that their love and sacrifice has been rejected. They can believe that they were taken advantage of by those they sought to served. They can feel that the more they give the less they receive in response. They carry an emotional burden—a heavy heart—mourning and weeping.

Relief is found in knowing that in sincerity before God they are wanting to please him. They learn to leave the response of others in the hands of God. The missionary must humbly commit all his ways unto him—the giver of life and the final judge.

Martin explains how Paul reminded the Corinthians of his sincere ministry:

> The Corinthians should have a reason to boast, namely, that he is an example of God's handiwork. But their doubt of Paul's sincerity forces him to place before them the facts, which consist of an asseveration that he has worked hard and openly for the Corinthians. Paul faces a dilemma in that there is nothing else for him to do but to remind them of his upright ministry.[7]

The missionary, like Paul, must find emotional stability in knowing the reality of his life and ministry before God. Missionaries are to feel deeply but they are also to feel according to the "facts" of their lives. Their emotions cannot be controlled by circumstances and the opinions of others.

Like Paul, a dilemma is brought upon the missionary when the sincerity of his calling is brought into question. The missionary must choose to remain humble, knowing in his heart his unending need for grace. He can then stand upon the "facts," as a servant who by the grace of God only desires to please God in everything.

Unfortunately, as Paul experienced, humility and sincerity can be seen by some as weakness and be taken advantage of and used against the missionary as self-seeking individuals seek their own agendas. Like Paul, the missionaries must find peace—a calmness of body, mind, and soul in

---

7. Martin, *2 Corinthians*, 118.

their relationship with God in knowing in their hearts their one desire to see the grace of God multiplied in the lives of men.

There must be an equilibrium of emotion through a foundation of understanding one's own humble, dependent sincerity, not being swayed by either criticism nor approbations of men. The messenger of God must know what he believes, whom he serves, and who has called and authorized him. He must go forward to carry out God's will as revealed in the word of God, undistracted by the voices of doubters, living as ambassadors of Christ.

The opinions of men will vary—some will be very pleased, while others will be resentful. God's sent servants cannot let their emotions be controlled by the displeasure or pleasure of men. Rather there must be an unwavering peace in their hearts that by the grace of God they are doing the will of God with a clear conscience knowing that it is to their Lord that they will one day give an account of their lives (2 Cor 5:10).

"Paul, in sharing the lot of the downcast, is lifted up at the arrival of Titus, for both the message and the messenger were a source of comfort and joy for Paul. . . . Titus was a heaven-sent 'means' for the renewal of Paul's spirit. . . . Yet it was not Titus's arrival that cheered but the uplifting news that came with that arrival (so Bultmann, 57), and the fact that Titus had come from Corinth where he had succeeded in his mission."[8] "For Paul this must have been a heartwarming event. The news of Titus has raised him 'from the trough of his former apprehensiveness to the crest of a great wave of consolation' (Hughes, 274)."[9]

During the trials of missionary life and ministry that lead to discouragement and despondency "heartwarming news" of God's faithfulness breathes new life into the soul. God in his faithfulness often sends his servants a messenger of consolation, assuring that all is not lost—what seemed like an impossible situation, a mountain that stood in the way, has now been overcome. God's merciful intervention has brought the change that was needed. The gospel truth has penetrated hearts—someone has repented—restoration has come—prayer has been answered and the kingdom of God is advancing.

In the moments of great discouragement, being downcast, God comes to his sent ones warming their hearts with the news of his faithful

---

8. Martin, *2 Corinthians*, 225.

9. Martin, *2 Corinthians*, 234, citing Bultmann, *Zweite Brief*, and Hughes, *Second Epistle*.

working as walls of resistance come down. The heart is uplifted as he has brought "godly sorrow," repentance, and restoration.

In following Paul's example, as one who refused to retaliate against his accusers, missionaries can be peacemakers—a stabilizing force—calming emotions, bringing understanding and conflict resolution. Out of the love of God in their hearts they bear all things, believe all things, hope all things, endure all things (1 Cor 13:7). Out of their maturity in Christ, they refuse to pay back evil for evil, rather impart good to every wrong received (1 Pet 3:9).

Throughout the book of 2 Corinthians, you sense Paul deliberately controlling his emotions while under attack. He does not lash out in anger. When his emotions are stirred, he continues to live by faith trusting in the faithfulness of his sovereign God.

He is not compulsive, letting his emotions run wild. He writes, giving counsel with great patience always seeking and hoping for repentance from those who have strayed, wanting full restoration. He understands that being slow to anger is refusing sinful anger (Jas 1:19).

There is no gospel engagement without emotional engagement. Living and preaching the gospel must come from the heart—a heart of passion. Paul is totally engaged—body, mind, spirit and emotions in bringing the gospel to the lost.

He prayerfully controls his emotions by committing his life and ministry to the one to whom he must give an account. He lives "before God" (2 Cor 3:4). He acts in the humility and kindness of Christ, seeking the wisdom of the Spirit, giving room for God in his mercy to intervene, believing God to bring a change of heart to his enemies and restoration to those who have strayed. He refuses to be compulsive and take matters into his own hands but rather commits the Corinthians into the hands of the almighty—the only one who can bring a person to humble repentance and bring lasting change.

MOTIVATE BY LOVE

Paul wrote, "For I wrote you out of great distress and anguish of heart and with many tears, not to grieve you but to let you know the depth of my love for you" (2 Cor 2:4).

This verse reveals the deep emotional connection Paul has with the believers in Corinth. Paul is not some detached observer. Rather, out of a heart full of love, he has deep concern for their spiritual condition. He has sorrow in his heart and is afflicted with the thought of them losing their trust in him and their straying from the gospel.

He tells them that he has an abundance of love for them. He is touched like a mother whose children are straying into dangerous waters fearing for their welfare.

In like manner, the modern missionary cannot be a detached observer. The souls of men call for a deep concern and emotional engagement. It calls for a heartfelt love—wanting to protect the flock of God—wanting to see those that come to Christ grow into mature followers of Christ.

The ambassadors of God must bring the gospel around the world out of a depth of love that God has placed in their hearts. There must be an emotional attachment to the people God has given them to reach with the gospel. They must love them in their broken condition—not judging or condemning—but loving them as they are in their lost condition.

"God so loved the world . . ." (John 3:16) must be the missionary's motivation. Every act of ministry and their daily manner of life must be motivated by the love of the Savior. Out of love, the missionary develops an emotional attachment to those to whom they bring the gospel. The missionary wants what is eternally best for those God has given them to love. Motivated by love, they make disciples, wanting them to know Christ and to mature in him.

Paul wrote, "You yourselves are our letter of recommendation, written on our hearts, to be known and read by all" (2 Cor 3:2 ESV). Concerning the words "on our hearts," Witherington writes, "The letter Paul refers to is about himself and the authenticity of his ministry, and he carries it in his heart . . . and since they are his letter of recommendation, it is not surprising that he would say that it was written in his heart. He can bring from his heart the example of the Corinthians as a basis for boasting and a testimony to his authenticity."[10]

"On our hearts" speaks of Paul's emotional attachment to the Corinthian believers. Because of his love and deep concern for them it was as if they were engraved on his heart. In love, he carried them around in his heart wherever he traveled.

Paul wrote. "When I came to Troas to preach the gospel of Christ, even though a door was opened for me in the Lord, my spirit was not

---

10. Witherington, *Conflict and Community*, 378.

at rest because I did not find my brother Titus there. So I took leave of them and went on to Macedonia" (2 Cor 2:12–13). As Paul traveled on his missionary journeys he carried in his heart his loving concern for the welfare of church in Corinth. Martin writes, "And Rissi (*Studien*, 16) sees in this decision to leave a successful mission enterprise in its early days an 'ultimate sign of his love' for the Corinthian church, about whose welfare Paul was deeply concerned. He was eager to rendezvous with Titus in order to learn from him how matters fared at Corinth."[11]

Paul wrote, "For Christ's love compels us, because we are convinced that one died for all, and therefore all died" (2 Cor 5:14–15). Sampley writes: "The verb translated 'compels' (NIV) or 'urges on' (NRSV) . . . has a semantic range from 'impels' to 'hold within bounds/control.' . . . Paul can be understood to claim that Christ's love drives him on."[12] Paul brought the truth of the gospel compelled by heavenly love.

"Paul is shut in as between two walls by Christ's love for him. Because of this love, Paul has one purpose—selfless devotion to God and his fellow human beings. . . . The point is that 'compels' signifies a positive force. Paul cannot but follow his plan of ministry because it is God's plan. What Christ has done for Paul is the basis of the apostle's life."[13]

"Because we are convinced" (v. 14). "This last point helps to paint a picture of a Paul who was sure, even after the test of time, that Christ's love, exhibited so tenderly in his passion, was the dominating force in his life."[14]

The great task of the missionary is the participation in God's plan of salvation and the only proper motivation for this God-given task is love. "The love of Christ constrains us" (5:14 NKJV). The two form an inseparable bond—the task (making disciples of all nations) and the proper emotion (the love of God) in carrying it out.

As ambassadors of Christ, missionaries must know the world's lost condition and its need to be saved (Acts 4:12). But joined to this knowledge is the need for their hearts to be moved by the passionate love of God that inspired salvation's plan.

God knew man's lost condition and was moved by love to act to save perishing humanity. In like manner God's sent servants who know the truth of the lostness of man as revealed in the gospel and must be

11. Martin, *2 Corinthians*, 42, citing Rissi, *Studien zum Zweiten Korintherbrief*.
12. Sampley, "Second Epistle to the Corinthians," 92.
13. Martin, *2 Corinthians*, 128.
14. Martin, *2 Corinthians*, 129.

compelled by love of God to bring to those without love the message of redemption.

Missionaries must be envisioned by the commission given them (Matt 28:19, 20) and be moved by the love that sent redemption's victim to the cross to bleed and die for lost humanity. They bring the message that "there is no other name under heaven given to mankind by which we must be saved" (Acts 4:12) which is joined to the message that "God so loved the world that he gave his one and only Son" (John 3:16).

In the gospel, lost humanity is met with endless love and truth. The missionary is an ambassador of love and truth representing the God of love and eternal truth. As his spokesmen, ministers of reconciliation, speak the truth in love (Eph 4:15).

Truth and love must be the foundation of every missionary's life and ministry. Without love our proclaiming becomes legalistic and harsh. Without truth our proclamation becomes human sentimentalism—powerless to save and transform. Love and truth fused together become the power of God bringing eternal salvation (Rom 1:16).

Paul wrote, "I do not say this to condemn you; I have said before that you have such a place in our hearts that we would live or die with you" (2 Cor 7:3). Martin explains: "He now extends and deepens this commitment to them by relating to what extent he will go to preserve the relationship intact. . . . 'To die together' and . . . 'to live together' are two verbs that both tell how much the Corinthians mean to Paul"[15]

Paul expresses his love for the Corinthians with emotionally charged words. Paul's concern for the Corinthians went beyond the thought of simply losing what he had planted—a futility of labor. Rather being joined emotionally with them he loved them from the heart—their dying would be his dying, and their living is his living. His only desire was to bless them and see them spiritually prosper, going on to maturity in Christ.

To truly live out the gospel in another culture among people that are in many ways different than the missionary, God's servant must be emotionally joined with them through the love of Christ, living and dying with them—holding them dear in their hearts, wanting them to be blessed of God in every way—wanting Christ to be formed within them. Paul was devoted to the Corinthians—so missionaries must be devoted to those God has given them to love.

---

15. Martin, *2 Corinthians*, 219.

Paul's heart was passionately attached to his converts in Corinth. It was the deepest desire of his heart that they would remain in the faith and be totally reconciled to himself. This is Paul's apostolic spirit—a missionary spirit that reflects the call of a "sent one" to a particular people who live in a certain place in a God-chosen foreign land.

God in his grace places his own love in the missionary's heart for a people who are yet without the gospel. His love holds them in its grip. It is a constraining force. Love seizes the missionary's heart and controls the mind, directing every step.

God's worldwide witnesses are left with no other choice but to love—to love those to whom God has sent them—to give the love they have been given. Because of his love within them—that has captured their hearts—they labor to see lives transformed and the church established—followers of Christ becoming the living thriving body of Christ.

Paul loved the Corinthians because God in his love had sent him to them. Missionaries live and minister the gospel because of the love that God has placed in their hearts for a people who live in a certain place—the place where God in his providential plan has sent them.

"Paul has preached the true Gospel and asked nothing in return (11:9), except to be loved. The Corinthians should open their hearts to Paul, for he has done nothing to injure them. When compared with his opponents the apostle is the only one who truly deserves to be in the Corinthians hearts."[16]

Paul wanted to have a reciprocal bond of love between himself and the Corinthians. For Paul this was of utmost importance—a necessity. In his understanding, the love of God must form an unbreakable bond between himself and his converts.

He believed that love was the only worthy emotion that could truly bind them together as they both embraced and lived out the gospel of love. He knew if they could not learn to love him, who in all sincerity had brought them the gospel, they would never become a loving community.

As they were both joined with Christ through the love of the cross, so the love of Calvary within their hearts must also be the force that binds them together in mutual understanding and care. Paul argues that there is no reason for the Corinthians to reject this bond of love because he has in all sincerity, with pure motives and godly actions, as a loving father to his children, presented to them the gospel of life.

---

16. Martin, *2 Corinthians*, 214.

Love must always be the binding force of missionary labor. If there is an attempt to replace the power of Christ's love in our missionary activity with something less, his servants abandon the only God-given force that can bind God's people together in a Christ-exalting, kingdom-building manner. It is the love of God that is poured out into his sent ones' hearts by the Holy Spirit (Rom 5:5) that can join missionary with disciple and thereby build a growing faith in a community that will last for all eternity.

When in the missionary endeavor there is a striving for unity through another means—through human means—a bond is formed that will prove to be easily broken. Like the apostle, those sent to far-off lands must labor in love and teach those who are loved the importance of responding in like manner.

In reading through 2 Corinthians, the reader is presented with a bond of love between Paul and his co-laborer Titus. They brought each other encouragement and were dependent on each other's faithful support (2:13; 7:6, 13:13; 8:6, 23; 12:18).

One of the great blessings experienced on the missionary field is for the missionary family to experience unity through mutual love. This shared caring community brings great encouragement as love is experienced through mutual prayer, uplifting fellowship, and shared ministry.

This love often is seen not only in one's own mission organization but also in the shared fellowship between missionary organizations. Many times missionaries receive a lifeline of generous care and practical help from missionaries outside their own mission—often from veteran missionaries who are willing to share practical wisdom with those new on the field.

Love causes missionaries of different denominational backgrounds to emphasize those beliefs and practices held in common and to minimize the differences. There is a realization that God's sent servants are all working for the same master, and all are working for the same cause. It becomes a community of humble, loving, mutual service of those who are not looking for personal recognition but only looking for the advancement of the kingdom.

THE EMOTION OF JOY

Paul found the secret of having joy amid distress and in all the battles he faced in his ministry. Even in his most difficult times, when he despaired of life, having been beaten with rods, he had a supernatural joy that sustained him. "There were many events in Paul's life that inevitably brought him grief. The lost state of his own people, the Jews, caused him no little pain (Rom 9:2). Other churches for which he cared were a source of concern (2 Cor 11:28). But no doubt the Corinthians were a major cause of his sorrow."[17]

For Paul the emotions of sorrow and joy walked together. In every circumstance of Paul's life and ministry he refused to take the attitude of defeat. He had an always present fountain of joy. He often called upon the Christian community "to rejoice always" (Phil 4:4) for he knew it to be a great source of sustaining power in the Christian life.

He found joy in knowing and sensing the nearness of God. Joy remained in his heart because he found God completely faithful—always at his side. He had joy because he truly was living for what is not seen rather than the seen (2 Cor 4:18). His trust in God was a growing trust. God had never failed him, and he believed that God would never fail him in the future (2 Cor 1:10).

Paul had joy because he was committed to the greatest cause in which a man can participate. He had joy because God had called him and was using him, opening effective doors of ministry to proclaim the gospel (2 Cor 2:12).

He had joy because what he was doing was eternal and he had no desire to be involved in any other work. He had joy because nothing could stop him from knowing Christ in the fellowship of his sufferings and in the power of his resurrection (Phil 3:10).

Joy was his because he had entered the river of God's grace and was daily drinking of the life of the Spirit—he was tasting of the life of the powers of the world to come (Heb 6:5 KJV). He had joy because he had an eternal hope, believing in the resurrection of the dead (2 Cor 5:1–8; 13:4).

Joy is measured out to the servant of God who lives for the eternal rather than the temporal (2 Cor 4:16–18). Paul had joy because he lived only to please his Lord (2 Cor 5:9).

Paul indicates that his greatest joy came in his greatest times of suffering. " I am filled with comfort. I am exceedingly joyful in all of our tribulations" (2 Cor 7:4). It is in the midst of Paul's greatest trials that

---

17. Martin, *2 Corinthians*, 183.

supernatural joy springs up in his soul, sustaining him, giving him hope and strength to endure.

It appears that for Paul the fullness of heavenly joy could only be known in the participation in the sufferings of the Savior. It was during his greatest trials and hardships that sustaining joy would flood his soul renewing his hope. As a part of his commendation through suffering Paul writes "as sorrowing, yet always rejoicing" (2 Cor 6:10; see also 8:2). Paul knew that sorrow leading to joy was the experience of the "Suffering Servant" (see Heb 12:2).

Joy and sorrow often met in Paul's life and ministry. Therefore, joy in a time of difficulty should be expected as a part of the experience of every missionary as they bring the words of life to a lost and dying world. Today's ambassadors for Christ can know that God in his faithfulness will not only meet them with his comfort in the moment of suffering (2 Cor 1:3–7), but he will come by his Spirit and flood their hearts with inexpressible joy (see 1 Pet 1:8).

Second Corinthians teaches us that joy is a celebrating heart that rejoices in times of trial and difficulty. Real joy is a work of the Holy Spirit that springs forth from his servants' hearts in times of trial and suffering. It is in the moment of suffering for Christ's sake that uplifting, faith-filled joy is needed (2 Cor 1:24). It is the messenger of God who, like Paul, lives a cross-centered life that experiences supernatural, sustaining joy (2 Cor 8:2).

God-given joy in times of suffering brings glory to God as the reality of faith is demonstrated. In that moment, joy becomes an overcoming, God-given force to keep God's sent servants from the sin of doubting and becomes a means (armor) to crush the devil's head (Rom 16:20), rendering his attacks impotent (Eph 6:10, 11).

For Paul, God was his source of joy that he drank deeply from in his time of hardship on his many missionary journeys. Today's ministers of reconciliation, during their missionary journeys, have available the same well of everlasting joy during the most difficult times of life and ministry. Joy is God's supernatural provision to sustain the missionary, causing them to overcome in this fallen world. The missionary has this gift of supernatural joy given by the Holy Spirit to uplift his soul as he faces spiritual battles when the enemy wars against this soul (Rom 14:17).

The Bible says concerning Jesus, "looking to Jesus, the founder and perfecter of our faith, who for the joy that was set before him endured the cross, despising the shame, and is seated at the right hand of the throne of God" (Heb 12:2). Joy and sorrow were first joined together in the Savior as he suffered and died on the cross. Though there was great sorrow there was also great joy in knowing the result of the Savior's sorrow and grief. The sorrow brought redemption and the transformation of lives, bringing many sons unto glory.

In the same manner, in missionaries' lives and ministry joy springs forth from their souls in the midst of the sorrows of difficult ministry, finding joy's root and foundation in the Lord's own joy of bringing redemption to a lost world. It is supernatural joy given by the Holy Spirit, given at the moment of need, overflowing from their lives for the glory of God.

This joy comes as missionaries pray in the Spirit—as the Spirit prays through them—interceding in their behalf and on the behalf of a lost world. This joy springs up in their souls in knowing that as the Spirit prays according to the will of God, he is bringing into being the will of God (Rom 8:26, 27).

Joy is a uniting force. The missionary with the believing community rejoices together (1 Cor 1:24). It is rejoicing together in the grace of the gospel that brings a unity of faith in a maturing community of faith (Phil 4:4).

EVALUATING EMOTIONS

Missionaries are wise to consider their emotions. Everyone has emotions and at various times during the day and in various ways those emotions are expressed. This is normal since our emotions are given to us by God.

We see in Paul's life a wide range of emotions. Paul experienced deep anxiety, fear, sorrow—relief, joy, and love. Emotions properly harnessed can drive us on into productive labor in God's kingdom. Missionaries harnesses their emotions for God's purposes by letting the emotion of love be the foundational force of all their emotional expressions.

Emotions often expose what is in the heart. A person experiences the force of his or her emotions by what he has treasured in his heart. Jesus taught us that a person lives out of their hearts (see Luke 6:45). God's messengers therefore must often ask God to purify their hearts and to give them emotions motivated by the love of God within them.

Unrestrained emotions must not rule our lives. As missionaries the Bible calls us to disciplined lives, living out of the life of the Spirit within and the fruit of self-control that he produces (Gal 5:22, 23). Untamed emotions that are not submitted to the life of the Spirit can be destructive to relationships and to the cause of Christ. Emotions must always be tempered by God-given wisdom that does not react but seeks in humility to act in a manner that honors God based on true understanding and evaluation.

J. Alasdair Groves and Winston Smith in their book *Untangling Emotions* explain the importance of evaluating our emotions. They explain that our emotions point to motivations. What people "feel" about they care about. Emotions show that something inside (desire) is "pushing" a person. To have God-honoring emotions "we need new hearts more than new emotions."[18]

J. Alasdair Groves and Winston Smith explain the human struggle with emotions:

> Unfortunately, this kind of heart-centered response to our emotions is rare. Our instincts run mostly in the opposite direction: reflexively we attempt either to change the emotions themselves or to escape from them. To control the situation or run from it. While no one can deny that control or escape can temporarily secure more comfortable emotions, it's the worship of our hearts rather than our emotions or our situations that most often need changing. Emotions are simply not meant to be turned off and on at will. They are meant to be dealt with at the source. . . . Scripture is adamant on this point: our biggest need is for new hearts with new loves and reorientated worship, not for more comfortable emotions.[19]

The authors explain the process of evaluating our emotions:

> Once you have identified that something is happening inside of you and examined what is going on in that feeling, you're ready to take the next logical step: Figuring which aspects of what you are feeling are good and godly and which are destructive or selfish. This is hard to do! You will rarely find only good in your emotions or only bad. Instead, you'll almost always find good and bad mixed together. And you have a lot at stake; you wouldn't be feeling emotion about it if you didn't. . . .

They go on to further explain:

---

18. Groves and Smith, *Untangled Emotions*, 79.
19. Groves and Smith, *Untangled Emotions*, 80.

> When you know *that* you are feeling, have named *what* you are feeling as best as you can, and have decided *which* aspects of the feeling are good and which are bad, you are finally ready to act. While the options for action are endless, proper responses to emotions fall into two fundamental categories. On the one hand, we want to embrace and nurture the loves of our heart and the behaviors that are good. On the other hand, we want to resist and even starve loves and actions that are bad.[20]

Missionary John Bower finds himself comparing himself to Bob Stevens, who happens to be the director of their shared mission. John often questions the decisions that Bob makes, believing in his own mind that better decisions could be made and that he is the person who could make the better decisions. John often feels anxious and becomes irritable in field meetings as in his mind he places himself in Bob's position and feels he has better ideas and solutions. John loves Bob and prays for him, but he cannot stop comparing himself with Bob and seeing himself in his mind being a better leader than Bob.

John knows that Paul the apostle warns against the danger of comparing oneself with others (2 Cor 10:12) and tries to blot out of his mind his sinful comparisons, but they just keep coming back. What should John's emotions of being anxious and irritable around Bob tell John? How should he evaluate his own emotions? What is going on in his heart that is "driving" his emotions?

John has times of good emotions when he feels the love of God in his heart for Bob. But his negative emotions of being anxious and irritable are often present. John must ask himself what is provoking these negative emotions.

As John opens his heart before God, he begins to see a sinful desire ruling his heart. He longs for importance and recognition by others as being the most competent. John finds help through the gospel. He repents of his sinful desire to be important in the eyes of men and asks God to remove it and replace it with a heart of humility that desires only to love as Christ loves. He asks God to help him consider others better than himself (Phil 2:3), looking to serve rather than be served.

Destructive emotions must not control God's servants. Christ's messengers must allow the Holy Spirit to create within them God-honoring emotions by asking God to purge their hearts of selfish desires and fill

---

20. Groves and Smith, *Untangled Emotions*, 97–98 (emphasis original).

them with gospel-centered motivations. They must be ever watchful over the emotions as indications of hidden motivating desires.

Missionaries whose hearts have been renewed and sanctified by the Spirit will produce God-pleasing emotions that will be a positive force in advancing God's purposes. God does not want to rob us of our emotions. He wants to bring our emotions under the control of his word and Spirit.

God's sanctifying grace gives us new desires as idolatrous desires (the love of other things more than God) are rooted out of our hearts and replaced with God-honoring desires. It is selfish longings for other treasures—both desiring sinful things and loving good things too much—that drive our destructive emotions.

To understand our emotional responses, we must dig deeper than the emotional responses themselves and by God's help discern the motivations (controlling desires) driving our emotions and behavior. Understanding our hearts' desires that are "pushing" our emotions is essential for proper Christlike behavior.

Though Paul had a wide range of emotions, his emotions were always driven by a desire to see others know Christ and for them to grow into maturity in him. His emotions were submitted to his desire to please God and to honor him in everything.

THE EMOTION OF ANGER

Paul exhorted the Corinthians, "This will be my third visit to you. 'Every matter must be established by the testimony of two or three witnesses.' I already gave you a warning when I was with you the second time. I now repeat it while absent: On my return I will not spare those who sinned earlier or any of the others" (2 Cor 13:1–2). Keener writes, "Paul is treating his next visit to Corinth as a courtroom battle."[21]

One emotion that missionaries must put to death is sinful anger. While there is such a thing as righteous anger (God's anger is always righteous), most of our anger is selfish, sinful, destructive anger. Sometimes our anger can be a mixture of both. In reading the above verses (2 Cor 13:1–2) in the context of the entire letter, Paul appears to be acting in righteous anger as he warns of his third visit.

Missionaries, no matter where God leads them—wherever he has placed them—are called to use their emotions for the glory of God and

---

21. Keener, *IVP Bible Background*, 552.

for the advancement of his kingdom. Missionaries must be aware of their emotions and the effect that they are having on others.

Living in a fallen world the messengers of God are often exposed to provocations (irritants) that can lead to sinful outbursts of anger. Every culture presents its own set of provocations. A missionary's own cultural expectations of right and wrong—what is acceptable or unacceptable—will encounter contrary expectations and behaviors in the foreign country where they live. This can lead to interpersonal clashes and hurtful misunderstandings.

The missionary in his daily interactions must guard his emotions. If sinful emotions arise to the surface, the missionary must pause and ask the Holy Spirit to help them know what desires within are provoking these emotions.

People like to justify sinful anger, blaming their outbursts on the faults of others or difficult circumstances they have encountered rather than controlling treasured desires within their hearts. God's servants must daily humble themselves before God in prayer asking for every idolatrous desire within the heart to be exposed and purged by the sanctifying work of grace.

Robert D. Jones recounts an episode between two prisoners in the book *One Day in the Life of Ivan Denisovich*, written by Alexander Solzhenitsyn: "The titled character questions how his fellow prisoner Alyosha, a Christian, can cling to a God who leaves him in prison, hungry. Ivan challenges his Christian friend to ask God to provide food. Alyosha's response stuns the skeptics. Instead of asking God for food, Alyosha tells Ivan that they must pray, 'that the Lord Jesus would remove the scum of anger from our hearts.'"[22]

Missionaries who grew up in homes where anger was a "normal" part of life can have anger deeply lodged in their hearts. Those given to anger must daily in prayer yield to the miracle of grace that reaches all the way to the heart, asking God to "surgically" remove anger from the heart and the desires that provoke it. "As divine image-bearers, we are not passive machines but active moral responders, accountable to God."[23]

Like other emotions, anger finds its root in "beliefs and motives."[24] "The root of anger lies in unsatisfied ruling, 'I-wantsies,' unmet demands,

---

22. Jones, *Uprooting Emotions*, 48–49.
23. Jones, *Uprooting Emotions*, 47.
24. Jones, *Uprooting Emotions*, 48.

and fallen heart-idols. Cravings cause conflicts."25 This is why God's sent servants must allow God's eternal word to do its work of judging the thoughts and intents of the heart (see Heb 4:12). God's messengers need enabling and transforming grace to act as Christ would in a fallen world.

Jones further explains,

> It is divine grace to "help in the time of need" (Heb. 4:16). It is powerful grace that is "sufficient" in times of weakness (2 Cor. 12:9–10). His grace enables us to forgive those people whose offenses would otherwise provoke anger. It empowers us to progressively overcome long-term patterns of judgmentalism, venting and clamming. God's grace nourishes, guides, and strengthens us even when our bad circumstances continue.26

Jones continues, "We must forsake the 'my rights, my kingdom, my will,' type of pride that spawns anger."27 Often this takes a radical decision to forsake the anger that controls us, knowing that it is an offense to God and a hinderance to his kingdom (Matt 5:30).

The devil will uses selfish, sinful desires that rule within and that lead to hurtful expressions of emotion to divide coworkers and to hinder the work of God. God's servants must not give any place to the devil (Eph 4:27). They must yield to the Spirit and his sanctifying power for the renewal of their hearts (2 Cor 3:18), asking God to make them peacemakers (see Mat 5:9).

The ambassadors of God must give every emotion of life over to the controlling power of the Spirit. In such a surrender a missionary's emotions and underlying motivations become a God-honoring force for the advancement of God's kingdom on earth.

---

25. Jones, *Uprooting Emotions*, 57.
26. Jones, *Uprooting Emotions*, 68.
27. Jones, *Uprooting Emotions*, 66.

4

Identification with Christ

"When I discover who I am, I'll be free."
RALPH ELLISON, "INVISIBLE MAN"

"Define yourself radically as one beloved by God. This is the true self. Every other identity is illusion."
BRENNAN MANNING, "ABBA'S CHILD: THE CRY OF THE HEART FOR INTIMATE BELONGING"

"We have to be braver than we think we can be, because God is constantly calling us to be more than we are."
MADELEINE L'ENGLE

"I, John, your brother and companion in the suffering and kingdom and patient endurance that are ours in Jesus, was on the island of Patmos because of the word of God and the testimony of Jesus." (Rev 1:9)
JOHN THE REVELATOR

PARADE OF VANQUISHED

Boris Egorov gives us a description of the "parade of the vanquished"—the marching of German prisoners of war by the Russians through the city of Moscow. The Nazis always dreamed of marching through the streets of Moscow, but they never thought that they would be forced to march through the city as war prisoners. "Almost 60,000 Wehrmacht prisoners-of-war took part in the so-called "parade of the vanquished" on the streets of the Soviet capital."

The Red army, in the summer of 1944, afflicted heavy "catastrophic" losses on the German arm—making it the worst defeat for the Germans in history. In the offensive in Belarus (Operation Bagration), the Germans lost half a million troops, with some other formations that invaded "Soviet lands" ceasing to exist.

While the Bagration battles were still being fought, the Russians decided it was time to celebrate by holding a parade in Moscow, a parade "centered on the vanquished, not the victors." They wanted to lift the morale of the Russian people and show the world just how great the Russian successes were.

The Russians chose fifty-seven thousand of the strongest German soldiers for the long march through the city. To give them strength for the march they fed them well. They refused to allow them to bathe—wanting them to appear to be in a "wretched condition."

In secrecy, trains began to arrive carrying in the vanquished. Early in the morning on the day of the display, the residents of Moscow were informed of the procession. The crowds gathered and witnessed the prisoners "marching in large columns of 600 men, 20 per row." The generals came first outfitted in their uniforms and medals, followed by "more than 1,000 officers, and a host of ordinary infantry."

Most of the crowd watched in silence. A few cursed and some threw stones—but were immediately stopped. The Russian soldiers, being compelled to march, had their own reactions. Some stared back at the onlookers in hatred, others seemed to be looking at the surroundings with interest. But most of them simply stared ahead and marched without emotion.[1]

VANQUISHED CAPTIVES

Jesus was displayed vanquished upon the cross, perceived by the fallen world as a moment of failure—a broken forsaken savior who was proven false. But in God's eyes—according to his infinite plan and purposes, the cross was place of victory—the forsaken and shamed Messiah was

---

1. Egorov, "How German Soldiers Marched," paras 1–8.

enthroned, being victorious, redeeming humanity—being raised from the dead, breaking the power of sin and crushing the head of the serpent.

God chose a "weak means" to conquer evil. Brokenness brought complete recovery. The one despised was exalted. What seemed to be a failure was God's unending victory, imparting the gift of everlasting life to the one who believes.

In like manner missionaries follow the way of the cross. They are despised as he was despised. They are persecuted as he was persecuted. They are perceived as weak—as a people preaching a foolish gospel (1 Cor 1:21). They suffer and sacrifice as our Savior suffered and became the ultimate sacrifice. Jesus was mocked and jeered for his apparent helplessness, so his sent ones are mocked for their lack of self-assertion—living and ministering in the gentleness and humility of Christ (2 Cor 10:1).

Paul writes of a "missionary parade" of vanquished captives: "Now thanks be to God who always leads us in triumph in Christ, and through us diffuses the fragrance His knowledge in every place. For we are to God the fragrance of Christ among those who are being saved and among those who are perishing. To the one we are the aroma from death to death, and to the other the aroma from life to life. And who is sufficient for these things?" (2 Cor 2:14–16 NKJV).

Conquering Roman generals would march in a victorious procession after a victory in battle. They would return with some captives who would be marched through the streets and mocked as helpless slaves. The procession was performed as an act of worship to their god (Jupiter) who had granted victory in battle.[2] The triumphant general was honored to the place of making him appear to be a god. "It seems as if Jupiter himself, incarnated in the triumphator, makes his solemn entry into Rome."[3]

Witherington further explains,

> Several ancient Roman, Greek and Jewish writers mention the Roman triumph. Dionysius of Halicarnassus writes (30-32 BC) that n the victory procession "the trophies" were carried and that the procession was concluded with "the sacrifice that the Romans call a "triumph" (2.3). The triumph was to honor a conquering general who "drove into the city," that is, Rome, "with the spoils, the prisoners, and the army that had fought under him, he himself riding in a chariot drawn by horses with golden

---

2. Witherington, *Conflict and Community*, 367.
3. Witherington, *Conflict and Community*, 368.

bridles and arrayed in royal robes, as is the custom in the greater triumphs" (8.67.9f).[4]

There was an accompanying fragrance of burning incense in a Roman triumphal procession. It was a fragrance that covered up the stench of the captive slaves that were being paraded in humility before the people. Keener writes, "In the ancient world, incense was burned to offset the stench of burning flesh (cf. Ps 141:2), and the same would have been true at Roman triumphal celebrations."[5] Normally as was the custom, after the procession the prisoners who were led in triumph were put to death.[6]

In Paul's understanding, there is no salvation without suffering. Suffering brought about salvation in the very presence of the then greatest kingdom of this world—the Roman Empire. Jesus was rejected, mocked, and crucified by the order of Pontius Pilate, the representative of Rome, in an apparent victory of ruling injustice. But it was the rejected, mocked, crucified Savior who was the true victor, bringing eternal salvation to lost humanity. In like manner, the servants of the suffering Savior must also participate in the same suffering at the hands of the "ruling kingdoms" of the present fallen world.

"Paul seems to have frequently used the imagery of the Roman triumph to describe his experience as an agent of God.... God is the author of the death verdict who leads his own agent through the empire in order to reveal his own presence, precisely through the weakness of his agent."[7]

Paul saw his calling, life, and ministry as a person being led as a captive in the triumphal procession of Christ—a victory that came at the cross, the place of suffering and rejection. As a slave of Christ, he carried a stench with him—the same stench of the Savior who suffered the cruelty of the cross.

But Paul's stench of a vanquished captive was having an effect. To those who had open hearts and were seeking truth Paul's stench pointed them to the stench of the cross where they found the forgiveness of their sins. But to those who hearts were closed and whose minds were blinded the stench of the cross brought them death, leading to eternal loss (2 Cor 2:16–17).

---

4. Witherington, *Conflict and Community*, 367, citing Dionysius of Halicarnassus, *Roman Antiquities*.

5. Keener, *IVP Bible Background*, 503.

6. Witherington, *Conflict and Community*, 367.

7. Witherington, *Conflict and Community*, 368–69.

"The prisoner knew that the procession led to a violent death. It is not only through Paul's words but also through the very course of his life that he reveals God, because his life reveals the message and meaning of taking up one's cross to follow Jesus. Here we are at the heart of one of the great Pauline paradoxes: power in weakness, victory through death, and a victory procession that leads to death."[8]

Keener writes, "The Roman senate normally decreed public thanksgivings before the triumphant processions, so they were great celebrations for the victors and great humiliations for the defeated. Most of the captives were executed after the triumph. . . . Paul glories in the image of Christians as peoples taken captive by Christ . . . and this prisoner of war himself, who identifies with Christ's death . . . offers the thanksgiving!"[9]

Sampley elaborates.

> Paul's picture in vv. 14–17 does not portray him, and the representatives with whom he there counts himself, as *themselves* triumphing always. To the contrary, Paul here describes himself and his fellow ministers of the gospel as the conquered captives who, in the practices and according to the cultural values of his time, would normally be counted failures, who, at the parade's conclusion, would be slaughtered. It is *God* who always triumphs; those who are led are not themselves triumphalists—a picture that accords very well with what Paul says about himself and other apostles in a passage he had earlier written to these Corinthians: "For it seems to me that God has put us apostles on display at the end of the procession, like men condemned to die in the arena." (1 Cor 4:9–13 NIV). . . . Paul pictures himself as the one who, like captives on display, are led along by God in God's processional, captives who nevertheless are the ones through whom God is spreading the fragrance of God's salvific presence across the world. It is at one a humble and an exalted portrait of Paul and his ministry; Paul is not in charge, and yet through him God spreads the gospel.[10]

The messengers of God who are despised as a stench-filled procession of captives become an aroma of Christ (2 Cor 2:14–16). Martin explains, "Paul is the conquered slave exposed to public ridicule (1 Cor 4:9,10,13)

---

8. Witherington, *Conflict and Community,* 369.
9. Keener, *IVP Bible Background,* 503.
10. Sampley, "Second Epistle to the Corinthians," 59–60 (emphasis original).

... and at the same time, 'he is the joyful participant in Christ's victory celebration. It is, in fact, just the kind of paradox Paul loved!'"[11]

The vanquished captives share in the victory of the victor. Like the Savior who brought in a glorious new unending covenant (2 Cor 3:6–11) the missionary's testimony to that new covenant cannot be extinguished. The Spirit speaks through the missionary's humble life, and it becomes a powerful testimony to the risen Savior.

The lives of the ministers of reconciliation bring the world to a fork in the road. Everyone must choose and the choice determines eternal destiny (2 Cor 2:16). We are a fragrance (NKJV) among those being saved and among those who are perishing (2 Cor 2:15–16). His servants' lives, as they mirror the Savior's life, give humanity an opportunity to escape death—eternal death.

PAUL'S CONFIDENCE

Paul asks the question, "And who is sufficient for these things?" (2 Cor 2:16b). The work of the gospel is the work of sin-marred men trying to help other sin-marred men. Missionaries has no sufficiency in themselves.

Paul further writes: "Such confidence we have through Christ before God. Not that we are competent in ourselves to claim anything for ourselves, but our competence comes from God" (2 Cor 3:4–5). Messengers of God must go and make disciples with confidence (see Matt 28:19–20). But their confidence must be in God not in themselves. It is a confidence they have through Christ that they live out before God.

They are confident that they have a Savior who bled and died and three days later rose from the dead, bringing salvation to a lost world. They have confidence in the message that God has given them, knowing that the gospel is the power of God unto salvation to everyone who believes (Rom 1:16). They have confidence that Jesus is with them (see Heb 13:5) and that they go in the power of the Spirit, being filled with the Spirit (Eph 5:18). They have great confidence, not because of anything that resides in them but because of all the sufficiency that resides in the risen Savior.

Paul's confidence is in finding strength in weakness. He is "weak" and therefore cannot claim any confidence in anything that resides in his own life. He refused to claim anything exceptional about himself. He

---

11. Martin, *2 Corinthians*, 46.

is as weak as any other human. He lives with a remaining fallen nature (Gal 5:16–18). He had many positions, academic claims, and religious affiliations and achievements before knowing Christ. But now he saw that all he gained was of little value in the kingdom of God. He counted it rubbish. He set it all aside to gain the knowledge of Christ his Lord (Phil 3:4–9).

His confidence now was that he was in Christ, dressed not in a righteousness of his own but in the righteousness of Christ, having had all his sins washed away. Christ had called him and gave him the ministry of an apostle. He knew that his calling and ministry was not derived from a human source but directly from Christ his Lord (Gal 1:1). He now lived to honor the name of the one who in his mercy met him on the Damascus Road.

He lived his life not before the eyes of men but before God (2 Cor 2:17; 3:4; 7:12). Paul never claimed sinless perfection, but he did know that he was committed to Christ and to his cause. He lived every day before God, before his all-seeing and knowing eyes. He was a minister of the gospel who was consumed by the knowledge of the grace of God that sets free (2 Cor 3:17). He lived and breathed the grace of the cross and by that grace he lived for the glory of God (2 Cor 1:3; 13:14). His sole desire, through the enablement of the Holy Spirit's transforming power (2 Cor 3:18), was to live a life pleasing to God (2 Cor 5:9).

Missionaries must not depart to their field of God's choosing self-confident. They must go Christ-confident. If they are pridefully self-confident, they will glorify the power of the flesh—their fallen nature—and end up bringing honor to themselves and thereby rob God of his glory.

God's global witnesses must place their total confidence in God, knowing that their competency is found in him because of what he has done in Christ. Their lives must be hidden behind the cross. They must labor under the shadow of the cross. They must live as one crucified with Christ yet alive as he lives his life through them (Gal 2:20).

In their weakness they find strength through the one who lives in their hearts by faith (Eph 3:17). Though God's servants will fail, God will never fail. Therefore, God's sent servants must put their total confidence and find their competency in the overcoming one (see John 16:33).

For Paul the ministry that succeeds is a ministry given by God by a person called of God (2 Cor 1:1). It is a ministry that has been drained of trust in personal endowments and has learned to rely on the all sufficiency of God.

Paul had a life and ministry that submitted to suffering as the discipline of God (2 Cor 12:9) and allowed the trials and difficulties experienced to put to death self-reliance so that he could rely on the all sufficiency of God. He died with Christ on the cross so that Christ might live within him and through him in resurrection power (2 Cor 12:9).

Paul gave his faculties over to the Holy Spirit for him to produce his fruit (Gal 5:20–22) and grace-gifts through his life (1 Cor 12:1–10). He died to self so that as God's servant his own will was moved out of the way to make room for God to step in and reveal his glory and power.

Paul died with Christ on the cross. Dead men cannot fight their own battles. Dead men cannot do their own wills. Dead men cannot practice sin. Dead men cannot self-glory. Dead men can only glorify the one who raises them from the dead in newness of life (Rom 6:4 ESV). Paul lived as a dead man and so must every ambassador of Christ.

When missionaries are weak then are they are strong (2 Cor 12:9–10). God works to strip away pride and self-trust from his servants' lives. Only when God's sent servants are devested of their sinful selves can they truly be instruments of his grace to a lost and dying world. It is God's purpose that those who are crucified with Christ be the ones who carry out the "Great Commission."

It is only when God's ambassadors are emptied of themselves that the Holy Spirit can come and empower them to bring life to others. It is only the missionary who has been crucified with Christ that can make the kind of disciples that will truly advance the kingdom of God on earth.

God's sent servants are crucified with him, being dead unto themselves—to be truly "weak"—so that they can be resurrected to a life of strength in him. This is the kind of minister and the kind of ministry that God seeks. It is in "weakness" God's global witnesses can clearly demonstrate that their authority comes from God and not from themselves.

The missionary finds his complete identification in the Savior because it is he who calls, he who empowers, he who leads, he who opens doors, he who opens hearts, and he who builds his church (see Matt 16:18). It is such missionaries that a lost and dying world awaits.

PAUL'S BOASTING

Paul uses present day conventions of what Plutarch called "inoffensive self-praise"[12] to defend himself against his enemies that have infiltrated the Corinthian church claiming to be very special "apostles" and therefore should be followed rather than following Paul. "Paul makes it clear that the Corinthians should have undertaken this exercise for him, and then he would not have been forced to do so (cf. 1:12–14; 2:3; 12:11)."[13]

Witherington further explains, "Paul wants his converts neither to adore nor to ignore him, so he will praise himself in a way that is consistent with his own principle that the Christian boaster should boast in the Lord (1 Cor. 1:30f). This means that he will boast of his own weakness and sufferings in order to show that his triumphs must result from God's work through him."[14]

Paul is "boasting" not only to defend his apostolic ministry and to guard and sustain the church he has established in Corinth. He does what he feels is necessary to bring the Corinthians to their senses—attempting to help them through his letters to discern truth from error—the true servants of God from the false "super-apostles" (2 Cor 11:5; 12:11). He feared that the false apostles who had begun to disrupt the church for their own purposes by pulling people to their side would destroy the church.

Paul identifies with the "weaknesses" of the Savior—Christ's sufferings on behalf of the world. He uses his own "weaknesses" as an example of a true apostle and argues that it must be God who is at work using such a "weak" and dependent vessel (2 Cor 4:7). He points to the results of his ministry—the signs of an apostle (2 Cor 12:12)—to show that it is God who is at work through a fragile vessel. He is therefore properly boasting in God (2 Cor 10:17).

JARS OF CLAY

"But we have this treasure in jars of clay to show that this all-surpassing power is from God and not from us" (2 Cor 4:7). In this verse, Paul claims that God uses the "weakness" of his humble servants to accomplish his

---

12. Witherington, *Conflict and Community*, 385, citing Plutarch's *Moralia* 539E–545B.

13. Witherington, *Conflict and Community*, 385.

14. Witherington, *Conflict and Community*, 385.

salvific plan on earth. "Paul adverts to his just-described new-covenant ministry and the glory of God represented within it with his generalizing phrase 'this treasure.' . . . So grand a treasure borne in such a menial, frail, seemingly inept container makes it unmistakable that the power enabling the whole enterprise is 'from God and not from us' (4:7)."[15]

Paul gives the Corinthians a profound illustration of "strength in weakness" (2 Cor 12:9). Paul compares God's messengers to a very frail, cheap piece of pottery—a thin clay lamp that appears to have been in abundance in Corinth. These lamps were easily discarded since they were made of a cheap readily available material.

Witherington explains:

> Having such knowledge is a great treasure, even though it is kept in earthenware vessels (v. 7). This may be a reference to cheap pottery lamps made in Corinth and used for walking about at night. Precisely because of their thinness, these vessels let out more light. This frail form also makes it clear that the light comes from another source, so Paul adds that in his case his frailty ought to make obvious that the power is coming from God and not from himself.[16]

The pottery was used as an instrument of light but had no light in and of itself. All that the clay lamp could do was contain the light and defuse the same. It is its thinness and frailty that lets the light shine through it. A heavy non-fragile lamp of clay would have blocked the light.

God has made it so that his servants' frailty glorifies him as they yield their "thin clay" selves to him for his use. His purpose is to shine light through his witnesses in a dark and dying world. But they can only truly shine when they remember their frail condition and surrender their "cheap" selves over to his infinite grace—becoming vessels of his powerful light.

The Son of God came to earth born of a frail virgin. He was incarnate, taking on the weakness of human flesh, demonstrating forever that strength and victory over evil can only come through a weak vessel. Jesus in weakness was rejected by men and persecuted by the religious leaders. He was mocked, beaten, and crucified as a criminal. But the crucifixion that led to resurrection was God's strength to bring redemption's power to a lost world.

---

15. Sampley, "Second Epistle to the Corinthians," 81.
16. Witherington, *Conflict and Community*, 386–87.

In like manner, missionaries go on the journey that God sends them, acting like a clay vessel of light. In this life the missionary will never stop being a thin, cheap, fragile clay jar. There becomes a constant reminder that the "all-surpassing power is from God and not from us."

Savage explains that the power of God residing in earthen vessels is often unrecognized by the world:

> The glory emanating from Paul's ministry could thus scarcely be more brilliant. Still, many miss it. They fail to see the splendour of the new life in Christ irrupting in the hearts of those formerly engulfed in darkness. That is because the new life comes to expression in the humility of faith, a trait viewed with scorn by those absorbed in the self-exalting outlook of their day. Far from seeing the glory of Paul's ministry, the radiance of new life spreading to more and more people, they see only 'weakness.'[17]

Like Paul and his co-laborers, God's sent servants must self-identify as thin fragile "jars of clay" in order to be usable instruments in the hands of the Redeemer, knowing he can only use one who is "weak." They must accept that his light will only shine through a thin clay vessel that is dependent on heavenly grace and resurrection power.

Savage sees Paul's use of "jars of clay" as pointing most clearly to the cross of Christ:

> Yet his most vivid instruction in this truth would have come from the cross of Christ itself. There, in the most humiliating of all forms of execution, Paul discovered the surpassing power of God (cf. 1 Corinthians 1:23–24). Moreover, he realized that it was especially in the cross that the power of God *could* dwell. Had it appeared in some other place arrogant humans would have been tempted to usurp it for themselves and to treat it as an object of personal boasting. In the first century the cross was simply too repugnant to be exploited for personal gain.[18]

It is when a missionary forgets his frail humanity that he fails the most. God has purposed that the heavenly treasure, the new covenant that is filled with glory seen in the face of Jesus Christ, be contained in a deposable clay vessel. In this manner, in God's wisdom, the power demonstrated is recognized as being totally from above.

---

17. Savage, *Power Through Weakness*, 185–86.
18. Savage, *Power Through Weakness*, 168 (emphasis original).

Without this humility and dependance, God's minsters of reconciliation are always in danger of misrepresenting the gospel. They expose themselves to the possibility of damaging their own souls as they deny the meaning of cross where the Son of God in weakness poured out his life unto death as the only means of salvation. "The apostle's conviction [is] that it is only in human weakness that the power of God *can* be manifested."[19] When his messengers accept their humble, dependent "earthen vessel" status, there comes a release of resurrection power in saving the lost for glory of God (2 Cor 12:9–10).

Earthen vessel is Paul's metaphor for human weakness.[20] "The implication is clear: earthen vessels are *both* weak *and* inferior, fragile *and* expendable. Perhaps Paul has chosen the metaphor precisely because it can bear two meanings, because it forms a tidy contrast in verse 7 with both 'treasure' and the 'power of God.' . . . The glorious gospel is borne about by those who are comparatively inferior, the powerful gospel by those who are weak"[21]

Missionaries are but earthen vessels. In the work of the advancement of the kingdom of God on earth they find themselves in the place of weakness and dependency. The fulfillment of God's will on earth—the salvation of a lost world—is not contingent on anything that resides within God's sent servants. Their talents and the abilities that he has given them—the educational and life-experience skills we have obtained—are of no value unless they are nailed to the cross as the missionary himself is crucified with Christ.

Savage further explains the metaphor "jars of clay":

> A helpful commentary on this verse is found in 2 Corinthians 12:1–10. There Paul reveals he has received from God both superlative revelations and a thorn in the flesh (12:1–7). The thorn, he acknowledges, was given to humble him, to prevent him from boasting on the basis of his revelations (v. 7). This humility in turn served a supremely exalted function: it became the necessary pre-condition for the indwelling power of Christ (v. 9). In other words, *the very existence* of Christ's power in Paul was conditioned on the apostle's prior humility and weakness.

---

19. Savage, *Power Through Weakness*, 164.
20. Savage, *Power Through Weakness*, 165.
21. Savage, *Power Through Weakness*, 165–66.

This would confirm the literal sense of 2 Corinthians 4:7, that it is only in Paul's weakness that the power may *be* of God.[22]

The Savior has chosen by his resurrection power to live and act through his chosen world-wide witnesses. He has purposed to act through humble lives that know the frailty of their own existence. Self-seeking, self-glorifying, and the prioritizing of self-protection must be crucified, buried with him in his grave so that his sent servants can arise with him with his resurrection power within them and flowing through them.

LIVING DEATH

Paul wrote of his living death that led to the revelation of the life of Jesus. "We always carry around in our body the death of Jesus, so that the life of Jesus may also be revealed in our body" (2 Cor 4:10).

"Paul is manifesting the spectacle of the dying or killing of Jesus in his own life and is thus being conformed to Christ's image even in this horrible way. Living believers are always being delivered over to death because of Jesus. . . . But the effect of all this is that, in spite of such sufferings, indeed through such sufferings, the life of God shines."[23]

God's redemption can only be revealed through a "weak" life. It is as we participate in his sufferings that Jesus' life is revealed through us. Suffering is never wanted nor sought but is accepted as the portion of the messengers of God. "It is important to observe that Paul did not regard suffering as an end in itself. He was intent on a higher purpose—that of manifesting the life of Jesus in his body."[24]

Suffering for the gospel points to a world in darkness that often hates the light of the gospel. It is as the missionary, because of their commitment to the gospel, "manifests the spectacle of dying or killing of Jesus"[25] in their own lives that their lives are conformed into his.

Paul seems to be saying that the transmission of life that he addresses in this verse ("revealed in our body") can only happen in the crucible of Christ's suffering and that for every ambassador of Christ there is the same participation requirement. It is the fiery trials of life and ministry that come upon his servants that becomes the means where the Spirit

22. Savage, *Power Through Weakness*, 166–67 (emphasis original).
23. Witherington, *Conflict and Community*, 387.
24. Savage, *Power Through Weakness*, 175.
25. Witherington, *Conflict and Community*, 387.

touches his ministers in their weakness, allowing Jesus to be revealed in their mortal bodies.

Missionaries must be stripped of themselves through hardship, and thereby make possible the transmission of the life of the resurrected Savior to those living in death. Like Paul, God's ministers of reconciliation must bear in their bodies the dying of Jesus to see the life of Jesus manifest in their lives and ministries.

"All of his suffering has the effect of revealing Jesus."[26] For Paul there is no revelation of the Savior without the joining into his sufferings. Suffering is at the very heart of the gospel: God's "suffering servant" (see Isa 53) and his suffering servants. His messengers must take up their cross and follow after him. Without the self-denial of suffering there is no real following after him. Paul wrote to Timothy: "Yes, and all who desire to live godly in Christ Jesus will suffer persecution" (2 Tim 3:12).

In addressing 2 Cor 4:1–12 Witherington writes,

> This section of Paul's argument already foreshadows what he will say in 12:10 and 13:4. He believes that the resurrection life or God's power is already manifested in this life, and this is especially evident when one is afflicted, suffering or weak. Furthermore, his labors and sufferings are not just the unfortunate cost of apostleship or occasions to demonstrate his faith, but they are at the heart of his witness. . . . Over and over again, Paul describes his ministry in apparent paradoxes—strength in weakness, glory through shame, life through death, riches through poverty. He creates these paradoxes partly to show that there are two opposing powers struggling in this world for the control of humankind—God in Christ, and the god of this world, Satan, who has blinded unbelievers and can afflict even *apostoloi* like Paul. Yet strangely, this pattern of apostolic suffering can also be seen as a matter of being conformed to the image of Christ. . . . Perhaps most striking of all, Paul seems to believe that "the very existence of Christ's power in Paul depends on his humility and weakness." Where there is arrogance and boasting of the wrong sort, by definition there can be no divine power. Paul believes this because he believes that the power to change the world has come through the cross and through the preaching of it in the preacher's life and words. 12:10 must be taken as Paul's basic conviction: When he is weak, then he is strong. When he empties himself or is emptied of all but Christ, then indeed he becomes a true and open vessel, a true conduit of power, light and

---

26. Witherington, *Conflict and Community*, 389.

life in Christ. The Corinthians needed a whole new conceptual framework to evaluate what did and did not amount to being a true agent of Christ.[27]

Paul believed that the closer a person walked with God and the more dedicated he was to the cause of Christ the more he would be called upon to identify with the cross of Christ. God's servant would identify with the cross of Christ through humility, self-denial, and the acceptance of suffering and the rejection of this world.

"If I must boast, I will boast of the things that show my weakness. The God and Father of the Lord Jesus, who is to be praised forever, knows that I am not lying. In Damascus the governor under King Aretas had the city of the Damascenes guarded in order to arrest me. But I was lowered in a basket from a window in the wall and slipped through his hands" (2 Cor 11:30).

Paul uses this story as a prime example of his living death. In Paul's time, his getting lowered through a widow was a humiliating experience. Paul had to escape like a common criminal, being lowered helplessly out a window and down a wall to escape. He was willing to suffer this humiliation for the salvation of others.

There is no life without death. In the kingdom of God, life does not bring forth life. Rather it is death that brings forth life. The missionary dies so that others might live. The more that we are dead the more we can transmit resurrection life to others. The more that we are alive the more we obstruct the release of the life of the resurrection to others.

To be a true servant of the gospel, God's sent one's must find themselves nailed to the cross, sharing in its shame, suffering as the Lord himself suffered. It is this experience of humiliation that releases the power of the resurrection to bring new life to those still in the darkness of death.

In like manner, Jesus himself warned his disciples, "Remember the words I spoke to you, 'No servant is greater than his master.' If they persecuted me, they will persecute you also. If they obeyed my teaching, they will obey yours also" (John 15:20). To follow Christ is to be crucified with Christ and to be crucified with him is to enter into tribulation, shame, and suffering—his tribulation, shame, and suffering—finding one's total identification in him.

---

27. Witherington, *Conflict and Community,* 390; the quotation is from Savage, *Power Through Weakness,* 204.

It is only in "weakness" that the power of resurrection grace is released into the world, and because it is released through "weakness" it brings glory to God. Human glorification is extinguished, and all eyes are turned in amazement to glory of the gospel seen in the face of Jesus Christ.

POVERTY BRINGS RICHES

"For you know the grace of our Lord Jesus Christ, that though he was rich, yet for your sake he became poor, so that you through his poverty might become rich" (2 Cor 8:9). Jesus left all the eternal glories and riches of heaven that he shared with the Father and the Holy Spirit in all eternity past and for the sake of fallen humanity set it all aside and entered the poverty of human existence so that by his humbling a lost world could know all the riches of God's eternal and unending grace and love.

Paul is saying that only poverty can bring riches and that the grace of Jesus is the supreme example of poverty being turned it into an overflow of riches to others. Blessing flows to the entire world through the chosen poverty of the Savior. In the same fashion, the missionary too must become poor to participate in making the world rich.

Paul emphasizes to his readers where lasting wealth is found. Paul uses Christ himself as the ultimate example of grace as one who had all the riches of heaven but entered earthly poverty so that by the poverty he experienced, the Corinthians might be rich. This also explains Paul's abandonment of the riches of this world, riches of which some may have thought he deserved (2 Cor 6:10).[28]

Jesus is the ultimate example of sacrificial, generous giving with the purpose of enriching of others. In following the example of the Savior, the missionary's life must be a generous life. Missionaries receive great spiritual wealth in knowing Christ. God's sent servants receive so that they might give. Grace received is grace to be given. The missionary receives spiritual riches so that they can enrich those who are yet spiritually poor.

Just as weakness brings forth strength so only poverty brings forth riches. Both are the working of the grace of God. This is how the grace of God is revealed. This is how the grace of God saves and delivers. There is no salvation outside weakness and poverty. Weakness and poverty

---

28. Sampley, "Second Epistle to the Corinthians," 24.

release the riches of the power of Christ's resurrection life into a world of complete poverty to make many rich.

STRENGTH MADE PERFECT

"But he said to me, 'My grace is sufficient for you, for my power is made perfect in weakness.' Therefore I will boast all the more gladly about my weaknesses, so that Christ's power may rest on me. That is why, for Christ's sake, I delight in weaknesses, in insults, in hardships, in persecutions, in difficulties. For when I am weak, then I am strong" (2 Cor 12:9–10). "Paul depicts his weakness as a perfect avenue for God's power."[29]

Paul receives the response to his prayer to remove the thorn in the flesh: "'My grace is sufficient; my power is perfected in weakness' (12:9). It is God's nature to display power in weakness, to place divine treasures in earthen vessels (4:7). God's power is perfectly suited to human weakness."[30]

God has chosen to show his glory and reveal his salvation through human weakness. It is the way he has chosen to bring redemption to the world.

Witherington points out the differences between Paul's catalogs of struggles with the same sort of catalogs given by the Stoic or Cynic sages. "While Seneca defined a sage as one who was fortified against all the slings and arrows of outrageous fortune . . . Paul makes no such claim. Rather he admits his weaknesses. Nor does he claim to be self-reliant or self-confident, as the Stoic or Cynic might, but rather he argues that he is God-reliant and God-confident"[31]

The cross is the supreme demonstration of "weakness" imparting salvation. In the same manner God uses his sent servants in their frailty and brokenness to bring about the revelation of his plan to save the world. It is in this manner all the glory and praise arise to his heavenly throne as the only one with power to save the lost and downtrodden.

It was at the cross where God's power was made perfect through weakness. The brokenness and suffering of the cross, the place where the Son of God in humility bled and died, was the place where God revealed his saving, transforming power.

---

29. Sampley, "Second Epistle to the Corinthians," 27.
30. Sampley, "Second Epistle to the Corinthians," 27.
31. Witherington, *Conflict and Community*, 388.

At the cross, ultimate weakness and self-emptying become the means of the redemption of humankind. Weakness and rejection brought reconciliation. "Weakness" is God's chosen means of saving a rebellious and lost world.

The natural desire is to be strong, but God calls his messengers to weakness. He calls them to dependance on his enabling grace. Like Paul, God works to strip his ambassadors of their trust in personal strength so that they will learn to trust him. Stripped of their human resources God's sent ones find the resources of the cross. They find that when being separated from self-reliance God releases resurrection power through them for the salvation of men.

A demonic thorn in the flesh was a painful experience for Paul (2 Cor 12:7). He prayed three times for God to remove it. But in the end Paul found the "thorn in the flesh" to be a blessing from God. He grasped the truth that God's strength is "made perfect in weakness." Missionaries must first know through the hardships of missionary life and ministry that his grace is sufficient for their lives so that they can then offer the sufficiency of Christ to others.

In identifying with the cross, missionaries often face trial and hardship. Governments are unstable. There are coup d'états. Civil wars beak out. They work in places that are overrun with poverty and crime. They face drought, famine, earthquakes, and typhoons. They often suffer infectious diseases and ongoing tropical illnesses. They witness religious persecution and the destruction of church properties. Some pay the ultimate price in losing their lives for the cause of Christ. Many are looked down upon as propagating a foreign religion—as destroying ancient culture.

The manner of missionaries' lives—the sacrifices they make and the suffering they endure—point to their willingness to take up that cross and follow him. Vital to the gospel message is the reality of suffering experienced.

No one can even begin to calculate the measure of suffering Jesus endured to bring humanity salvation. His intense and brutal physical suffering was vastly surpassed by his spiritual suffering as he became sin—taking on himself the sins of the world.

Jesus' ultimate sacrifice cries out for the missionary to take up his cross. The cross speaks of the ultimate sacrifice of God's only Son. Missionaries accept to participate in the sufferings of the Son of God to find strength in weakness so that others may escape eternal death. Without the sacrifice of suffering there is no participation in the redemptive plan of God.

"For to be sure, he was crucified in weakness, yet he lives by God's power. Likewise, we are weak in him, yet by God's power we will live with him to serve you" (2 Cor 13:4). Paul's entire life, his total existence is lost in the death and resurrection of Christ. It is his total identity—what he lives for. He lives to know Christ in his death so that saving resurrection power might be released through his life for the redemption of lost humanity. It must be the same for ambassadors of Christ.

5

Incarnating Christ

"By being partakers of Christ incarnate, we are partakers in the whole humanity which he bore. We now know that we have been taken up and borne in the humanity of Jesus, and therefore that new nature we now enjoy means that we too must bear the sins and sorrows of others."

C. S. Lewis, "Mere Christianity"

"Man's maker was made man that He, Ruler of the stars, might nurse at his mother's breast; that the Bread might hunger, the Fountain thirst, the Light sleep, the Way be tired on its journey; that Truth might be accused of false witness, the Teacher be beaten with whips, the Foundation be suspended on wood; that Strength might grow weak; that the Healer might be wounded; that Life might die."

Augustine

"There they offered Jesus wine to drink, mixed with gall; but after tasting it, he refused to drink it."

Matthew 27:34

AN INCARNATE LIFE

J. Hudson Taylor was a missionary who embodied the principle of strength in weakness as he lived to incarnate the Savior to the Chinese people. Having arrived in Shanghai, China, on his tenth visit to China, J. Hudson Taylor fell ill and had to remain in his room. During this time of confinement Taylor wrote: "Ah, how much pains the Lord takes to empty us and to show us He can do without us!"[1]

On November 1898, Taylor, having recovered from his illness, headed to Chongqing for a West China missionary conference. "The journey took them hundreds of miles up the Yangzi, first by steamer and then by more primitive boats negotiating mid-winter rapids."[2]

In the middle of the trip Hudson received tragic news of the death of the first China Inland Mission (CIM) missionary to die as a martyr. His name was William Fleming from Australia.

Steer writes,

> Down in the south-west province of Guizhou, Fleming had been murdered together with his friend and assistant Pan Shoushan, a convert from the black Miao tribe. "How sad the tidings!" Taylor wrote to John Stevenson. "Blessed for the martyrs but sad for us, for China, for their friends. And not only sad, but ominous! It seems to show that God is about to test us with a new *kind* of trial: surely we need to gird on afresh 'the whole armour of God.' Doubtless it means fuller blessing, but through deeper suffering. May we all lean hard on the Strong for strength . . . and in some way or another the work be deepened and extended, not hindered, by these trials." These were sadly prophetic words.[3]

THE THEME DEVELOPED

Some writers believe that the theme of 2 Corinthians is "strength-in-weakness," a theme Paul develops throughout the letter.[4] Paul's commitment to "weakness" as the manner to convey the gospel brought him into conflict with those in Corinth. Black tells us, "The writer employed the idea of weakness as a central motif in these letters because he had no choice: the concept had become an element of the serious disturbances at Corinth and demanded redress."[5] He further explains, "For when all the arguments are condensed and combined, the difference between Paul

---

1. Steer, *J. Hudson Taylor*, 349.
2. Steer, *J. Hudson Taylor*, 349.
3. Steer, *J. Hudson Taylor*, 349.
4. Martin, *2 Corinthians*, 46.
5. Black, *Paul*, 127.

and his adversaries is essentially this: one represents an apostolate in weakness, the other in (false) glory."[6]

Savage gives further explanation:

> The things which the Corinthians find so objectionable about their apostle—his failure to boast, his timid personal presence, his amateurish speech, his refusal of support—all represent deliberate attempts by Paul to remain humble before an exalted God. . . . Paul accepts this caricature but adds the stunning qualification that it is precisely in such 'weakness'—in his mind, such humble faith—that true power, the power of God, becomes effective in his ministry.[7]

The inspiration for this conviction comes from the cross of Christ itself, where the principle of power working in what the world regards as a place of abject weakness receives its most striking manifestation. As a minister of Christ, the same principle must operate in Paul. He, too, must appear hopelessly "weak." He, too, must suffer because of weakness. Indeed he labours on the brink of total ruin, hard pressed, despairing, persecuted, struck down—yet precisely because he does, because he carries about in his body the dying of Jesus, the life of Jesus springs into action, rescuing his mortal flesh from ultimate destruction, commuting life and hope to increasing numbers of people and channeling the power of the new age into the gloom of the old.

Every missionary will bring a self-identify—how he perceives himself and his ministry—to the missionary field. Missionaries will either identify as weak or strong—being strong in self-reliance and thereby setting aside the weakness of the cross or weak in taking up their cross so that they can be strong in Christ. From the Pauline perspective, it is the "weak" missionary that will advance the kingdom of God because it is through weakness God has chosen to save the world.

GRECO-ROMAN WORLD

There was an overriding world view in the Greco-Roman world. "A spirit of the age or an outlook of the time, a sort of habit or fashion of thought which a person might assimilate subconsciously merely by living within a

---

6. Black, *Paul*, 85.
7. Savage, *Power Through Weakness*,185.

certain society or culture,"[8] that was the polar opposite to the world view portrayed in the gospel.

Savage further explains how this world view conflict was particularly pronounced in Corinth:

> Of all the cities of the Graeco-Roman world, none engendered an atmosphere of self-centeredness more striking than Corinth. Energized by upwardly mobile freedmen and their sons, for whom status was an obsession and self-boasting a daily ritual, arrogance and haughtiness were so commonplace that they could easily have been described as the 'wisdom of the age.' . . . 'Words of wisdom' are simply a verbal manifestation of the 'wisdom of the world', and audible expression of the proud, self-reliant, God-less outlook of the day. . . . He is opposing the sort of forceful and arrogant speech which springs naturally from the self-regarding wisdom of his day. It is because he fails to indulge in rhetoric of this kind that he incurs the criticism of his converts.[9]

Savage believes it is the conflict between Paul's own perspective on life and ministry and those of the Corinthians that causes Paul to further clarify his Christ-centered view:

> In each of the areas in which the Corinthians find fault with Paul—his boasting, his physical presence, his speech and his support—we have discovered not only that his converts are drawing inspiration from the social outlook of the day but also that Paul responds by adopting a position which represents the exact antithesis of what they would have desired in a religious leader. While the Corinthians will find his position offensive, Paul insists that it actually works for their good. The reason for this fundamental disagreement between Paul and his converts would seem to boil down to a conflict between two opposing perspectives: the worldly outlook of the Corinthians and Paul's own Christ-centered viewpoint. This is a critical observation, for it is precisely out of this conflict that Paul's teaching of power through weakness in 2 Corinthians seems to emerge—that is to say, it is the radical disjunction between the secular prejudices of the Corinthians and his own conception of Christ which spawns his paradoxical description of the Christian ministry.[10]

---

8. Savage, *Power Through Weakness*, 77.
9. Savage, *Power Through Weakness*, 78.
10. Savage, *Power Through Weakness*, 99.

"IN CHRIST"

Paul was very conscious of how he represented the gospel and the great responsibility to demonstrate the truth of the gospel in his manner of life and in his communications with the Corinthian church. Paul refused to adopt what was in Corinth the culturally preferred manner of self-boasting that was contrary to the gospel and to the example of the Savior. "The weakness about which he has been criticized (11:21) is really for him the only subject for boasting, for it is in weakness—his humiliations and sufferings—that Paul demonstrates his likeness to Christ, who was 'crucified in weakness' (13:4)."[11]

The theme of "strength-in weakness" becomes for Paul his way to theologically explain his understanding of incarnational living and ministry. Paul lived and ministered the gospel out of a belief that he was a person "in Christ." It was because he was "in Christ" that he could incarnate Christ.

As being a person "in Christ," Paul found his total identity as one who daily participated in the death and resurrection of Christ.

Savage writes concerning Phil 3:2–9:

> As a Pharisee he placed confidence in the flesh, now he boasts in Christ (v. 3); formerly he sought prestige for himself, now he loses honour for Christ's sake (v. 7); once he pursued his own righteousness through law, now he seeks the righteousness of God through Christ (v.9). It is obvious that Paul is contrasting a former life in which his focus was squarely on himself to a present existence in which his eyes are firmly on Christ. He was formerly too self-absorbed to give proper honour to Christ.[12]

Savage further explains: "This caused a *transformation of his mind* and forced him to concede that his own self-centeredness had made a mockery of the divine image. His mind was thus renewed according to the image of God. . . . By sharing in the judgement of the cross Paul's mind had been purged of adamic pride and refashioned according to the self-giving image of God."[13]

---

11. Black, *Paul*, 93.
12. Savage, *Power Through Weakness*, 135–36.
13. Savage, *Power Through Weakness*, 151 (emphasis original).

INCARNATION

Paul's participation in Jesus' death and resurrection was the means for him to incarnate the Savior in his own life and ministry. New creation (2 Cor 5:17) had come through Jesus' death and resurrection and it was Paul's desire to reveal that new creation life through his own life as one who died with the Savior and had risen with him to experience resurrection grace and life. This resurrection life is released into the world through Paul's ministry, persuading men to be reconciled with God (2 Cor 5:18) so that they themselves can enter into resurrection, new creation life.

Frank D. Macchia wrote, "Moreover, humanity does not need to relinquish that which is human to be ruled by the divine. To the contrary, humanity was made for the divine presence, to be its tabernacle and to be fulfilled by this! *Humanity was made for incarnation.* . . . Christ revealed God primarily by being one with the Father in essence but also by being perfectly human, for humanity was created to be the visible revelation in flesh of the Word of the Father."[14]

Incarnating the Savior becomes the task of the missionary. Missionaries must be a "visible revelation" of the Savior who left the riches of heaven, becoming poor by taking on human flesh so that the world might be rich (2 Cor 8:9).

The missionary must carry the reality of divine presence—the inbreaking of resurrection new creation power into the world—as they live embedded in the death and resurrection of Christ, calling others into the same reality, a reality that all men were created to know and live.

THE SENTENCE OF DEATH

Paul wrote, "Indeed, we felt we had received the sentence of death. But this happened that we might not rely on ourselves but on God, who raises the dead." (2 Cor 1:9). Paul's life-threatening hardships caused his faith to grow in a God who can bring the dead back to life.

God uses every trial of life that his servants suffer for the gospel to strip them of self-reliance and to further teach them how to walk by faith and not by sight. The missionaries' feet are swept out from under them as they realize that all human wisdom and strength will fail them. By

---

14. Macchia, *Tongues of Fire*, 215 (emphasis original).

faith they come to a deeper trust in the faithfulness of God. Missionaries receive "the sentence of death" to learn to rely upon the God who "raises the dead."

In laboring for the gospel, his messengers are to remain in the state of weakness. Like Paul missionaries are to carry about in their bodies the dying of the Lord Jesus. This is to be the way, the manner, the mindset, the attitude, and the reality of experience in their gospel-centered life and ministry.

The missionary embodies the cross and resurrection—they incarnate the crucified and risen Savior to the people God has sent them to reach. Weakness is the missionary's manner of walking by faith in full identification with the message he preaches.

The way of the cross must be internalized within the lives of the messengers of the gospel so that the resurrection life of the Savior might be manifest in bringing life to those living in death. It is in the identification with the death of the Savior that they become an instrument of resurrection life to others.

It is God's will that his servants be delivered over to death through the sufferings and trials of gospel ministry. In this death, resurrection life springs forth from their lives as the resurrected Christ lives and reveals himself through them.

Paul's call to incarnate the Savior began on the Damascus Road (Acts 9). With his encounter with the resurrected Savior, Paul is made completely helpless—his strength leaves him; he is blind for three days—in humility and self-emptying he does not eat or drink for three days. It is in this humbled, weak state of being that he is then ready to receive his calling from a man named Ananias who has received a vision telling him to go to lay his hands on Paul so that Paul may regain his sight.

Paul finds strength in the mist of his weakness. Everything is stripped away so that in that weakness he can clearly hear how God has chosen him to be the chosen vessel to bear the "name of God to the Gentiles, kings, and the children of Israel" (Acts 9:15 NKJV).

Paul will bear the name of Jesus in weakness. God tells Ananias: "For I will show him how much he must suffer for my name" (9:16).

Paul's apostolic ministry was to be a ministry that could not be carried out in human strength but rather one that would drain him of all trust in his own strength—learning in his utter weakness to depend upon the strength, help and guidance of the Holy Spirit. All his accomplishments in life—all his confidence as a law-keeper—was to be swept away, being nailed to the cross so that in his newfound weakness he would find the surpassing grace and power of the resurrection. "The vocation to a suffering apostolate is freely acknowledged, and Paul finds no reason to hide it, even if his detractors scorned his frailty and ragged demeanor (10:10)."[15]

It is this profound understanding of weakness that prepares a missionary to go and make disciples (Matt 28). It is the crucified missionary—who incarnates the crucified one in his own body—the one who has given up trust in the flesh—who has been brought by God to the realization of the complete futility of human striving—who has no desire for human achievements or the accolades of men—who is ready, no matter the cost, to go as a messenger of the gospel to a lost world.

Missionaries must continually turn their eyes to the "suffering servant" (Isa 53) and gaze upon him to keep their spiritual equilibrium and God-honoring perspective and to maintain their proper motivation. With the crucified one as the center of their attention missionaries find grace in their weakness and their weakness becomes strength as his resurrection power is released through their lives.

Like Paul, the missionary must first be drained of self so that God can fill them with himself. God's sent servants must be those who have learned and understand in their hearts that the flesh profits nothing (see John 6:63); that the flesh must be crucified (Rom 6:6); that God's messengers must become weak so that they can find God's strength to perform the ministry that has been given them of reaching a world lost in darkness.

THE CONTENT OF PREACHING

"For what we preach is not ourselves, but Jesus Christ as Lord, and ourselves as your servants for Jesus' sake. For God, who said, 'Let light shine out of darkness,' made his light shine in our hearts to give us the light of the knowledge of God's glory displayed in the face of Christ" (2 Cor 4:5–6). Martin records, "Of the various temptations which beset the Christian minister, one of the chief and deadliest is the temptation to preach himself."[16]

---

15. Martin, *2 Corinthians*, 80.
16. Martin, *2 Corinthians*, 81.

To preach oneself is to seek importance for oneself through the ministry. The preacher moves himself into the center of attention, desiring self-gratification and the accolades of others. Like the "super-apostles" (2 Cor 11:5) in Corinth when one preaches oneself the gospel is used for one's own self-advancement.

Preaching oneself leads to the deafening of one's spiritual ears. Instead of hearing from heaven and obeying, life becomes calculations and arrangements of one's own choosing based on one's own fleshly wisdom. Such people incarnate themselves rather than embodying the humble Savior. This was the manner of "ministry" of Paul's enemies at Corinth.

As with the false teachers in Corinth, so with those who preach themselves, every day is planned for self-promotion with a constant covering of their carnality with a "gospel façade." Acting as religious politicians they learn how to say the right things at the right time with a purpose of moving their life upwards, wanting more and more recognition. Every decision is made by first looking to the right and the left, surveying every opinion, seeking the easiest path of least resistance that will promote self-boasting.

The desire for importance in the eyes of men becomes a controlling force in the person's life. Being insatiable, importance becomes an addiction as it controls the heart and mind like a drug. Unfortunately, too often, behaving like Paul's opponents, missionaries who preach themselves are found on many mission fields.

Savage clarifies,

> Paul is distancing himself from arrogant speech as well as abusive speech. This provides an even firmer basis for supposing that he is rejecting the vulgar rhetoric of his day and not the classical speech of the intellectual elite. It also serves to confirm that the Corinthians are criticizing him for not attaining this more popular standard. They want assertiveness and demagoguery, high-falutin rhetoric. He gives then only words of weakness and humility.[17]

Paul says that the ministry of a missionary and all ministers of the gospel is not the preaching of oneself but rather the preaching of Jesus Christ the Lord. This is preaching "on a bended knee." This is preaching from a submitted heart. This is preaching from a surrendered life—surrendered to Jesus as Lord—preaching done for the glory of God—preaching of the

---

17. Savage, *Power Through Weakness*, 73.

death and resurrection of the Crucified Savior—the power of God unto salvation to everyone who believes (Rom 1:16).

Savage further elucidates 2 Cor 4:5 where Paul says that he preaches "Jesus Christ as Lord and ourselves as your servants." He says that the first part of what Paul says entails his preaching, since Jesus as Lord must have been a "standard formula in Christian worship in Paul's day."[18] He goes on to say, "What is striking is the second half of the proclamation, 'and ourselves as your slaves'" Paul indicates that a central part of his message "was his own humble service."[19]

God's sent servants can only see the Lord's glory through humble eyes. They can only be used by a humble Savior if they have a humble heart.

Savage tells us: "Here, then, are least two ways in which Paul's humility works out in practice: in willingness to submit to suffering and in his service to others. We may now be more precise about the way in which divine glory works out in the ministry of the apostle Paul. It works out in the same way in which it did in Christ—in humble suffering and sacrificial service."[20]

Savage joins 2 Cor 4:5 with 1 Cor 1:23 to show that "in Paul's mind this is a unity between preaching Jesus as *Lord* and proclaiming Christ as *crucified*."[21] In Phil 2:5–11 Paul clarifies that "it is precisely in dying the death of a slave . . . on a cross that Jesus demonstrates what it means to be Lord. . . . At the heart of the kerygma thus lies a paradox which draws together two seemingly contradictory features about Christ, his humility and his lordship."[22]

It then becomes clear why Paul preached himself as a slave of all (2 Cor 4:5). "The gospel which he preaches is being worked out in his life. He is being transformed into the likeness of Jesus Christ, a likeness which, as we have seen, comes to expression pre-eminently in self-giving service. Paul's behaviour among the Corinthians thus embodies the message he is proclaiming. His 'service' is indivisible from his preaching. He must, 'because of Jesus' . . . (4:5) preach himself as slave of others."[23]

---

18. Savage, *Power Through Weakness*, 153.
19. Savage, *Power Through Weakness*, 153.
20. Savage, *Power Through Weakness*, 153–54.
21. Savage, *Power Through Weakness*, 153.
22. Savage, *Power Through Weakness*, 153.
23. Savage, *Power Through Weakness*, 153.

Paul followed the example of Jesus who carried out his salvific ministry "in humble suffering and sacrificial service." It is the same service that is the definition of what Paul meant by "when I am weak." Weakness becomes strength for Paul because it is this manner of service that God chose to demonstrate his glory in saving a lost world.

IMPLICATIONS OF SERVANTHOOD

As God's ambassadors strive to serve God and men faithfully on the field of God's calling, teaching and living out the truth of the gospel, conflicts can arise as deeply embedded cultural traditions are challenged. One area of tension that can arise when the gospel truth of servanthood is taught (see Matt 20:26), includes counting others better than oneself (Phil 2:3).

Missionaries bring a message and way of life that demonstrates that the ground is level before the cross and all human divisions that place one group above another are sinful. This message often brings missionaries into conflict with those within the church who want to maintain their long held cultural positions of power and control.

Missionaries themselves and their teachings become a threat to the established cultural hierarchy, where certain groups are at the top and others are seen as less and placed below. This is prevalent where there is tribalism and caste systems but can appear most anywhere.

In wisdom and love missionaries must stand fast in their knowledge of the Bible and their convictions of what is pleasing to God, knowing that God is no respecter of persons and that such divisions come from the evil one. Through patience, biblical teaching, and modeling humble service—praying and trusting for the Holy Spirit to work the human heart—God in his infinite grace will do what no man can do.

COMMENDING TO MEN'S CONSCIENCE

"Rather, we have renounced secret and shameful ways; we do not use deception, nor do we distort the word of God. On the contrary, by setting forth the truth plainly we commend ourselves to everyone's conscience in the sight of God" (2 Cor 4:2). Paul embodies the paradox of weakness leading to strength with a clear conscience. Paul repeatedly emphasizes his clear conscience before God and men.

Savage writes,

> Paul has little option but to try to explicate the paradox for them. Accordingly, he commends *himself* to the conscience of his readers, calling attention to the very humility which they disdain (2 Corinthians 4:2). His aim is not principally to defend himself or even his ministry but rather to edify and restore his wayward converts (2 Corinthians 12:19; 13:9). Since he embodies in himself the truth about Christ (. . . 2 Corinthians 4:2) he regards their assessment of himself as a telling indication of their spiritual condition. Paul hopes they will judge him accurately (. . . 2 Corinthians 13:6 and see 2 Corinthians 1:13; 5:11), for if they do so they will proceed towards salvation and life, but if not towards perdition and death (2 Corinthians 2:15–16; 4:3). He never ventured to identify who is and is not in the process of being saved. He merely poses an implicit question: Do you see that my ministry bears the glorious imprint of the cross?[24]

The death of the Savior, which brought the world life, set the "standard" of redemption's work and gave us the perfect example of how to take up our cross and follow after him. "The dying of Jesus is archetypal. Henceforth all righteous suffering will bear a specifically Christological imprint"[25]

The call of the missionary is to bear "the glorious imprint of the cross." God's sent servants must present their lives and ministries to the consciousness of those they are reaching as messengers of God who have nothing to hide—as those who live solely for the honor of Christ.

Like in Corinth such humility will often incur misunderstanding and insult from those who seek importance, exposing the importance-seekers' own spiritual deficiencies. But the sincere missionary must take heart (2 Cor 4:1, 16) in knowing that it is in following the way of the cross that life-saving grace and power is transmitted to lost humanity (2 Cor 3:12).

God's sent servants' lives must point to the cross—the place of hope and redemption. The goal must be to incarnate the crucified Christ—his self-giving sacrifice for lost humanity. The imprint becomes evident when the missionary lives in the "atmosphere" of the new creation and in that reality is transformed "from glory to glory" by the Holy Spirit (2 Cor 3:18). The missionary brings the gospel by incarnating the gospel—its humility that imparts resurrection power.

---

24. Savage, *Power Through Weakness*, 163 (emphasis original).
25. Savage, *Power Through Weakness*, 174.

"JARS OF CLAY"

"But we have this treasure in jars of clay to show that this all-surpassing power is from God and not from us. We are hard pressed on every side, but not crushed; perplexed, but not in despair; persecuted, but not abandoned; struck down, but not destroyed. We always carry around in our body the death of Jesus, so that the life of Jesus may also be revealed in our body. For we who are alive are always being given over to death for Jesus' sake, so that his life may also be revealed in our mortal body. So then, death is at work in us, but life is at work in you" (2 Cor 4:7–12).

Missionaries are nothing more than "jars of clay." As fragile "earthen vessels" (NKJV) missionaries incarnate the one crucified for the sins of the world. In knowing that the all-surpassing power of God is only revealed through jars of clay, God's messengers cling to the weakness of the cross in daily facing the trials of the cross so that resurrection life may be revealed through their lives. Missionaries submit to the way of the cross—dying daily—so that life may come to those dead in their sins.

God's sent servants must stand in the shelter the cross of Christ and live every day in its shadow (Ps 91:1). The sufferings and insults of identifying with the crucified one enables his sent servants to remain hidden there as "jars of clay."

In these verses is found Paul's "apostolic testimony." "Paul's intimate association of his apostleship with Jesus' death is a major theme of his ministerial life."[26] This is how he describes his weak incarnate life and ministry as an itinerate missionary. "The 'body' . . . is thus both the locus of Paul's commitment to the Gospel of a crucified Jesus (Gal 6:14) and the medium of the display . . . of divine power."[27] Savage clarifies that Paul "is thinking of a process of dying, a putting to death, rather than the final condition of death."[28]

Savage further explains, "By claiming to carry about 'the dying of Jesus' Paul is thus making the remarkable assertion that he endures the same sufferings which marked the cross of Jesus. . . . He also endures it physically, 'in the body' (v. 10), 'in our mortal flesh' (v. 11). In short, Paul experiences—continually and physically—the sufferings of the cross. His affliction is an extension of Christ's."[29]

26. Martin, *2 Corinthians*, 87.
27. Martin, *2 Corinthians*, 87–88.
28. Savage, *Power Through Weakness*, 172.
29. Savage, *Power Through Weakness*, 172.

Savage continues, "There is a supreme purpose in carrying about the dying of Jesus—namely, to turn back the forces of death and to open up a whole new way of life. Just as human weakness is a prerequisite for divine power (2 Corinthians 4:7), so carrying about the dying of Jesus precedes a manifestation of the image, the glory, the new age and the fullness of life of Jesus Christ (2 Corinthians 4:10–11)."[30]

Carrying the death of Jesus is the calling of the missionary; to not only proclaim the truth but to embody it; to not only tell of the great sacrifice that brought redemption but to be willing to sacrifice all for the salvation of the lost. Like the apostle, missionaries must carry around "the dying of Jesus" in their own bodies through "always being given over to death for Jesus' sake."

The cross cries out "only death brings life!" Missionaries' lives and ministries must give forth the same cry on every missionary field: "I am here to die that you might live!"

There are not two missionary paths to choose from. There is only one path, one means of bring life into a world of death. Ministers of reconciliation must be given over to death so that life may be revealed in their mortal bodies—life that they offer to others.

TWO OPTIONS

Explaining 2 Cor 4:7 Savage asks the question, "Is it possible that Paul means exactly what he says that it is only in weakness that the power may *be* of God, that his weakness in some sense actually serves as the grounds for divine power?"[31]

Savage further elaborates, "Paul became convinced that there were two mutually exclusive options available to people: the way of human arrogance and the way of divine power. . . . If there is to be a demonstration of the surpassing power of God it will be in human self-negation (hence the message of 2 Corinthians 4:7). As Paul puts it in 2 Corinthians 12:10, 'it is when I am weak that I am strong.' . . . Why *must* the glory of God be revealed in human shame? The apostle answers, it is because only in shame can there *be* a demonstration of divine power."[32]

---

30. Savage, *Power Through Weakness*, 177–78.
31. Savage, *Power Through Weakness*, 166.
32. Savage, *Power Through Weakness*, 168–69 (emphasis original).

It is only in accepting "self-negation" that there comes to God's servants the possibility of resurrection power being released through their lives. It is in self-humbling that our hearts are opened to an intimacy with Christ and receptive to his resurrected life and power.

Messengers of God must choose: Do they want human affirmation and personal boasting which leads to a life empty of Christ's effective power? Or will they, by the grace of the Savior bestowed upon them, accept the humility and shame of the cross as their own, boasting only in the Lord, living for his glory and honor and thereby know the power of his resurrection?

To live in the shadow of the cross in admitted weakness will not lead to the receiving of accolades from others. Paul was accused by the false apostles who had infiltrated the Corinthian church of being of no importance and not a true apostle—someone to be rejected.

Men often like to associate with "important" people. They believe their associations is what gives them importance. They want "strong" people to encircle them to "strengthen" the perception of others concerning their own personhood and ministry.

It is for this reason that the one who ministers through the participation in the sufferings and rejections of the cross of Christ will not be readily accepted nor appreciated. It is easy to disregard someone who is perceived as weak and unimpressive.

"Weak" missionaries are often shunned and counted as unimportant. Those with fleshly minds will insult those deemed below themselves. Humble missionaries will be seen as unworthy of the attention of others.

God's servants are often ostracized because of their lack of worldly influence and inability to augment the egos of others. As Paul knew so well, this kind of treatment adds to the suffering of those who want to walk the way of the cross. It is a hardship that comes not only from rejection but comes from having to bear the burden of observing the unending carnal pursuits of so many (Phil 2:21).

The missionary has the privilege of "taking pleasure" (2 Cor 12:10 NKJV) in such treatment as being an opportunity to join the Savior in his sufferings—the Savior who himself was rejected and was put in the category of one who associated with "tax collectors and sinners" (see Mark 2:16).

MAKING DISCIPLES

It is the participation in hardship for the cause of Christ that most qualifies a missionary to make disciples and lead others into maturity in Christ. It is the "weak" missionary that can say follow me as I follow the crucified, risen savior (1 Cor 11:1).

If God's sent ones live in the weakness of the cross, every occasion becomes an opportunity for God to work. It is in weakness that his worldwide witnesses walk in the will of God, creating an opportunity (an atmosphere of faith) for the Holy Spirit to work in revealing the Savior's saving grace, opening the door for the making of many disciples.

It is God's sent servants' acceptance to participate in the sacrifice and suffering of the cross through the hardships of gospel ministry that becomes the means for God to work in marvelous and powerful ways, bringing many sons to glory (see Heb 2:10). Transforming, resurrection power is released through his servants' lives as they join with the Savior's suffering, as they take up their cross and follow after him.

The true heroes of the faith are the forgotten names of pastors, in distant lands, living out in remote villages, separated from modern conveniences and medical care. These are prime examples of those who incarnate the Savior in their lives and ministry.

They are fearlessly bold in going to the unreached; often in very difficult and resistant places, experiencing persecution—they pray, fast, boldly proclaiming the words of life to lost and bound souls. They proclaim the truth in meekness, demonstrating a God-honoring dependency on the Holy Spirit. They suffer much and learn to believe God to do what is humanly impossible. As the writer to the Hebrews records, "Of such men and women the world is not worthy" (see Heb 11:38).

The missionary must adopt the same God-honoring character and manner of labor. All must flow out of weakness as God's sent ones join hands with their national brethren in total dependence on God and together proclaim the riches of Christ.

APOSTOLIC AUTHORITY

"For to be sure, he was crucified in weakness, yet he lives by God's power. Likewise, we are weak in him, yet by God's power we will live with him in our dealing with you" (2 Cor 13:4). Being "weak in him" must be the identity of every missionary—the truth that controls their lives and ministries.

Paul plans to make his third visit to Corinth (13:1), planning to implement, if necessary, the needed corrections. Paul acted in humility in his identification with the cross but acted boldly in God-given resurrection authority when discipline was called for. Paul believed that weakness was a sign of apostolic authority.

Black explains,

> The only incontestable vindication of apostleship is weakness and humility in Christian service. According to this criterion, Paul can lay claim to superiority, not simply equality, over his rivals.
>
> Paul, therefore, accepts the charge of his opponents that he is weak, for weakness is a sign of apostleship. Christ himself was "crucified in weakness, but lives by the power of God" (13:4). Far from contradicting the gospel, the sufferings, limitations, and weaknesses of the apostle are wholly consistent with it because sufferings, limitations, and weaknesses of Jesus compromise the very core of the gospel's message.[33]

Missionaries, like the apostle, act in the authority of the crucified one. It is the humble sent one who is authorized to act to keep the church pure, bringing correction to the wayward (1 Tim 5:20; 2 Tim 4:2).

WEAKNESS PROVOKES SUFFERING

In addressing 2 Cor 13:4 Savage writes, "To be weak in Christ means to share in his un-self-striving, self-negating, servant-like, God-centred faith. Here Paul enunciates the related teaching that it is precisely 'because of' such weakness that Christ was crucified. In other words, it was the 'weakness' of humble faith that provoked the self-exalting of this world to afflict Christ with ridicule and scorn, and ultimately crucifixion. Accordingly, those who are 'weak in him' can expect their humble faith to precipitate a suffering like his."[34]

Missionary service demands the missionary to be a lifelong learner. It also demands a life of labor filled with many daily duties that must

---

33. Black, *Paul*, 90.
34. Savage, *Power Through Weakness*, 174–75.

be performed. But unless God's servant brings to the field of service a Christ-centered weak life, all energies spent will be in vain.

BUILDING A STRONG FOUNDATION

Paul wrote about the foundation he laid in Corinth: "I am jealous for you with a godly jealousy. I promised you to one husband, to Christ, so that I might present you as a pure virgin to him" (2 Cor 11:2). Paul was very concerned with laying a strong foundation of gospel truth in the lives of the Corinthians—a strong foundation that could be built upon. He wanted to see the church grow and spiritually prosper so that the grace of God would have free course to reach more and more people (2 Cor 4:15).

Those missionaries who, like Paul, slowly but assuredly lay a firm foundation on Christ and his eternal word, being careful to incarnate the message they themselves proclaim, will reap a strong, spiritually minded church that will have a firm foundation to grow and reproduce in a God-honoring manner all for his glory.

GOD'S POWER MADE PERFECT

"Each time he said, 'My grace is all you need. My power works best in weakness.' So now I am glad to boast about my weaknesses, so that the power of Christ can work through me. That's why I take pleasure in my weaknesses, and in the insults, hardships, persecutions, and troubles that I suffer for Christ. For when I am weak, then I am strong. (2 Cor 12:9, 10 NLT).

Since Calvary, only death can bring life. Only "dead men" who live in weakness can be infused by resurrection power to be ministers of reconciliation. God's power "works best in weakness." Black writes about the requirement of weakness (Gr. *astheneia*): "His overall objective is to show that God's power is more clearly seen in weakness than in Paul's own strength, for *astheneia* is not a hinderance to God's working, but the requirement for it."[35]

The Greek word translated "rest on" (2 Cor 12:9 NIV) has the meaning of abiding upon someone or something. Black tells us that it has the meaning "to take up residence in a tent."[36] That reminds us of "the

---

35. Black, *Paul*, 95.
36. Black, *Paul*, 101.

shekinah glory that filled the Old Testament tabernacle of Jehovah (Ex 40:34)."[37] Paul is telling us that a special anointing rests upon his life as he participates in and endures the same sufferings that Christ suffered.

It was in the times of his trials that Paul experienced the "overshadowing presence" of the Holy Spirit empowering his life.[38] Paul lived with this paradox in his life and ministry. "Only when Paul is weak in human power can he be strong in divine power."[39] It is in the moment of suffering as Christ suffered that the missionary finds heavenly power and grace descending upon his life, releasing saving grace to a lost world.

A CALL TO INCARNATE

Living in weakness is a call to incarnational living and ministry. God's sent ones live among the people to whom God has called them, learning their language and their many customs, discerning their religious traditions and demonic practices that have veiled their minds. Because of living among them and learning their ways, missionaries can identify with them, understanding their daily struggles. Enculturation becomes a part of incarnation—making the gospel understandable and applicable to daily struggles.

Missionaries must go as empty vessels that God has filled with his life and love. It is when a committed life and the eternal message of the cross meet, and weakness is filled with glorious resurrection strength, that the gospel has an eternal effect, seeing transformed lives ushered into God's kingdom.

The work of God in seeing a God-honoring advancement of the kingdom of God, will always be brought forth by servants of God who share in the humility of the shameful cross of Christ. The messengers of God must minister out of weakness and dependance on God.

Without this weakness the gospel proclaimed is distorted as the missionary's life fails to point others to the humble one who suffered, bled, and died for a lost and dying world. It is only in internalizing the weakness and shame of the cross that missionaries can be faithful messengers of God as they are sent to the ends of the earth.

---

37. Black, *Paul*, 101–2.
38. Black, *Paul*, 102
39. Black, *Paul*, 102.

Without the self-awareness of sharing in the humility of the cross, missionaries are in danger of bringing another gospel—a man centered message—and end up preaching themselves rather than preaching the Christ of the gospel (2 Cor 4:5).

As it has been often said, "You cannot separate the message from the messenger." Paul embodied the gospel—he was crucified with Christ (Gal 2:20). It was in suffering and sacrifice that he learned that when he was weak in himself, he found a profound strength in his Lord. For Paul this was essential to his life and ministry as one sent by God. It cannot be less essential for one sent by God today.

The gospel of a crucified Savior will only have its eternal effect when it is carried by those who have accepted their own weakness, living crucified lives. Like Paul, God's weak messengers will then see the glory of God in the face of Jesus, and his glory will become their glory shining on their own faces, empowering them to become the light of the world to a world yet in darkness.

Personal boasting must be crucified. Like Paul, missionaries must carry about in their bodies the "dying of Jesus." They must go and make disciples as those who are participants in the new creation, who have been purged of self-seeking and human boasting.

God has chosen to act through a paradox. He takes the weak things of this world to confound the wise. He takes the unknown, unrecognized, to reveal his plan of salvation. He chooses the weak to display his power. He takes his eternal treasure and places it in earthen vessels. He chooses ones willing to suffer to bring healing to a broken world. He uses the dying to reveal resurrection life.

The church must send to the ends of the earth men and women who have taken the cross as their own, who carry it in their hearts, who confess their weakness and dependency on the crucified Savior. It is through these servants that resurrection saving grace and power will be released for the salvation of many.

6

Glorious Gospel

"The gospel is not a doctrine of the tongue, but of life. It cannot be grasped by reason and memory only, but it is fully understood when it possesses the whole soul and penetrates to the inner recesses of the heart."

JOHN CALVIN

"That one of the greatest privileges and advancements of believers, both in this world and unto eternity, consists in their beholding the glory of Christ."

JOHN OWEN, "THE GLORY OF CHRIST"

"The Lord Jesus received is holiness begun; the Lord Jesus cherished is holiness advancing; the Lord Jesus counted upon as never absent would be holiness complete."

J. HUDSON TAYLOR

"Sing to the Lord, for he has done glorious things;
let this be known to all the world."

THE PROPHET ISAIAH

GLORIOUS MUSIC

The world-famous violinist Fritz Kreisler generously gave away most of the fortune he had made from his concerts and compositions. When he came across an "exquisite violin" on one of his trips, he wanted to buy it but lacked the funds.

Later when he had the funds he returned to the seller, wanting to purchase the "beautiful instrument." But upon his return he found that the instrument had already been sold. He went to find the new owner who was a collector and asked to purchase the instrument from him. The new owner refused.

"Keenly disappointed, Kreisler was about to leave when he had an idea. 'Could I play the instrument once more before it is consigned to silence?' he asked. Permission was granted, and the great virtuoso filled the room with such heart-moving music that the collector's emotions were deeply stirred. 'I have no right to keep that to myself,' he exclaimed. 'It's yours, Mr. Kreisler. Take it into the world, and let people hear it.'"[1]

The world needs the glorious gospel that the apostle Paul preached. As God's means to save the world, the gospel of our Lord Jesus Christ remains the "glorious music" of eternal hope to the human soul. Missionaries are compelled by God's love go to the four corners of the earth so that every man can hear it.

TWO ROADS

Paul believed in only two roads in life and that everyone is on one road or on the another (see Matt 7:13–14). There is the road to salvation and there is a road to perdition. Martin writes, "At all cost, it must not be watered down, and so falsified. The hearers must be confronted with an 'either . . . or decision.'"[2]

Missionaries must live with the sobering fact that every person they meet is on a road to an eternal destiny. They are either on the road to eternal life or the road to eternal death.

Martin explains that the two present participles in 2:15

> denote "those on the way" to either "salvation" or "perdition" (4:3; cf 1 Cor. 1:18; Phil 2:18; 1 Pet 2:7). . . . Paul's Gospel proclamation was intended to lead to the hearer's "salvation." . . . It is an eschatological term, announcing that the day of God's promised deliverance for Israel [cf. 6:2] has arrived, to be greeted by faith and with gratitude: see Rom 10:1, 11; 11:14; 1 Cor 9:22; 10:33; 1 Thess 2:16. But it is given a wider application by Paul as "apostle to the nations" [Rom 1:15] to include Gentiles [Rom

---

1. Innes, "Beautiful Music."
2. Martin, *2 Corinthians*, 56.

10:12–17]. The converse is . . . "destruction, ruin, loss," also an eschatological codeword for existence apart from God.[3]

The one road that leads to life is available to all men who will be willing to leave the road of death (through repentance) and begin a new life on the road of life. Every man begins life on the road to death and destruction (see Ps 51:5) and must escape the road of death through the finished work of Christ. The road to death is a path of destruction and despair—hopelessness and fear. The road that leads to life grows brighter every day as his disciples move forward in faith with eternal hope of an everlasting reward (see Prov 4:18).

Paul the missionary was transformed on the Damascus Road. Jesus in his mercy met him and forgave him of his sins and gave him a new life. He entered into the new creation (2 Cor 5:17).

There was laid upon Paul a burden for lost humanity and as a former persecutor of the church (1 Cor 15:9) he sees himself as a debtor to all men (Rom 1:14 NKJV). His life ambition was to bring the message of eternal life to those still in darkness. "Paul's primary goal in life was to glorify his Lord by winning men and women to the gospel, and this desire dominated everything he did or said."[4]

ACCOMMODATION

"I do not say this to condemn you; I have said before that you have such a place in our hearts that we would live or die with you" (2 Cor 7:3). Out of love for the Corinthians Paul was willing to set aside the right to his own life so that they might continue in the grace of God they had received (2 Cor 6:1).

Paul was willing to set aside his own personal preferences and privileges so that others might come to know Christ. "To the weak I became weak, to win the weak. I have become all things to all people so that by all possible means I might save some" (1 Cor 9:22). "Paul's ultimate purpose in accommodating himself to others is the preaching of the gospel and the consequent conversion of non-believers. . . . Paul voluntarily brought himself under bondage and was willing to accommodate his actions to

---

3. Martin, *2 Corinthians*, 48.
4. Black, *Paul*, 75.

others if only he might see some of them won to the gospel, for whose sake he does all things."[5]

Missionaries travel to far-off lands realizing that the darkness has not yet lifted. Men and women, boys, and girls, are still walking in the darkness of their sin, being blinded by the god of this world (2 Cor 4:3–4). Therefore, like Paul, they often "accommodate" by giving up their own personal preferences and privileges so that others unhindered (removing every unnecessary obstacle) hear, understand, and receive the gospel.

AROMA OF CHRIST

"For we are an aroma of Christ to God among those on the road to salvation—and among those on the road to ruin" (2 Cor 2:15);[6] "a deadly fume that leads to death" (2:16);[7] "a life-giving fragrance that leads to life" (2:16).[8]

Martin explains,

> The Torah is often called a medicine or drug . . . which may bring benefit or harm according to the circumstances of its use. In fact, the medicine is unchanged—it is the Torah; but those who come into contact with it find it to be either an elixir of life . . . or a deadly poison. . . . To Israel it is life, to the Gentiles it is death. . . . Paul's apostolic work is to offer Christ as the repository of divine knowledge (cf. Col 2:3), which may either be accepted as life-conferring or rejected (in which case it is death-dealing). In Christ is the remedy for sin; if it is taken, it is a life-giving medicine; if it is refused, the apostle's ministry acts like poison.[9]

Missionaries obey the "Great Commission" (see Matt 28:18–20), spreading "fragrance" (NKJV) of Christ to a world that is perishing. They call men to leave the path of perdition and join the multitude of other followers of Christ on the path of life.

As God's sent servants live in communion with the Savior—being filled with his grace and love—walking in the fellowship and power of the Holy Spirit, their lives put forth a scent of the gospel that has an effect

---

5. Black, *Paul*, 77.
6. Martin, *2 Corinthians*, 44.
7. Martin, *2 Corinthians*, 44.
8. Martin, *2 Corinthians*, 44.
9. Martin, *2 Corinthians*, 48.

on every man. God's messengers' aroma brings men to the crossroad of their life.

All must decide how they will receive ("breathe in") the gospel as a "life-giving fragrance that leads to life" or receive the aroma of the gospel as a "deadly fume that leads to death." Men encounter the aroma coming out of God's servants' lives and to those who accept it, by believing, the aroma becomes an elixir that leads to life. But to those who reject the message of the gospel it becomes a fume of death.

The salvation of God is known through those that carry this saving message in vessels of clay (2 Cor 4:7). Though these messengers are far from perfect, they are being progressively transformed by the message of grace they proclaim (2 Cor 3:18). It is God's purpose that his transformed messengers be the fragrance of the gospel in this world, imparting life to all who receive it.

Missionaries who live by the grace they have received are a fragrant aroma of Christ. They become an aroma of delight to those who bow the knee and accept the Savior. But the same aroma, because of the rebellious darkness of sin in the human heart is despised and rejected becoming an aroma of death.

This is a reality for every missionary on every field of labor. Missionaries pray for those to whom they are bringing the gospel, hoping for an openness to the message proclaimed. By God's help, they live before men as humbly as they know how. But God's servants know that it is the receptivity of those who hear that decides how the aroma of the gospel will be accepted. Only the hearer can decide if it is a "life-giving fragrance" or a "fume of death."

This spreading of gospel fragrance often calls for great patience, knowing that there is a time of planting and a time of sowing and only then can a harvest come (1 Cor 3:6–8). Sometimes, in God's infinite wisdom and mercy, this "farming process" happens rapidly, but other times it may take many years of faithful labor before there is a harvest. Missionaries must daily pray that the aroma that exudes from their lives will truly be to others the sweet smell of Christ, leading to life.

PROCLAMATION

> But having the same spirit of faith, according to what is written: "I believed; therefore I spoke," we also believe, therefore we also speak. (2 Cor 4:13 NASB)

The missionary must use every honorable means available to bring the gospel to every nation of the world. "Paul concedes as a premise (2:14) that God in Christ has launched a victory campaign, of which the end is not in doubt. The good news of messianic triumph has to be proclaimed, and men and women have to be called to share in the new age of the Spirit."[10]

Missionaries go in faith to the place where God has led them to preach the gospel and make disciples. It is a life of faith that is carried out in daily steps of faith, living by what is unseen rather than what is seen (2 Cor 4:18).

Sampley explains Paul's call to preach the gospel:

> Christ has died and been raised; believers currently share his death and confidently expect to share his resurrection at the end of time, at the parousia. At the center of this gospel is Paul's affirmation of God's grace, by which he means God's freely given, unmerited gift of new life in Christ . . . a grace that by its very inner power means that it abounds to more and more people. And how does it do that? The answer is only implied: At least in part, it is by Paul's doing what he is called to do—spread the gospel just as he has done to the Corinthians.[11]

It is by faith that Christ's servants obey and go to the lost proclaiming the death and resurrection of the Savior. By faith they are "given over to death for Jesus' sake" so that his life might be revealed in their mortal bodies (2 Cor 4:11), being willing to suffer for the sake of lost humanity, so that others may be brought to life.

Christ's sent ones speak of a Savior who gave his all in pouring out his life to redeem rebellious humanity. They speak as messengers who have experienced transforming grace and offer that same grace to others.

Missionaries speak a paradoxical message of shame being glory and weakness being strength, of a wisdom of God that surpasses all the wisdom of this world (1:25). They bring a foolish message that confounds the wise (1 Cor 1:26–29).

Missionaries proclaim a message that gives all glory to God. They are compelled by love (2 Cor 5:14) to speak, knowing that it is the only message that can bring hope to a broken world that is desperately lost in sin (2 Cor 4:13). They commit themselves to follow the example of the

---

10. Martin, *2 Corinthians*, 55.
11. Sampley, "Second Epistle to the Corinthians," 82.

Savior—to suffer; to serve; so that others may escape the darkness and join in the fellowship of the children of light (Eph 5:8) in following the Savior.

Savage explains how Paul used Ps 115 to explain his faith to preach:

> Clearly, it is faith which moves Paul to preach. In this he is taking up the mantle of the psalmist, quoting verbatim the words of LXX Psalms 115:1 "I believed, therefore I spoke." ... The entire psalm is of relevance to Paul. Its author laments the horrific nature of his affliction (LXX Psalms 114:3, 8), and yet because of the firmness of his faith he continues to speak, even though he knows it will mean further suffering. The same reality would seem to be etched in Paul's mind. In spite of his affliction, he too will speak; his faith compels him to do so—a faith borne of the conviction that in carrying about the dying of Jesus the life of Jesus will also spring powerfully to work in his ministry.... Faith thus initiates a remarkable cycle in Paul. By faith Paul preaches the gospel, which in turn brings affliction, which then produces in him greater faith, which in turn creates greater boldness of speech, which then provokes additional affliction. For the minister of Christ, the pattern of believing—speaking—suffering is inescapable and perpetual.[12]

Missionaries speak because it is in hearing that faith comes alive in a dead human soul (Rom 10:17). The Spirit takes the truth of the message and in his own mysterious and powerful way breaks through the hardness of the human sin-filled soul and brings new life—new creation (2 Cor 5:17; Titus 3:5). Concerning "new creation" Martin explains: "With Christ's coming a new chapter in cosmic relations to God opened and reversed the catastrophic effect of Adam's fall which began the old creation."[13]

Missionaries persuade men (2 Cor 5:11) to enter into the new creation that was brought into being by the death and resurrection of God's Son. They call them to escape the ravages of this dark, fallen world and be translated into the kingdom of God's dear Son (Col 1:13 KJV). They offer their hearers the forgiveness of sin and the gift of everlasting life.

---

12. Savage, *Power Through Weakness*, 180–81.
13. Martin, *2 Corinthians*, 152.

A MESSAGE FOR ALL MEN

Missionaries preach the gospel with the full assurance that the gospel is a message for all men. In addressing 2 Cor 5:14b, 15 Witherington writes, "The word 'all' should be taken quite seriously here. Christ died for the sins of the world, not merely the elect."[14]

Concerning Paul's words "then all died" (2 Cor 5:14), Martin explains that the gospel is for all men because all men died in Christ—the world's "progenitor of a new race, the representative of the new humanity."[15] God in Christ has made a way for all men to be saved. The "Second Adam" (Rom 5:12–21; 1 Cor 15:47–49) paid the penalty of every person's sin. On the cross he represented us all, taking our place. Each man can be saved by appropriating for his own life the benefits of the free gift of God that was bought at the cross and brought into delivering fruition through the resurrection.

The sacrifice of the Savior was a substitutionary death on behalf of all humanity. His death was more than sufficient for the sins of all of humanity. Therefore, missionaries go with a powerful message of full assurance. All can be saved because God's Messiah died in the place of every fallen man. Every sin was paid for so that all of humankind has the potential of being saved. All that is required is that they hear from the missionary preacher (Rom 10:14), repent and believe the gospel. All must hear because all can be saved.

EVERY NATION

Paul's use of "all" is also very important in clarifying the scope of the missionary enterprise. The gospel is the good news that must be proclaimed to every nation. Jesus died for every man and therefore every person in every community must have an opportunity to hear the saving message of the forgiveness of sin through the death of God's Son.

The price was paid for all of humanity of all ages. Therefore, it behooves the missionary to take the saving message to a lost world so that they can hear the liberating message and escape eternal judgment (see Matt 25:46; Rev 20:10).

---

14. Witherington, *Conflict and Community*, 394.
15. Martin, *2 Corinthians*, 131.

URGENCY OF RESPONSE

Like Paul, each missionary must live with the urgency not only for the proclamation of the message, knowing that faith comes in hearing the message (Rom 10:17), but also with the urgency of a response. "Behold, now is the accepted time; behold, now is the day of salvation" (2 Cor 6:2b).

From a heart compelled by love (2 Cor 5:14) God's global witnesses express an urgency—compelling the lost to enter the "ark of safety" (see Luke 14:23 NKJV). It is not the time to put off a response—tomorrow is not assured—hearing the gospel calls for a decision. Missionaries ask God for mercy, and they urge their hearers to respond to mercy in repentance.

Paul had a growing faith placed in his heart by God that compelled him to preach the gospel. He has a deep conviction that it is only in the dying of God's servants as they join in the sufferings of Christ that they can become a vessel of "inherent truth" to those perishing in their sins (2 Cor 4:12). "Christ's messengers are consigned to a life of humiliation and risk. And this is in order to leave the unmistakable impression that the power of the message does not derive from the ingenuity and skill of the pleaders but comes solely from the inherent truth of the message of God's word."[16]

In Ivory Coast deacons are trained by a pastor of a mother church to go and plant cell churches in neighboring villages. This multiplication process begins with open-air evangelism, gathering in a harvest of those that become the core of the new church planting. Deacons are then chosen to go and supervise the training of the new converts.

Every Saturday the deacons are taught by their pastor the lesson they are to teach on Sunday morning in the newly planted "cell churches" they are supervising. The teaching and supervision they receive from their pastor not only prepares them for the weekly teaching and care of the converts, but over time, as they have a growing understanding of the word of God and the work of the ministry, they become prepared for further responsibility. Under the pastor's direction, many of these deacons become themselves pastors and church leaders. The pastors who were trained through this process then carry on the same practice of multiplication through ever-expanding church planting.

---

16. Martin, *2 Corinthians*, 94.

GOSPEL WRITTEN ON HEARTS

> You show that you are a letter from Christ, the result of our ministry, written not with ink but with the Spirit of the living God, not on tablets of stone but on tablets of human hearts. Such confidence we have through Christ before God. Not that we are competent in ourselves to claim anything for ourselves, but our competence comes from God. He has made us competent as ministers of a new covenant—not of the letter but of the Spirit; for the letter kills, but the Spirit gives life. Now if the ministry that brought death, which was engraved in letters on stone, came with glory, so that the Israelites could not look steadily at the face of Moses because of its glory, transitory though it was, will not the ministry of the Spirit be even more glorious? If the ministry that brought condemnation was glorious, how much more glorious is the ministry that brings righteousness! For what was glorious has no glory now in comparison with the surpassing glory. And if what was transitory came with glory, how much greater is the glory of that which lasts. Therefore, since we have such a hope, we are very bold. We are not like Moses, who would put a veil over his face to prevent the Israelites from seeing the end of what was passing away. But their minds were made dull, for to this day the same veil remains when the old covenant is read. It has not been removed, because only in Christ is it taken away. Even to this day when Moses is read, a veil covers their hearts. But whenever anyone turns to the Lord, the veil is taken away. Now the Lord is the Spirit, and where the Spirit of the Lord is, there is freedom. And we all, who with unveiled faces contemplate the Lord's glory, are being transformed into his image with ever-increasing glory, which comes from the Lord, who is the Spirit. (2 Cor 3:3–18)

Paul in these verses is alluding to both the lives of the prophets as well as to Moses (see Exod 34:35). Martin writes, "A final appeal is made to OT prophecy, specifically Ezekiel's hope (11:19; 36:26) that one day God's word would be engraved, not on stone tablets ... but on the 'fleshly tablets of the heart.'"[17]

Paul explains to the Corinthians that conversion is a miraculous work of God anticipated by the prophets of old. Paul is calling on the Corinthians to remember the miracle work of God that the Holy Spirit has done in their lives and not allow the false teachers who have infiltrated

---

17. Martin, *2 Corinthians*, 45.

the church to rob them of all that God has done. The Spirit had reached into their lives through the gospel of Christ and wrote not on tablets of stone but on tablets of "flesh" (meaning a sensitive, receptive person).

Paul is describing, using the Old Testament, the promised and awaited new birth in Christ. The gospel is proclaimed, through the ministry of God's chosen servants. Grace prepares the heart, making it receptive to the truth. A believing life is set free as the truth penetrates and liberates as the gospel is written deep within the human soul.

Paul wants to make clear to his converts in Corinth that the impartation of heavenly life is not the work accomplished by men. It is outside the realm of human endeavor. It is a miracle of the Spirit of God that they must cherish.

Paul's description of new birth reminds the missionary that gospel ministry is not accomplished through human capacities. There must come a revelation from God to awaken the heart that has become dull (2 Cor 3:14) and the mind that has been blinded by demonic darkness (2 Cor 4:3–4).

Rather than a letter of recommendation, the means by which his enemies in Corinth used to "accredit their mission," Paul says that they themselves are his letter of recommendation; a letter not written on stone, but a letter that is the work of the Holy Spirit, who has written the truth on their hearts.[18] Concerning 2 Cor 3:3 Witherington comments, "The point is that Christ, through Paul, is the ultimate author of this letter. It was written not with ink but by the Spirit of the living God, not on tablets of stone but on tablets of fleshly . . . hearts"[19]

Christ is always the author of the letter that God writes deep within the soul. When the truth of the gospel is proclaimed, the Spirit takes the life-giving message and writes it on the human heart. God looks for any open, searching, believing heart and when he finds such a heart he begins to write—he writes the gospel message of grace and forgiveness deep within, setting the soul free.

God's timing of when he opens a heart is a mystery of his own eternal providence. The awakening of the soul often takes persistent prayer (Col 4:2) and the sowing of seed over an extended period of time (see Matthew 13:1–9). The soil of the human heart becomes receptive as the truth is sown and patiently watered. A heart must be prepared to receive

---

18. Martin, *2 Corinthians*, 45.
19. Witherington, *Conflict and Community*, 378.

the truth; and only God can make that preparation through his word and Spirit.

Often a person hears the gospel from multiple sources (gospel literature, radio, internet) and has personal encounters with followers of Christ over a period of years before the person's mind understands and the heart finally cracks open to saving love and mercy. A light must be turned on and only God in his merciful patience can throw the switch (see 2 Pet 3:9).

There must be a watchfulness by God's sent ones, continuing to stand in faith, believing for what often seems like an impossibility—always needing a miracle. God's sent servants must believe that hard ground will be softened and that the veil of the darkness of the power of sin will be lifted (2 Cor 3:16). Like farmers, missionaries continue to sow and pray for awakening rains—rain to soak the dry and resistant land of the human heart and miraculously bring forth a crop to be harvested for the glory of our Lord and Savior Jesus Christ.

Ambassadors of Christ go to their God-chosen field of labor trusting in the faithfulness of God. They stand upon the promise that the truth of the gospel never returns empty but accomplishes the purpose of God in saving and liberating souls from sin and Satan (see Isa 55:11).

This calls for endurance and faithfulness on God's messengers of reconciliation. When a great harvest on a missionary field of labor is seen, often forgotten is all the sowing and watering that took place over many years, which now is bearing fruit. Missionaries must believe Paul's exhortation to not become weary in doing good for God is faithful and they will reap a harvest if they do not faint (Gal 6:9).

Only God, by his Spirit, can write the gospel on the human heart. God created us to live from the motivations of our hearts (Luke 6:45). Men change when their heart changes. Only as God writes eternal truth upon their hearts can men become obedient children of God.

As missionaries go around the world to make disciples they must go with a sensitivity to the Holy Spirit and a profound belief in the message of the gospel. God's sent servants empowered by the Spirit (see Acts 1:8) with the word of God stored like fire within their bones (see Jer 20:9) proclaim the gospel, believing God to write it on "the tablets of human hearts."

It is the word of God in the proclamation of the gospel joined to Spirit empowerment that sets the souls of men free. For men to be saved, the Spirit must do a miracle by engraving the truth on the human heart.

Like Paul, God's Spirit-filled missionaries fulfill their calling despite their frailty, refusing to rely on human devices, surrendering mind, soul, and body to the Holy Spirit and his eternal dynamic power. In the power of the Spirit, their lives conform both inwardly and outwardly to the gospel as they daily demonstrate the gospel's power in their own lives as a testimony to the reality of saving grace.[20]

Paul's description of the Corinthian converts as "letters of recommendation" is a reminder of the power of world missions. Lives are changed in profound ways. Change comes deep within the human heart, leading to Christlike living. Through changed lives whole communities are then affected.

This effect occurs as those that have had the gospel written on their hearts are observed by neighbors in their communities. Often knowing the person before their conversion, observers are amazed at the dramatic change that has taken place. They realize that the change they see in the person's life must have come from a powerful source, leading to the opportunity for witness and for more "letters" to be written.

GLORIOUS NEW COVENANT

Martin comments about Paul's view of the "new covenant": "So Paul paradoxically gives a certain measure of approval to the OT idea of the Sinai covenant as expressing God's glory. But the good is now replaced by the better; indeed, by the best, which elsewhere Paul puts in more personal language: 'the surpassing . . . worth of knowing Christ Jesus my Lord' (Phil 3:8)."[21]

Concerning Paul's description of the relationship of the old covenant to the new Sampley writes, "He knows that the old covenant had glory, but, being convinced that the new covenant's glory (and, therefore, his ministry) so exceeds the earlier glory, he says that the new glory is so dazzling as to make the earlier glory seem to be no glory at all (3:10)."[22]

Martin explains 2 Cor 3:13: "Moses' face was lighted up with a radiance, and it was such an aura that repelled the Israelites. The same radiant brilliance required the placing of a veil over his face . . . ('to prevent the Israelites from fixing their eyes [to see] the significance of what was about

---

20. Black, *Paul*, 65.
21. Martin, *2 Corinthians*, 64.
22. Sampley, "Second Epistle to the Corinthians," 28.

to be done away').":23 Keener addresses the same verse: "Moses' glory had to be covered (Ex 34:30, 33–35)—unlike Paul's forthright speech (v. 12)—and would always fade away—unlike the glory of Paul's message, revealed through the Spirit who came to reside in believers."24

Paul's point is that we must leave what has faded and less glorious for the glory that "excels" (NKJV). Law-keeping could not produce the righteousness (2 Cor 3:9) that God required and therefore in God's wisdom it was replaced by something much more glorious and lasting.

Now is the time of infinite grace and liberty. Missionaries proclaim a glorious gospel based upon the "best" covenant.

The gospel that God's servants proclaim is glorious because it is based upon a glorious new covenant. They offer the world a glorious gospel of grace that awakens the dull mind and lifts the veil of spiritual darkness (2 Cor 3:14–16) and brings to the whole world a glorious Savior who gloriously sets the captive free.

God's sent servants must not allow their hearts to return to the old fading glory, turning to that which will always fail (2 Cor 3:6). God's sent servants must cling to the cross of Christ and to the freedom that the cross daily imparts to the human soul.

The truth of the gospel and the freedom it imparts to minds and hearts will never fade or pass away. This liberty, freely given by God, is a glory that will last for eternity. It is the liberty of the freedom of sins freely forgiven based on the eternal covenant, which is infused with the radiant life of the Spirit. Living in this freedom, missionaries can impart freedom.

SPIRIT FREEDOM AND DEPENDENCY

"Now the Lord is the Spirit, and where the Spirit of the Lord is, there is freedom" (2 Cor 3:17). Witherington gives clarity concerning this verse: "Paul is saying, 'Now when I say "Lord," I mean the Spirit.' That is, it is the Spirit of the Lord that unveils the human heart and lays it open to receive the truth and to gaze intently on the face of Christ. . . . The Israelites must turn to the Spirit, the Spirit of the Lord, if they wish to change, for only the Spirit gives life and freedom."25

---

23. Martin, *2 Corinthians*, 67.
24. Keener, *IVP Bible Background*, 504.
25. Witherington, *Conflict and Community*, 382.

Missionaries must live Spirit-filled lives, living in God-honoring, grace-filled freedom (2 Cor 3:6,17). God's servants must be progressively and gloriously transformed by the Spirit (2 Cor 3:18).

Spirit-filled missionaries (Eph 5:18) must walk in the freedom of grace in order to impart freedom to others. To be filled with the Spirit is to walk in the freedom of the Spirit. God's sent servants must set aside every form of legalism (outward and inward) that leads to death (2 Cor 4:6) and surrender to the Spirit who imparts life.

Spirit-empowered missionaries live in liberty to obey the word of God out of a love for the Savior to whom they belong, wanting to please him in everything (2 Cor 5:9). Because they are indwelt by the Spirit (2 Cor 5:5), and they have been baptized in the power of the Spirit (see Acts 2:1–4), God's global witnesses put no confidence in the flesh (Phil 3:3), seeking daily to surrender themselves to the Spirit of the living God.

The missionary is to go as one who is dependent on the Holy Spirit. "Paul succeeded in his ministry in spite of his weaknesses because he discarded mere human helps and relied solely upon the divine *pneuma* and *dynamis*."[26] Missionaries must daily seek his guidance to be led of the Spirit, knowing his voice and direction (see Acts 16:6–10).

God's global witnesses walk daily in the Spirit, being led by the Spirit (Gal 5:16–18). They must wait in prayer for the Spirit to come and fill them, empowering them (Acts 1:8), being refilled with the Spirit according to the spiritual urgency of the moment (see Acts 4:29–31).

God's sent ones need the Spirit to lead them into all truth (see John 16:13). They need his daily comfort in all their trials (se John 16:7 KJV). They must have the wisdom of the Spirit, including the gift of the word of wisdom (1 Cor 12:8).

God's sent servants can experience edification—the building up of their faith—by praying in the Holy Spirit (1 Cor 14:4; Jude 1:20). They are to be people full of the Spirit (see Acts 7:55), producing the fruit of the Spirit (Gal 5:20–22).

Missionaries are to develop a sensitivity to the Spirit, believing that the Holy Spirit will manifest his gifts through their lives according to his will and purpose (1 Cor 12:7). They must surrender to the Holy Spirit, asking and believing that he will glorify the name of Jesus through their lives (see John 16:14). Ambassadors for Christ are to be channels for the

---

26. Black, *Paul*, 66.

Holy Spirit, proclaiming the gospel, believing that he will confirm the word of God with signs following (see Mark 16:20).

God's ambassadors should be known as people of the Spirit, who live in the freedom of the Spirit, always conscious that the letter kills and that it is the Spirit that gives life (2 Cor 3:6). They are to speak in the boldness of the Spirit (see Acts 2:14) so that when the word of God goes forth through their lives, bondages are broken, and men and women set free.

SANCTIFICATION

"And we all, who with unveiled faces contemplate the Lord's glory, are being transformed into his image with ever-increasing glory, which comes from the Lord, who is the Spirit" (2 Cor 3:18). This is one of the most profound verses in Scripture concerning sanctification through the transforming power of the Spirit. Keener writes, "For Paul the divine image and glory obscured in Adam are restored in Christ."[27]

By faith, through the Spirit's help, God's ambassadors gaze upon the sinless Son of God and contemplate his glory and through that gaze they are changed. They see his beauty, and his perfection, and that daily beholding affects them—his perfection touches their souls and from deep within they are transformed.

Paul's description of transformation must be understood in the context of the experience of Moses. Moses was bathed in the very presence of God and by that glorious presence was changed—shot through with the glory of God.

The light of God, his kindness and goodness, had so touched Moses as he remained in his presence that the glory of God rested on him and something glorious happened to Moses. The supernatural light of God's glory could be seen on his face.

Paul tells us that those under the new covenant behold God's glory even more plainly than Moses (see Exod 33:20); thus, like Moses, they are transformed by the Spirit to reflect God's glory. As God's servants are changed as they wait upon God in the secret place of prayer on all the mission fields of the world. God's glorious presence brings ever-growing, Christlike change.

Missionaries not only preach a message of escape from eternal destruction, but a message that is glorious to transform. His messengers

---

27. Keener, *IVP Bible Background*, 505.

preach a glorious message based on a new glorious covenant sealed in Christ's blood (see Mark 14:24) that has power to save and transform, thereby imparting Christlikeness.

The weakness of the missionary's flesh (see Mark 14:38) calls for continual transformation in the process of daily sanctification. God's sent servants' weakness is transformed into strength as the grace of God by the Spirit of God removes the old and replaces it with the new (Eph 4:22–29).

Savage helps us understand the phase "are being transformed into the same image" in 2 Cor 3:18. He wonders why Paul shifted from "glory" to "image" in explaining transformation since in the same verse (2 Cor 4:4) Paul is clearly referring back to the glory of the Lord.[28]

Savage explains that in using "image" rather than "glory" Paul is

> drawing attention to the visible character, the salient image, of Jesus Christ. He is underscoring the fact that Christ, in his resolve to live for God's glory and not his own, and in his act of consummate self-sacrifice on the cross, demonstrates not only what God is like but also, dramatically, what humans ought to be like. They ought to manifest the same self-emptying character which Christ displayed on the cross. They ought to be "transformed into the same image."[29]

It is vital for missionaries who bring the gospel to a lost world to be committed to progressive sanctification. God's sent servants bring a gospel that empowers for change—a change that includes self-emptying—the old self being nailed to the cross and by the working of the Spirit of grace, transformed to take on the character of the Crucified one.

Sanctification of God's messengers is from glory to glory (3:18)—God imparting his glory within his sent ones, making them more like his Son. Through the working of the word of God (see Heb 4:12) and the life of the Spirit within them (1 Cor 6:19) there comes a renewing of the mind (Rom 12:2) and a strengthening of moral conscience with an ever-increasing desire to please God. In this process there comes the putting to death of the sin that still remains within us (Rom 8:12–13).

Sampley explains,

> Believers are works in progress; they are being transformed. The rhetorical climax of the Letter to the Romans grounds its appeal for a life appropriate to the gospel by affirming a metamorphosis

---

28. Savage, *Power Through Weakness*, 147.
29. Savage, *Power Through Weakness*, 151–52.

(using the same Greek term found in 2 Cor 3:18), a transformation, which in this case focuses on a renewal of the mind so that the Roman hearers can make appropriate moral decisions such that God is properly honored (Rom 12:1-2).[30]

Concerning 2 Cor 3:18, Sampley sees the "mirror" as being Christ and "Lord" to be God. The image that a follower of the Savior must be conformed to is Christ (2 Cor 4:4). "Thus the transformation Paul here celebrates is that all believers are (ideally) becoming ever more Christ-like."[31]

Sampley further elaborates:

> Imitation of Christ is a theme of massive proportions in the Pauline letters and is evinced here. In Paul's view, God's plan includes believers' being "conformed to the image ... of God's son (Rom 8:29). Paul is convinced that believers will "wear the image of the one from heaven," Christ (1 Cor 15:49). In all of these passages, 2 Cor 3:18 included, Paul regularly thinks of believers as being conformed to Christ, but the expression "from glory to glory" indicates, as the NIV translation has rightly rendered it, that this association with Christ involves an "ever-increasing" glorification, or "from one degree of glory to another" (NRSV). The faithful life begins with the restored glory of God from which people had fallen short via sin (Rom 3:23), and it will end in the full, cosmic refurbishment wherein God's glory is once again fully manifest (Rom 8:18-21). So "from glory to glory" expresses, once more, in the most cryptic fashion, Paul's larger picture that the life of the Spirit is a life ever growing and increasing. As believers gaze upon the glory of the Lord, therefore, they actually look to their source and at the same time to their goal to which, gradually, as they become more like Christ, God's glory reflected, they become more identified with the glory of God.[32]

For the missionary, Christlike character is essential, and that essential character comes by living in the freedom of the Spirit leading to God-honoring transformation. God's sent ones must be free by living in grace through the enablement of the Spirit. This freedom of walking in the Spirit (Gal 5:16) leads to God-honoring renewal.

Missionaries will reproduce after "their own kind." It is for them to model the power of grace. Who they are and who they are becoming

---

30. Sampley, "Second Epistle to the Corinthians," 70.
31. Sampley, "Second Epistle to the Corinthians," 70.
32. Sampley, "Second Epistle to the Corinthians," 70-71.

through the life of the Holy Spirit within will be transmitted to their converts. This commitment to Christlike change will have long-lasting implications for the church planted on every mission field as it pertains to its growth, spiritual vibrancy and effectiveness in multiplying itself.

The missionary lives for the glory of God by being transformed by the Spirit of God. "Oh to be like him!" must be the cry of every missionary's heart.

Thomas O. Chisholm penned the hymn "O to Be Like thee":

> *Refrain*:
> Oh! to be like Thee, oh! to be like Thee,
> Blessed Redeemer, pure as Thou art;
> Come in Thy sweetness, come in Thy fullness;
> Stamp Thine own image deep on my heart.
> *Third stanza*:
> Oh! to be like Thee, lowly in spirit,
> Holy and harmless, patient and brave;
> Meekly enduring cruel reproaches,
> Willing to suffer, others to save.[33]

Witherington believes that Paul is speaking of the believer gazing upon the Lord:

> It is precisely because the Spirit frees believers that Paul feels it important to speak freely. All who have that Spirit gaze with unveiled face on the face of Christ (v. 18). Here the verb *katoptrizomai* can mean either "gaze on" or "reflect in a mirror," but the point is that believers are transformed into Christ's likeness by gazing intently on him, so this is surely the meaning of the verb here. They are transformed into his image, from glory to glory, just as he bears the very image of God, being God's mirror, God's Wisdom.[34]

According to Paul's glorious gospel, justification must lead to sanctification. The people of faith become a community of transformed people, shining forth the glory of Christ, becoming a powerful testimony in the world (Eph 5:27).

A progressively sanctified church is the church as portrayed in the book of Acts (see 2:42–47), and it is the church missionaries are called to establish in every land. God's sent servants are to establish transformed and "being-transformed" communities of faith that are a testimony to

---

33. Chisholm, "O to Be Like Thee."
34. Witherington, *Conflict and Community*, 382.

the power of the gospel of grace. Those who have accepted the gospel message and learn to wait in his presence in prayer, are to be changed by the Spirit from glory to glory. This work of the Spirit is to be evident in all the nations of the world.

In such a church the fruit and gifts of the Spirit are manifest. There is a fervent love for each other (see 1 Pet 1:22). There is an abundance of sharing and caring (see Acts 2:42–47). In this transformation, they become an instrument of drawing mankind to the Savior's grace and love.

RESTORATION

Missionaries go with a message of restoration. The Messiah has come to bring renewal. All of creation is groaning as if in labor, awaiting the coming of Christ when there will be complete restoration (Rom 8:21–22). Glorification will bring the total restoration of the image of God in the redeemed (1 Cor 15:51–54). "In the new age of eschatological fulfillment God's glory is found, not in the Old Testament or the Mosaic covenant, but in Christ who is the . . . 'image' of God."[35]

Salvation through the forgiveness of sin opens the door to the power of God's continuous healing grace. The redeemed who are being transformed in this life are being prepared for eternity. Eternity's work of complete restoration begins now as daily lives are being renewed. The deeds of the flesh are put to death and as his followers are vested with Lord Jesus Christ (Rom 13:14), growing in the fruit of the Spirit (Gal 5:22–23), and learning to glorify God in word and deed (1 Cor 10:31). This is the first fruits of total transformation in the age to come.

This is the message of restoration God's sent servants bring to a world suffering in sin's decay. Bondage can be broken—slaves of every addiction set free—free to a life of ever-increasing liberty as they are transformed from inside out through the eternal word of God and by the sanctifying power of the Holy Spirit (Rom 12:2), tasting of the powers of the age to come (see Heb 6:5).

Missionaries preach a gospel of salvation that leads to restoration. It is not only the restoration of the innocence in the garden—but more than that. Glorification will surpass the life experienced in the garden (1 Cor 15:47–49). The followers of Christ will be shot through with glory

---

35. Martin, *2 Corinthians*, 81.

(1 Cor 15:52–53). It will be glory that will last throughout eternity with ever-increasing glory (see Rev 22:1–5).

Ambassadors of Christ go with the assurance that the gospel can free and transform the darkest soul—the greatest sinner (1 Tim 1:15)—those blinded by the biggest lies—those farthest away from God and closest to hell—the ones caught in the greatest lies of the devil—those bound in addiction and demonic oppression and possession. The missionary must believe that God wants to save them, deliver them, and restore them—beginning the transformative process that will be completed at the moment of glorification when the redeemed will see him and be transformed as we see him as he is (1 John 3:2).

GOD'S GLORY REVEALED

> The god of this age has blinded the minds of unbelievers, so that they cannot see the light of the gospel that displays the glory of Christ, who is the image of God. . . . For God, who said, "Let light shine out of darkness," made his light shine in our hearts to give us the light of the knowledge of God's glory displayed in the face of Christ. (2 Cor 4:4, 6)

Martin explains, "The knowledge of God's glory is what the Pauline gospel is all about. And for him it is focused 'in the face' . . . or 'person' of Christ. The risen Lord is the subject who both illumines his servants and summons them to his service . . . and the object whom Paul and his associates are charged to make known and so to bring saving truth to light."[36]

Savage sees the background of Paul's discussion of God's glory in 2 Cor 3 and 4 coming out of the great discussion of the glory of God found in LXX Isaiah. Paul understands the glory that he has received directly from God and has permeated his ministry "as a fulfilment of prophecy and thus an eschatological light."[37] It is a light that has broken into history and displayed in the gospel, being seen in the face of Jesus Christ. It is the light of God's Kingdom. What Isaiah prophesied is now revealed as the Savior shines this powerful future light through the ministry of Paul.

In Isaiah, Israel is in darkness, not because there is a lack of light, rather their pride has blinded them to the light of God's glory. They exalt themselves and thereby rob God of the glory and exaltation that he alone

---

36. Martin, *2 Corinthians*, 200.
37. Savage, *Power Through Weakness*, 112.

deserves. "Israel proudly concentrates on its own activity (42:17; cf. 17:8), taking full credit for its own achievements. . . . By neglecting the Lord and cultivating a self-focus (cf. 17:4), Israel effectively denies the most fundamental truth of its existence, namely, its total indebtedness to God. . . . Israel is guilty of far more than merely encroaching on God's domain. It is effectively casting God from his domain."[38]

Because of this pride, God pronounces severe judgment. But the judgment will bring with it hope. They will be purged of their pride and self-exaltation. "For in the painful experience of fear and suffering Israel's pride will be crushed. It will be in judgment that Israel will regain a proper humility before God."[39]

"In other words, divine judgement will serve to open Israel's eyes to its own lowliness before an exalted God. No longer will the people stumble along blindly in search of their own counterfeit glory (cf. 59:10). Instead they will humbly *see* the true glory of God (cf. 35:2–5). . . . And in seeing his glory, they will also reflect it!" (Isaiah 60:1; 58:8).[40]

Commenting on Isa 60:1, Savage tells us,

> The people of God thus come themselves to manifest the eschatological light. In this way their suffering and judgement will work paradoxically for *their* glory!
>
> The remarkable nature of this prophecy becomes even more dramatic when we consider the sheer magnitude and the startling effect of this light. According to LXX Isaiah, it will be seven times brighter that the sun (30:26), eclipsing both sun and moon (60:19), and will emanate directly from God himself ('the Lord will be your everlasting light,' 60:20). It will precipitate an upheaval greater in scope and power than anything since the first light penetrated the primeval chaos. It will devastate the supposed 'light' of Israel's self-centeredness and show it to be the profound darkness that it really is. It will reveal Israel's wisdom to be foolishness, its strength weakness and its truth a lie . . . Never again will Israel pursue its old self-serving ways, but will in fear seek the vastly different ways of its Maker—trusting him, not men, glorifying him . . . not itself.[41]

Savage continues to explain:

---

38. Savage, *Power Through Weakness*, 117.
39. Savage, *Power Through Weakness*, 121.
40. Savage, *Power Through Weakness*, 122.
41. Savage, *Power Through Weakness*, 123–24 (emphasis original).

> Paul is drawing broadly on the theme of glory in LXX Isaiah when he writes 2 Corinthians 3–4, his response to those who question the character of his ministry could hardly be more dramatic. The light which is shining in his heart (2 Corinthians 4:6) is none other than the unapproachable splendour of God's own glory, a brilliance surpassing that of the sun and a brightness not seen since creation. Indeed, it is the long-awaited light of the eschaton, heralding a new creation and commencing the day of salvation. As such it is a paradoxical glory, visible only to those whose pride has been shattered through judgment. . . . By drawing on LXX Isaiah Paul hopes to overwhelm his congregation with the fathomless dimensions of glory attending his ministry. Not only is it a light more brilliant than that of Moses and more powerful than that of creation, it is also the great eschatological glory foretold in the prophets and destined to consummate history by reversing the proud ways of humankind. The light radiating in his heart could scarcely be more pregnant with meaning.[42]

Paul clearly based his ministry on an understanding of the promised salvation seen throughout the Old Testament. The prophets foresaw a glorious revelation of the salvation of God—light breaking into this fallen dark world—bringing freedom to those who are bound, bringing an end to the proud unrepentant hearts of men.

The messengers of God in a glorious manner taste the powers and the glorious light of the age to come. As in Paul's life, messengers of God are to be channels of this eternal glory.

Missionary ministry is to be a glorious ministry. God's glorious light is to shine through his servants. This is supernatural ministry that flows through Spirit-filled missionaries as they yield their lives to the light and glory of the Spirit of God. The Spirit reveals the glory of the cross and the emptiness of human pride, including all attempts at boasting and self-glorification (see John 16:8).

Through Paul's suffering in choosing to follow the path of the humble Savior, he became qualified to be a channel of the glorious gospel of God; to see light cast out the darkness and men set free and transformed by the reality of eschatological Spirit-power that was being manifest in and through his life. "The god of this age perpetuates gloom; the God of a new age shines a great light. Since we now know this light to be the eschatological glory promised in Isaiah, we may conclude that the glory

---

42. Savage, *Power Through Weakness*, 126–27.

emanating from Paul's heart represents the light of the new aeon breaking into the old."[43]

Like Paul, ambassadors of the gospel (2 Cor 5:20) must be fully committed to the gospel of light. They must allow the suffering of the gospel to strip them of all pride and self-trust, seeking only to show forth the glory of the Savior who has redeemed them.

Savage continues to elucidate this truth by pointing out how Paul in 2 Cor 4:4, 6

> identifies the "light of the knowledge of the glory of God" with the "light of the gospel of the glory of Christ." . . . The eschatological light promised in Isaiah would thus seem to receive its consummate fulfillment in the gospel of Christ. Hence Paul makes the remarkable assertion that the glory which was beamed into his heart is that which appeared initially and with stunning effect on the face of Jesus Christ (v. 6).[44]

Like Paul, it is only a life that is been drained of seeking glory and stripped of self-glorifying boasting that can become a vessel of such radiant glory. Missionaries are called to be such vessels.

Was this not the experience of Steven? While being stoned to death for the impartation of the truth, all his remaining pride was crushed—eliminated from his life—and heavenly eschatological glory came down and rested upon him, God placing the glory that is on the face of Jesus upon his face (Acts 6:15).

Like Paul and Steven, God's sent servants must have the glory of Christ on their faces as they bring the message of this glorious gospel to a lost world. This is a call to daily transformation—waiting in the presence of God until his glory becomes his servant's glory. It is then that his sent ones will be prepared to bring the light of the glorious, delivering, transforming gospel to a lost world still living in the darkness—those awaiting the light of God's glory seen on the face of Jesus his Son.

---

43. Savage, *Power Through Weakness*, 127–28.
44. Savage, *Power Through Weakness*, 128.

7
Reconciliation

"Forget, forgive, conclude and be agreed."
WILLIAM SHAKESPEARE

"It is faith that looks up at the creator God and knows him to be the God of love. And it is faith that looks out at the world with the longing to bring that love to bear in healing reconciliation, and hope."
N. T. WRIGHT

"The Cross is the ultimate evidence that there is no length the love of God will refuse to go in effecting reconciliation."
R. KENT HUGHES

"Come, all you who are thirsty,
come to the waters;
and you who have no money,
come, buy and eat!
Come, buy wine and milk
without money and without cost."
THE PROPHET ISAIAH

A MIRACLE OF RESTORATION

Shortly after the turn of the century, Japan invaded, conquered, and occupied Korea. Of all of their oppressors, Japan was the most ruthless. They overwhelmed the Koreans with a brutality that would sicken the strongest of stomachs. . . .

One group singled out for concentrated oppression was the Christians. When the Japanese army overpowered Korea one of the first things they did was board up the evangelical churches and eject most foreign missionaries. . . . The conquerors started by refusing to allow churches to meet and jailing many of the key Christian spokesmen. . . .

One pastor persistently entreated his local Japanese police chief for permission to meet for services. His nagging was finally accommodated, and the police chief offered to unlock his church. . . . for one meeting. . . .

The Korean church has always had a reputation as a singing church. Their voices of praise could not be concealed inside the little wooden frame sanctuary. Song after song rang through the open windows into the bright Sunday morning. For a handful of peasants listening nearby, the last two songs this congregation sang seemed suspended in time. It was during a stanza of "Nearer My God to Thee" that the Japanese police chief waiting outside gave the orders. The people toward the back of the church could hear them when they barricaded the doors, but no one realized that they had doused the church with kerosene until they smelled the smoke. The dried wooden skin of the small church quickly ignited. Fumes filled the structure as tongues of flame began to lick the baseboard on the interior walls. There was an immediate rush for the windows. But momentary hope recoiled in horror as the men climbing out the windows came crashing back in—their bodies ripped by a hail of bullets.

The good pastor knew it was the end. With a calm that comes from confidence, he led his congregation in a hymn whose words served as a fitting farewell to earth and a loving salutation to heaven. The first few words were all the prompting the terrified worshipers needed. With smoke burning their eyes, they instantly joined as one to sing their hope and leave their legacy. Their song became a serenade to the horrified and helpless witnesses outside. Their words also tugged at the hearts of the cruel men who oversaw this flaming execution of the innocent.

> Alas! and did my Savior bleed?
> and did my Sovereign die?

Would he devote that sacred head
for such a worm as I? . . .

The souls who left singing finished their chorus in the throne room of God. Clearing the incinerated remains was the easy part. Erasing the hate would take decades. For some of the relatives of the victims, this carnage was too much. Evil had stooped to a new low, and there seemed to be no way to curb their bitter loathing of the Japanese.

In the decades that followed, that bitterness was passed on to a new generation. The Japanese, although conquered, remained a hated enemy. The monument the Koreans built at the location of the fire not only memorialized the people who died, but stood as a mute reminder of their pain. . . . It wasn't until 1972 that any hope came. A group of Japanese pastors traveling through Korea came upon the memorial. When they read the details of the tragedy and the names of the spiritual brothers and sisters who had perished, they were overcome with shame. Their country had sinned, and even though none of them were personally involved (some were not even born at the time of the tragedy), they still felt a national guilt that could not be excused. They returned to Japan committed to right a wrong. There was an immediate outpouring of love from their fellow believers. They raised ten million yen ($25,000). The money was transferred through proper channels and a beautiful white church building was erected on the sight of the tragedy. When the dedication service for the new building was held, a delegation from Japan joined the relatives and special guests.

The song leader began the words to "Nearer My God to Thee." . . .

Something remarkable happened as the voices mingled on the familiar melody. As the memories of the past mixed with the truth of the song, resistance started to melt. The inspiration that gave hope to a doomed collection of churchgoers in a past generation gave hope once more. The song leader closed the service with the hymn "At the Cross." The normally stoic Japanese could not contain themselves. The tears that began to fill their eyes during the song suddenly gushed from deep inside. They turned to their Korean spiritual relatives and begged them to forgive. The guarded, calloused hearts of the Koreans were not quick to surrender. But the love of the Japanese believers—not intimidated by decades of hatred—tore at the Koreans' emotions. . . . One Korean turned toward a Japanese brother. Then another. And then the floodgates holding back a wave of emotion let go. The Koreans met their new Japanese friends in the middle. They clung to each other and wept. Japanese tears of repentance and Korean tears of forgiveness intermingled to bathe the site of an old nightmare. Heaven had sent the gift of reconciliation to a little white church in Korea.[1]

> Since, then, we know what it is to fear the Lord, we try to persuade others. What we are is plain to God, and I hope it is also plain to your conscience. We are not trying to commend ourselves to you again, but are giving you an opportunity to take pride in us, so that you can answer those who take pride in what is seen rather than in what is in the heart. If we are "out of our mind," as some say, it is for God; if we are in our right mind, it is for you. For Christ's love compels us, because we are convinced that one died for all, and therefore all died. And he died for all, that those who live should no longer live for themselves but for him who died for them and was raised again. So from now on we regard no one from a worldly point of view. Though we once regarded Christ in this way, we do so no longer. Therefore, if anyone is in Christ, the new creation has come: The old has gone, the new is here! All this is from God, who reconciled us to himself through Christ and gave us the ministry of reconciliation: that God was reconciling the world to himself in Christ, not counting people's sins against them. And he has committed to us the message of reconciliation. We are therefore Christ's ambassadors, as though God were making his appeal through us. We implore you on Christ's behalf: Be reconciled to God. God made him who had no sin to be sin for us, so that in him we might become the righteousness of God. (2 Cor 5:11–21)

RECONCILIATION DEFINED

Reconciliation is the act the bringing together of two parties who have been alienated. Martin writes, "Paul's ministry comes to his contemporaries with the news that God has taken the initiative and now offers peace."[2]

Further defining reconciliation Martin writes,

> God's decisive act in the person of Christ by which the world is returned to God from its estrangement. "Reconciliation" is

---

1. Kimmel, *Little House on the Freeway,* 56–61.
2. Martin, *2 Corinthians,* 148.

a word that rests on prior disagreement and animosity; but, in this case, on whose side? Undoubtedly the cause is double-sided. On God's side there is that manifestation of his holy love called his "righteousness" in the light of which the world stands both condemned and "lost"; it is alienated and under the foreign domination of evil powers. On the human side, there is all that is summed up in terms such as "enmity," "hostility," "bondage," "fear," "despair,"—language of the human condition, which is part of Paul's anthropology (Rom 5:1–11; 8:1, 2 12–17; Gal 4:3–9. . . . This barrier too must obviously crumble and fall if a genuine rapprochement is to take place.[3]

God in his love according to his eternal plan acted to bring relational peace between himself and a rebellious world. He saw us in our helpless separated state and in compassion moved toward us to bring us back unto himself.

"The three phases are represented in 5:21; phase 1 is the portrait of Christ as the one who did not know sin; phase 2 is Christ's being made (by God) sin on behalf of believers; and phase 3 is expressed in the purpose clause 'in order that we might become the righteousness of God in him.'"[4] The sinless Lamb of God (see John 1:29) was made sin, bearing the sin of the world in his own body (see 1 Pet 2:24), that believing souls might be made righteous, having their sins washed away, being completely forgiven.

The servants of God have been entrusted with the message of God's provided means of reconciling the world unto himself (2 Cor 5:18). The king of glory, the Son of God, the sinless spotless one, left heaven in carrying out the will of his Father, freely gave himself as a sacrifice for sin, becoming sin on behalf of all men, in order that the one who believes might become righteous, by the complete washing away of every sin and its stain (see Isa 1:18).

God had to do for mankind what they were totally incapable of doing for themselves. Peace (ending wrath Rom 1:19, 3:25) has already been established through the cross. The world is already reconciled through the death of the Son of God on the cross—it is applied to those who believe (Rom 5:1, 2).

Concerning 2 Cor 5:16–21 Martin writes, "a carefully prepared piece of soteriological credo, that is, a specimen of confessional statement

---

3. Martin, *2 Corinthians*, 148.
4. Sampley, "Second Epistle to the Corinthians," 96.

expressing in summary form what the first Christians believed about God's redemptive work in Christ."[5]

R. E. O. White writes, "The root idea (in Greek) is change of attitude or relationship."[6] White clarifies the importance of the understanding of biblical reconciliation when he writes, "Reconciliation that makes fellowship with God possible for all may be the central concept in Christianity."[7] He further explains, " The NT basis of reconciliation is the 'death of his Son,' 'through the cross,' 'by the blood of his cross, by Christ's physical body through death (Rom. 5:10; Eph. 2:16; Col. 1:20, 22)."[8] Martin clarifies, "Christ died as a proxy for all."[9]

Macchia explains,

> Humanity suffering under wrath are claimed by the cross, God lays claim to them in Christ. In that claim, God claims them for glory. God finds us in Christ and reveals to us the truth of our existence in him. The cross slays us and removes any chance that we can find our own way to glory. Only in being laid aside by the judgment of God at the cross can we by faith claim our place with Christ in glory. In accepting Christ, we accept that for which we were made. In rejecting Christ, we reject our own being as determined from all eternity in Christ. Rejecting Christ is a form of self-negation.[10]

White explains both the human and the divine requirements for reconciliation as seen in Scripture. Concerning the requirement for men he writes, "Human beings being made for fellowship with God, what is the difficulty requiring Christ's intervention? Since reconciliation means that God made Christ to be sin for us (2 Cor. 5:18–21), part of the answer must be sin.... 'You were alienated ... enemies in your minds because of your evil behavior' (Col. 1:21). This total attitude of humans needs to be removed."[11]

He then clarifies the requirement for God: "References to divine 'judicial' wrath (Rom. 1:18; 5:9; 12:19), and the whole case for divine condemnation (Rom 1–3) suggest also a barrier on God's side, precluding

---

5. Martin, *2 Corinthians*, 139.
6. White, "Reconciliation," 726.
7. White, "Reconciliation," 726.
8. White, "Reconciliation," 727.
9. Martin, *2 Corinthians*, 130.
10. Macchia, *Tongues of Fire*, 137.
11. White, "Reconciliation," 726–27.

fellowship ... whose removal requires Jesus's death, not merely his message or example."[12]

White explains the three-fold miracle of reconciliation that leads to contentment:

> "We were reconciled ... being reconciled ... we received reconciliation ... he reconciled us ... be reconciled" consistently apply reconciliation to humanity. Estrangement gives way to prayer, and fellowship, hostility becomes faith, and rebellion becomes obedience. Further, humanity is reconciled to humanity (Eph. 2:14) and also to life itself. We are reconciled to God's legitimate requirements, therein providing contentment.[13]

Sampley tells us, "Paul's most powerful delineation of reconciliation is found in 2 Cor 5:11–21, where the reconciliation is at once cosmic, communal, and personal."[14] For Paul reconciliation can be understood as cosmic because through Christ's death God was reconciling a decaying futile world unto himself (Rom 8:20–21; 2 Cor 5:19).

It is communal because the work of God in Christ is always collective ("us"). God has reconciled the world unto himself to form the family of the reconciled, who live out that reconciliation in a God-honoring community.[15] Followers of Christ experience the new life of joint reconciliation in Christian fellowship which will be experienced in its fullness when Christ comes for his church.

Paul also emphasizes that reconciliation is personal. Each individual believer through faith in Christ's death and resurrection finds himself "in Christ" now living under the Lordship of Christ.[16]

GOD'S INITIATIVE

Witherington emphasizes that reconciliation is God's initiative:

> All these things have happened because God has taken up the work of reconciliation (v. 18). God is the initiator of this process. Had God not sent the Son to die, humans could not have been reconciled to God, regardless of human desire or goodwill.

12. White, "Reconciliation," 727.
13. White, "Reconciliation,"727.
14. Sampley, "Second Epistle to the Corinthians," 29.
15. Sampley, "Second Epistle to the Corinthians," 29.
16. Sampley, "Second Epistle to the Corinthians," 29.

> Reconciliation then is chiefly something God must accomplish, before humankind can respond to the work of Christ. . . . In v. 18 Christ is the agent or means of reconciliation, but God the Father initiates it. . . . Here we find the ultimate expression of God as the great benefactor. Christ as the means of benefaction, and Paul as the human agent and ambassador of the largess of salvation. This in turn makes Paul's work the "ministry . . . of reconciliation." . . . Paul was appointed to make known all of this, not because it was his design but because it was God's purpose.[17]

Martin concurs with Witherington when he writes, "Consistently the stress falls, in the apostolic preaching, on God as the originator of the act of reconciliation; he is always the subject and never the direct object of the verb. He is never said to be reconciled to us."[18]

Reconciliation was required to bring peace because men are sinners and God is a holy God, separate from sinners. For God's intended purpose of bringing about a restoration of fellowship between sinful man and a holy God there was required a means of reconciliation—the shed blood of God's only Son.

Everything has changed because of God sending his Son to be humanity's ransom payment, reconciling the world unto himself (2 Cor 5:16, 17, 19). Christ's reconciling death brought the forgiveness of sins and restoration of fellowship.

MESSENGERS OF RECONCILIATION

God sends missionaries to proclaim deliverance from the enslaving power of sin, calling men to be reconciled to God (2 Cor 5:20), knowing that there is no other Savior that can free from sin's entrapment (see Acts 4:12). God's sent servants proclaim the means for a new relationship with God through the forgiveness of sin.

Those who put their faith in the finished work of Christ become children of God, and therefore know God as their heavenly father. Humanity was under wrath because of their rebellion but now, by eternal grace, they have experienced reconciliation.

Missionaries join hands with God in proclaiming the message of reconciliation. They make disciples, exhorting them to receive the

---

17. Witherington, *Conflict and Community*, 396.
18. Martin, *2 Corinthians*, 147.

message of reconciliation to find peace with God (Rom 5:1). God's sent servants go with a message of hope for the hopeless.

In the establishment of the early church, God raised up an apostolate to be entrusted with the ministry of reconciliation of proclaiming the gospel.[19] In the same manner today, God calls out men and women to be missionaries to the nations and gives them the ministry of reconciliation.

His sent servants proclaim the life-giving gospel to a desperate world. The powerful message of the gospel proclaimed by the called and sent messenger becomes God's means of bringing the hope of reconciliation to the far reaches of the planet.

THE FINISHED WORK OF CHRIST

Martin writes of the finished work of Christ,

> When Christ's work was done, the reconciliation of the world was accomplished. When men were called to receive it, they were called to a relation to God, not in which they would no more be against Him—though that is included—but in which they would no more have Him against them. There would be no condemnation thenceforth to those who were in Christ Jesus. . . . It means that God was putting away his own condemnation and wrath. When this was done, He could send, and did send, men to declare that it was done.[20]

Reconciliation is the message of Jesus' declaration on the cross, "It is finished!" (see John 19:30). All has been accomplished. The wrath of God has been turned away (appeased). Sin has been forgiven. Condemnation for past sins is removed—God is no longer against us—we have peace through the shed blood of God's dear son (Rom 5:1).

This message of complete deliverance from judgment has been given to his sent ones. God sends his preachers of peace (see Matt 5:9) into the entire world to make disciples of men who are reconciled to God through the sacrifice of Jesus. God is no longer against the world—condemnation and wrath has past (Rom 8:1)—there is now peace between God and man for those who will but accept the free gift of God (Rom 6:23).

Missionaries go to the ends of the earth to let the world know what God in his love has done to bring the world back unto himself. Sampley

---

19. Martin, *2 Corinthians*, 156.
20. Martin, *2 Corinthians*, 155.

writes, "Paul, who has been made 'ambassador for Christ,' is now the one through whom God's appeal is made in behalf of Christ: 'be reconciled to God' (5:20)."[21] Like Paul, every missionary has been made an ambassador for Christ. It is their task to call men and women of all ages in every nation of the world to come to the cross and be reconciled to a forgiving God.

Concerning the ministry of reconciliation White clarifies, "So too the church was commissioned, not as a cozy fellowship of the likeminded but as an agency of unification, to go *out* into all the world with Christ's reconciling message."[22] Man's need for the message of reconciliation was the reason why Paul reminded the church in Rome that every man needs a preacher (Rom 10:14).

Sampley explains that "to be an ambassador places Paul in a lofty position of responsibility, as one who must, in all his activities, represent the one in authority and, as here, speak for him."[23] In following in the footsteps of the apostle God's messengers have a "lofty position of responsibility." They carry the words of life—the only words that can bring peace between God and man.

Missionaries speak for God, calling men to abandon the way of destruction and be reconciled to the one who sent his only son to be the sacrifice for the sin of the entire world. As Christ's ambassadors, this must be the central focus of missionary life and ministry; daily engaging in their God-given authority to call men out of the darkness and into the light of the glory of Christ (2 Cor 4:6).

THE MESSAGE'S WARNING

Sent ministers of the gospel go to their place of calling not only with a message of reconciliation but also a warning of judgment for those who fail to be reconciled to God (2 Cor 5:10). "In the context of a plea for reconciliation, Paul as an ambassador urges the Corinthians to make peace with God the ultimate king; emperors normally took action against unrepentant client states that had offended them, and no one took such warnings lightly."[24]

21. Sampley, "Second Epistle to the Corinthians," 95.
22. White, "Reconciliation," 727.
23. Sampley, "Second Epistle to the Corinthians," 95.
24. Keener, *IVP Bible Background*, 508.

The God of the Bible, the true and living God, is the eternal king—the one before whom every man must give an account. Everyone must not only enter the ark of safety they must escape the flood and its destruction.

Like the apostle, missionaries plead with men to be reconciled with God (2 Cor 5:20). Their message is a message of the escape from eternal judgment as well the acceptance of eternal life. The Lord Jesus Christ is either the Savior who forgives sin or the eternal judge who will repay the unrepentant (see Matt 25:31–46).

MESSENGERS WITH AUTHORITY

Paul's request for prayer to the church in Ephesus must be the request of every ambassador of reconciliation: "Pray also for me, that whenever I speak, words may be given me so that I will fearlessly make known the mystery of the gospel, for which I am an ambassador in chains. Pray that I may declare it fearlessly, as I should" (Eph 6:19–20).

Speaking of Paul's ministry purpose Martin explains, "He will be concerned in 5:11–21 to show that the aim of his ministry is to aid in the reconciliation of the world to God (5:18–21). His ministry is an avenue through which God calls the sinful world back to himself."[25]

Missionaries that are called and sent by God are the present-day ambassadors through which God is now making his appeal. It is the most important appeal the world can hear because it goes forth with eternal consequences.

In explaining 2 Cor 5:18–21 Martin writes, "The note of authority runs through this statement, since those who are charged to undertake 'the ministry of reconciliation' are no less than 'ambassadors for Christ.'"[26] This is an authority from God to carry out his will on earth.

For the missionary, authority does not imply arrogance. Rather it invokes the thought of humility and dependance on God as a sent servant. This authority given to God's servants must come with a deep conviction and inner compulsion to proclaim God's means of reconciliation to a world that has gone astray.

Missionaries are ambassadors of Christ. They are not ambassadors sent by a country of this world. Their authority does not come from some

---

25. Martin, *2 Corinthians*, 119.
26. Martin, *2 Corinthians*, 146.

president, prime minister, or earthly king. They proclaim the gospel in the name of the King of Kings and the Lord of Lords (see Rev 19:16).

They go to carry out the command of the Lord of the universe to bring the precious message of the gospel—of the Son of God who bled and died so that the world might be saved. They go in the authority of Jesus' name and in the power of the Spirit to preach the everlasting gospel, healing the sick and casting out devils (see Matt 10:8).

Missionaries go and make disciples, planting thriving churches that are fully equipped to reproduce themselves in an ever-expanding (village to village, town to town, city to city) manner. They go in the name that is above every other name and they bring that powerful, delivering name to lost humanity that are bound by sin and the devil.

The words of his messengers of reconciliation go forth with power, as the Spirit-inspired proclamation flows through them, being followed, as Christ promised, with sign and wonders (Rom 15:19; 1 Thess 1:5). They go in this authority through bearing the shame and suffering of the cross, knowing that it is in this sharing of pain that God releases resurrection power, setting captives free (2 Cor 12:9).

LASER FOCUS

Missionaries must remain laser focused on their God-given ministry of reconciling the world unto God. The devil works through any and every means to distract God's messengers so that they lose sight of their God-given objective. Satan brings distractions ("noise") to redirect the mind and to overburden the emotions with earthly cares to keep God's servants from the most important task. He uses every diabolical means at his disposal to keep God's messengers from carrying out the "Great Commission" (see Matt 28:19–20).

It does not matter what specific ministry a missionary may have (evangelism, teaching, discipleship, church planting, pastoral preparation), the controlling factor of mind and heart must be the reconciliation of lost souls to their Creator through the precious shed blood of Christ. The missionary's steadfast aim in life and ministry must be to be an instrument of the Holy Spirit through which God calls the sinful world back unto himself.

It is for his servants to perform the responsibilities of an ambassador. They are God's official envoys, those who represent the ruler of the kingdom of heaven. They proclaim the message of reconciliation with God through the forgiveness of sins. They call men to come to the Savior, the only one who can wash away their sins and give them rest (see Matt 11:28).

Missionaries have been given a ministry of reconciliation. This is an all-encompassing reconciliation. Through the preaching of the gospel men are reconciled to their maker through the forgiveness of their sins. The wall of separation between gentile and Jew has been torn down (Eph 2:13, 14). The believer has peace with God, knowing that God's wrath no longer rests upon him (Rom 5:1). By faith followers of Christ have been adopted into the family of God (Rom 8:15), now living as fully accepted children of God.

Like Paul, Christ's sent ministers of reconciliation ask other believers for prayer (Rom 15:31). They know the spiritual struggle they face is against the powers of evil, which endlessly work to keep the world in darkness (Eph 6:12).

They know the weakness of their own flesh and the lack of courage that often besets them. God's sent ones therefore often ask for prayer for Holy Spirit given boldness to speak the truth—to proclaim the gospel fearlessly as God would have them speak (Eph 6:19; see Acts 4:29–31). Ministers of reconciliation willingly join in with the suffering of the Savior so that others will have the opportunity to make peace with almighty God (2 Cor 4:12).

A FELLOWSHIP OF THE RECONCILED

Keener in addressing 2 Cor 5:20 writes,

> Having established that he and his colleagues are Christ's representatives, Paul entreats the Corinthian Christians to be reconciled to God again by being reconciled again to himself (7:2; cf. Mt 10:40). Treatment of a herald reflected one's attitude toward the sender, and in ancient Mediterranean life (and especially in Roman party politics, well known in Corinth), one should be friends of one's friends and enemies to their enemies. If the Corinthians welcomed Paul's opponents, they were rejecting him; if they rejected Paul, they rejected the one who sent him.[27]

---

27. Keener, *IVP Bible Background*, 508.

In Paul's mind, as a representative of God—an ambassador of Christ—he could not separate the Corinthians reconciliation with God from a reconciliation to himself. To treat him badly and to reject him as an apostle sent by God was to reject the one who had sent him. To side with the false teachers was to reject him as their apostle.

In addressing 2 Cor 5, Martin writes,

> Paul's teaching on reconciliation seems to have incorporated and adapted traditional material already in existence. . . . It is remarkable that Paul has used kerygmatic idioms more suited to a preaching of the gospel to unbelievers outside the church . . . and is evidently explained by the secondary use Paul is making of the traditional preaching forms to enforce his concern for the Corinthians to be restored to good relations with himself as an apostolic leader.[28]

Paul not only brought a message, but he embodied the message he brought from the hand of God. The Corinthians must understand that his poor treatment by them did not bode well with God. In accepting Paul's opponents, they were rejecting Paul and therefore rejecting God himself who had sent Paul.

White emphasizes that the celebration of the Lord's Supper was from the beginning meant to be a meal that declared reconciliation: "When we recall that a shared meal was in Eastern eyes a means to unity, implying a covenant of friendship, we understand the Eucharist's original purpose: not as a celebration of Christian privilege but as an ever-repeated pledge and renewal of reconciliation to God and one another, enshrining the basic Christian commandment (uttered at the table) of mutual reconciling love."[29]

The body of Christ and the fellowship within that body is to be a testimony of the power of the cross to reconcile—reconciling man with their Creator and reconciling man with man within the fellowship of the followers of Christ. The body of Christ is to be a place of peace that points to the grace of the cross that has power to end enmity in all its forms. "The power of God is seen at its best when a relationship between two parties is restored, first, between an individual and God, and second, between two sets of human beings."[30]

---

28. Martin, *2 Corinthians*, 138–39.
29. White, "Reconciliation," 727.
30. Martin, *2 Corinthians*, 246.

Ministers of reconciliation present a fellowship of believers who have found God-honoring unity, loving each other fervently from the heart (1 Pet 1:22 NKJV). They invite those still on the outside to come and experience loving, soul-satisfying, meaningful, grace-filled relationships.

This is the missionary task. We go and make disciples, living exemplary reconciled lives in loving care for our fellow missionaries and in calling others to leave the divisive brokenness of a life of sin and enter into the same experience of blessed reconciliation. We invite those still on the outside to come and join the fellowship of the reconciled to begin to taste of the heavenly, freely given gift of shared life eternal.

The individually reconciled are brought into the family of the reconciled. It is a family where the reality of a reconciled life is lived out. It is here that the reconciled strive for God-honoring, Spirit-given unity in all their interactions within the body of Christ. They demonstrate that they are truly reconciled with God through humble serving relationships.

Missionaries are to be God's ambassadors of reconciliation showing a divided world how to find peace with God and with their fellow man through the liberating shed blood of the messiah. "When St. Paul says that God has given him the ministry of reconciliation, he means that he is a preacher of this peace. He ministers reconciliation to the world. . . . It is not the main part of his vocation to tell men to make their peace with God, but to tell them that God has made peace with the world. At bottom, the Gospel is not good advice, but good news."[31]

PEACEMAKERS

Missionaries, like the apostle, are preachers of peace. The missionary must live as a peacemaker, always carrying about with them a spirit of loving reconciliation. They must demonstrate that they are peacemakers through the message they proclaim and in all of their relationships. They must demonstrate that reconciliation received through the grace of the cross leads to loving fellowship in the community of the reconciled. The love of Christ should be the controlling force within the fellowship of believers—a love that is continually extended one to the other.

It is expedient for missionaries who labor alongside each other to exhibit the reconciling love of the cross in their labors together. They might not be the closest friends, nor should they expect to agree on

---

31. Martin, *2 Corinthians*, 155.

everything. But it is crucial that they love each other in Christ's name and that they demonstrate that love in seeking the very best for their fellow missionaries.

It is vital that there be a God-given peace between missionaries as they serve together on the field of God's calling. Missionaries live with a realization that the accuser of the brethren is always at work to divide, through misunderstanding and unforgiveness. No "opportunity" can be given for the devil to divide (Eph 4:27 NASB) resisting him steadfast in faith (see Jas 4:7). Loving, reconciling fellowship must be a constant priority, carefully and prayerfully guarded.

On the mission field, because of the state of our fallenness, misunderstanding and divisions will come. Every misunderstanding must be met with prayer, asking for wisdom from above (see Jas 3:17 NKJV). Humility must rule the heart. Each party must open his or her heart before God to the inspection of the Holy Spirit, asking him to show them their sinful part in what is now dividing. When they have failed, they must ask forgiveness from those offended.

There must come repentance and confession of the sin that has offended—believing and hoping that one sincere confession will lead to others. Any idol lodged in the heart, including the desire for importance, must be repented of, asking God to root it out and replace it with a desire to serve. The goal must be God-honoring restoration, knowing that it is in loving unity that they have strength to fight the good fight of faith (1 Tim 6:12).

Forgiveness must be given based on one's own experience of Christ's forgiveness (Eph 4:32). Love must cover a multitude of sins (see 1 Pet 4:8) and every disagreement must be followed by a move toward reconciliation and restoration of fellowship.

For a fellow servant that has sinned, having fallen into the hands of the devil, God's messengers must pray for him that God will bring him to his senses. They must pray he will see his need for repentance, freeing himself from the devil's grip (2 Tim 2:24–26).

Missionaries must have loving patience so that by the wisdom given by God they can see the undoing of the trap laid by the devil. They are to believe that as they humbly seek reconciliation with their fellow workers, God will enable them to come out on the other side united through full restoration.

In these painful relational trials missionaries must remain in prayer, asking God by his grace, to enable them to please him in their words (carefully chosen) and deeds. Their minds must be focused on the knowledge that they battle not against flesh and blood (Eph 6). They must seek to honor God by holding on in faith, believing that he will crush the devil under their feet (Rom 16:20). They must in all things seek to be ambassadors of peace (see Luke 2:14).

8

Commitment to the Cause

"Our only concern should be to keep the fight [for souls] aggressive and to win victory regardless of cost or sacrifice."

SAMUEL ZWEMER

"If Jesus Christ be God and died for me, then no sacrifice can be too great for me to make for Him."

CHARLES STUDD

"My burden was similar to that of a general who, on the eve battle, realized he will commit troops, some of which will become certain causalities."

J PHILIP HOGAN

"From now on let no one trouble me, for I bear in my body the marks of the Lord Jesus."

PAUL THE APOSTLE

IN DEATH'S GRIP

Sitting in a world history class in Bible school, the students gazed upon the sweetest of ladies—Professor Virginia Hogan. Virginia and her husband Philip had been missionaries to China. Philip now served as the Assemblies of God world mission's executive director.

No matter what historical subject was being discussed in the class that day, her mind would wander to thoughts of her beloved China and a lost world needing the Savior. And in those thoughts, she would often pause and begin to quietly weep in front of the class.

J Philip Hogan attended Central Bible Institute in Springfield, Missouri, where he met Virginia Lewis. "Virginia felt a call to missions from her youth and Hogan feared that her call would take her away from him. Showing a persistence that would mark his entire life, he proposed marriage and the two were wed in 1937."[1]

Philip and Virginia served in the pastorate in Missouri and Ohio and then a church in River Rouge, Michigan. During a mission's convention with missionary Leonard Bolton, both Virginia and Philip received a call to China. Virginia was deeply touched by the Holy Spirit during one of the services. "Weeping with the burden for souls that had been hers for many years, Virginia felt the Lord say, 'This (China) is the place.' She replied that God would have to call her husband to missions work as she could not."[2]

Philip too was touched by God. "Meanwhile, Hogan spent late hours talking to Bolton and found himself stirred toward the need of the nations of the world, as well. He began going to the Detroit Public Library and reading every book he could find on China. He also attended a Chinese mission in downtown Detroit on Sunday afternoons. In 1945, on a Christmas visit to their families in Springfield, J. Philip and Virginia Hogan met with Noel Perkin. . . . After a 30-minute meeting, they found themselves tentatively appointed to China. Returning home, they resigned their church and began taking classes in Mandarin at the University of California, Berkeley. In February 1947, they sailed for China."[3]

They arrived in Ningpo China at the beginning of the Communist Revolution where they were warmly welcomed.[4] They were engaged in teaching at the Bible school. Everett Wilson writes of the Hogan's ministry in Ningpo, "The Hogans lived in the unheated Bible school compound, barely surviving the bitter winter. . . . Causing most concern, however, was the foreboding news of the advance of the Communists in the northern provinces. . . . Then Hogan began to suspect that he was under surveillance. Communist operatives had begun to infiltrate the south, waiting for their opportunity to seize control."[5]

1. Oberg, "J. Philip Hogan," para. 4.
2. Oberg, "J. Philip Hogan," para. 5.
3. Oberg, "J. Philip Hogan," para. 6.
4. Wilson, *Strategy of the Spirit*, 38.
5. Wilson, *Strategy of the Spirit*, 39.

The situation grew more and more tense with growing violence. They made the decision to evacuate to Shanghai, where other missionaries from the north had begun to gather. Things went from bad to worse. "When the Cultural Revolution swept China in the 1960s the entire nation exploded in furry against all symbols of foreign influence."[6]

The Hogans evacuated China and moved to Taiwan to continue their work among the Chinese. "But they had scarcely settled on Taiwan when Virginia was advised by her doctor to return to Shanghai for medical attention before political conditions there deteriorated further."[7]

Virginia arrived in Shanghai only to fall and injure her back. Missionary doctors operated on her, "but the accident and the surgery left Virginia sedated and almost immobile."[8]

Philip "rushed to Shanghai to be with her. But the hospital directors, concerned about the worsening political conditions, urged him to return to Taipei immediately."[9] Hogan had been promised that Virginia would be evacuated by plane as soon as she was able to be moved, and so Philip returned to Taiwan.

The promised evacuation of Virginia evaporated as the crisis worsened. Wilson tells us, "Alone and in a rapidly deteriorating political situation, Virginia knew that she was in grave danger. Anxious hours followed; she had to place her life entirely in God's care."[10]

Virginia received a message to be at the airport the next day at 6:30 in the morning. The roads were crowded, and she feared she would not make her appointment. Arriving she was half carried to the ticket counter. She found that her passport was there, but she could not use the ticket given, "a ticket which had been issued to the attaché."[11]

Virginia was left alone next to the ticket counter. "Virginia felt dreadfully alone and frightened. . . . In too much pain to be concerned about her appearance she simply lay on a pile of luggage and watched as other passengers sought frantically to board flights."[12]

Virginia was urged to return to Shanghai but found it impossible since she had no money for a taxi or food. "So she simply lay down on the

---

6. Wilson, *Strategy of the Spirit*, 40.
7. Wilson, *Strategy of the Spirit*, 40.
8. Wilson, *Strategy of the Spirit*, 40–41.
9. Wilson, *Strategy of the Spirit*, 41.
10. Wilson, *Strategy of the Spirit*, 41.
11. Wilson, *Strategy of the Spirit*, 41.
12. Wilson, *Strategy of the Spirit*, 41.

luggage of a man sitting nearby and slept, intermittently drifting in and out of consciousness. In her feverish, bewildered state, Virginia prayed, 'Lord, you are the only one who knows I'm here. If this is the end, I don't want to suffer anymore. Just let me die.'"[13]

A man came and motioned for her to follow him. She managed to get to her feet. She was taken to a large room, and alone, she was locked inside. She leaned against a wall, "gripped by fear but determined somehow to survive."[14]

A man appeared and motioned for Virginia to enter an adjacent room that was filled with a group of Chinese with "somber expressions" on their faces. A man then opened the door and told everyone to run to an awaiting aircraft. Virginia, who had surgery two days earlier, found supernatural strength and began to run as the words from the prophet filled her mind, "They shall run and not be weary, they shall walk and not be faint." After everyone was aboard the plane began to taxi down the runway on its way to Taipei.[15]

GIVEN OVER TO DEATH

> "Indeed, we felt we had received the sentence of death. But this happened that we might not rely on ourselves but on God, who raises the dead. (2 Cor 1:9)

> The term for "death" here . . . is used in contemporary medical writings to describe dead or dying tissue. Paul employs it for dramatic effect . . . as a way of emphasizing the difficulties he has experienced for the gospel.[16]

In following in the footsteps of the apostle, it is the missionary's readiness to experience daily death that ignites a passion and gives growing faith to continue on during the trials and hardships of service as an ambassador for Christ.

"For we who are alive are always being given over to death for Jesus' sake, so that his life may also be revealed in our mortal body" (2 Cor 4:11). Paul was given over to death for the cause of Christ therefore his

---

13. Wilson, *Strategy of the Spirit*, 42.
14. Wilson, *Strategy of the Spirit*, 42.
15. Wilson, *Strategy of the Spirit*, 42.
16. Sampley, "Second Epistle to the Corinthians," 81.

life was now hidden in the crucified one. Being hidden in Christ, his life manifested the risen one.

His life was no longer self-focused. Self-preservation was eclipsed by Christ-glorification. Paul was constantly given over to death so that resurrection life might flow through his life for the salvation of the perishing.

The focus of his life was the proclamation of the gospel. He ordered his life with the goal of seeing the grace of God reach more and more people (2 Cor 4:15). His desire was that his life and ministry would be pleasing to God (2 Cor 5:9). He lived for the honor and glory of Christ.

"Known, yet regarded as unknown; *dying, and yet we live on*; beaten, and yet not killed" (2 Cor 6:9; see 2 Cor 1:8, 9; 4:10, 11). "Paul was constantly aware of death (noted by present participle) but God's power for triumph over death was also known to the apostle. . . . Paul was constantly both dying and living. . . . His ministry called him to die both 'physically' and 'spiritually,' yet the power of God enabled Paul to 'live' in triumph, both now and in what the future might bring him."[17]

"For whoever wants to save their life will lose it, but whoever loses their life for me and for the gospel will save it" (Mark 8:35). When God's sent ones count all lost for Christ's sake and for the gospel he has given them, they live as dead men—always willing, if God so chooses, to give their lives for the one who gave his all for them (see Matt 10:28). In this manner missionaries live the "weak" life, finding their meaning and very existence in following in the footsteps of the "suffering servant."

It is God's messenger who is "given over to death for Christ's sake" who can say with Paul "for to me to live is Christ and to die is gain" (Phil 1:21). It is the heart which is still attached to this world and to the lusts of this fallen world (see 1 John 2:15–17) that finds physical life difficult to relinquish for the cause of Christ.

Missionaries often live with the danger of death. They minister in unstable countries where haphazard violent uprisings and revolts can occur on any given day. They face diseases in the air and those transmitted through insect bites, in places where there are limited medical facilities. Care must be taken because the water they drink and the food they eat is often contaminated.

---

17. Martin, *2 Corinthians*, 181–82.

God's ambassadors face the dangers of wild animals and of violent men. There are dangers from those who practice their demonic inspired traditional religions—those who love the darkness and hate the light.

Like Paul, God's sent ones live not only with dangers but with the reality that God is able to deliver them (see Dan 3:17–18). Faith grows in their hearts as God intervenes and makes a way of escape, surrounding them with his angels of protection (see 2 Kgs 6:17–20), intervening at just the right moment, showing his loving hand of care and deliverance (2 Cor 1:10). Some do not escape, giving their lives for the Savior they love (see Heb 11:36–40), receiving an imperishable reward.

God's messengers count it a privilege to give their lives for the cause of the gospel—whether it is through disease or sword—the ultimate sacrifice for an eternal cause. They willingly pour out their lives (2 Tim 4:6) in some far-off land for precious souls for whom Christ died; being messengers "of whom the world was not worthy" (see Heb 11:38); living the "weak" life of the crucified one unto the very end; knowing that the world will not be redeemed without personal participation in the sacrifice and suffering of the Messiah.

In the manner of the ministry of Jeremiah, the weeping prophet (see Jer 9:1), Paul was a weeping apostle (see Acts 20:19,31; Rom 12:15; 2 Cor 2:4; Phil 3:18). He learned to weep because of his concern for believers' spiritual welfare, wanting them to endure in the faith until the end. He cared for his converts more than he cared for his own life (2 Cor 7:3).

Jesus was alive in Paul; the Savior living his life through Paul's crucified life (Gal 2:20). He lived for the lost and for the liberation of eternal souls from the blinding powers of darkness (2 Cor 4:4). He faithfully labored, often with a sentence of death, for the advancement of God's kingdom on earth.

The gospel was his sole passion. Prayer was his devotion (Col 4:2). In suffering he knew resurrection power (2 Cor 12:9). The heart of God for a lost world had become the consuming passion of Paul's life (Rom 9:1–3).

God's sent ones must live and minister out of a broken heart (see Ps 51:17). They must serve in humility, being willing to be given over to death for Christ's sake. They die in order to see the life of Calvary flow through them to a fallen and desperate world. Ministers of reconciliation live as dead men so that others might find life eternal (2 Cor 4:12).

PROVIDENTIAL LEADING

It was God who was directing Paul's steps, opening doors of effective ministry (2 Cor 2:12). God was the one who through his prevenient grace (2 Cor 4:6, 15) was opening the hearts of those who were hearing and believing the gospel message (Rom 10:17).

Paul sees the hand of God at work in all that befalls him. Because of his faith that sees the unseen (2 Cor 4:18). His life is never perceived as series of accidents or haphazard occurrences. Rather he saw God intimately involved in his life and ministry. God was at work purging self-trust from his life and teaching him to trust in God who raises the dead (2 Cor 1:9).

Life had clear purpose and direction. Paul lived for one who had died for him. He lived to bring the message of the death and resurrection of Christ to a lost world.

As Paul prayed with the spirit and prayed with the understanding (1 Cor 14:15 NKJV) he witnessed God confirm his word with signs following (2 Cor 12:12). Paul, through much suffering and hardship (2 Cor 6:4–10), found himself daily in the middle of God's will, preaching the gospel to those who had not yet heard.

God's sent servants must have the same trusting faith, seeing the hand of God in every instance as the Holy Spirit providentially leads them to accomplish his purposes. Missionaries must know that God has called them and laid his hand upon them to be servants of the gospel. They must believe that God daily will faithfully, in his own marvelous way, direct them to be instruments in his hands to bring about his eternal plan for the saving of the lost.

God's messengers must believe that he will open the right doors and close the wrong doors and make a way where there seems to be no way (2 Cor 2:12; see Rev 3:7, 8). Missionaries must be those who are filled with the Spirit (Eph 5:18) and are led of the Spirit (Rom 8:14) in doing the work of world evangelism.

Being deeply committed to the eternal word of God, God's ambassadors develop a sensitivity to the voice of the Spirit, sensing the prompting of the Spirit, knowing when to move, what to do, what to speak (see Matt 10:19, 21:1–11) and where to labor (see Acts 16:6–10) in order to see the unfolding of redemption's plan. They speak with boldness as Spirit-filled witnesses (2 Cor 4:13; see Acts 1:18; 2:36, 37), fearing neither man nor devil (see Matt 10:28).

Because of the command and commission of the word of God (Matt 28:18–20), God's ambassadors have the God-given task of world evangelism. Therefore, missionaries daily gird their minds and souls for the task given (1 Peter 1:13 NKJV).

God's sent ones wait upon the Lord for new strength (see Isa 40:31 ESV)—receiving an enduement of power from on high (see Acts 2:1–4). They wait with a listening heart to the wisdom of the Spirit (1 Cor 12:8) to carry out their God-given work, making the most of every opportunity (Eph 5:16). They seek the fruit of the Spirit (Gal 5:22, 23) and the gifts of the Spirit (1 Cor 12:7–11) actively work through them to see the manifestation of the glory of God in the face of Jesus Christ (2 Cor 4:6).

A COMMITMENT TO THE CROSS

Missionaries out of their commitment to the gospel take on the humble garb of the sufferings of Christ (Rom 13:14), knowing that it is only in participation in his sufferings that resurrection power is released.

Savage writes,

> In Paul's mind the problem boils down to a difference of Christology.... For Paul, drawing inspiration from the cross, it means conforming to a Jesus of humility and shame. On the one hand, few see anything impressive in the ministry of the humble Paul. On the other hand, Paul sees nothing impressive apart from humility. For the Corinthians, this represents an opaque paradox. For Paul, it is the mystery of Christian ministry.[18]

Missionaries must internalize Paul's "mystery of Christian ministry." This is a ministry that will be an "obtuse paradox"—something to be rejected by many as unnecessary in carrying out the will of God. The humility of the cross to many becomes an offense, bringing misunderstanding by men who, like Paul's opponents, have their own agendas.

God's sent servants who take up their cross and follow Jesus find themselves on the outside, seen as people who should be marginalized and forgotten. They are talked about as a kind of strange phenomenon—as those who have taken the truth too far.

Ambassadors of Christ are opposed by those who give lip service to the crucified life, but whose behavior and lifestyle speak of something different. Messengers of Christ are marginalized by those who seek the

---

18. Savage, *Power Through Weakness*, 162.

comfortable life that is filled with recognition and praise of men. They are rejected by those who preach and live a different gospel (one devoid of suffering), by those wanting to avoid the shame of the cross (Gal 6:12).

Like Paul, ministers of reconciliation become unwanted reminders to others of their own half-hearted commitment to follow the crucified one. Like the Corinthian false teachers, God's sent ones are opposed by those who want the type of glory given by this fallen world rather than the glory given by God through identifying with the one who was enthroned on a shameful cross.

Like Paul, God's messengers live with the burden of the feelings of rejection from those they would rightfully expect encouragement and affirmation. Like the false apostles in Corinth, the weakness of the cross is interpreted by opponents as failure and therefore rejected.

The conflict between Paul and the church in Corinth was constantly being reinforced. The more Paul lived out the humility of the cross the more he was rejected and belittled by those who had fallen under the influence of the "super-apostles" (2 Cor 11:5, 12:11). Paul response was to call them to repentance in returning to him and to his message (2 Cor 2:4; 6:11–13; 7:8–11).

Paul grieved for the Corinthians because he knew that the worldly glory that they sought was poison to their souls, being a denial of the truth of the gospel. He feared that the new teachings they were receiving were separating them from the Savior they had come to know (2 Cor 11:2–4).

They were accepting another gospel, and he knew that this "other gospel" would not get them into God's eternal kingdom. Therefore, he labored to remind them of the gospel he preached and the humble Savior they had come to know. Paul called them to walk by faith (2 Cor 1:24), putting their trust in the Crucified one.

Savage explains, "Paul draws inspiration from his gospel. In the cross of Christ he discovered not only that divine power had been manifested in human weakness, but also that it took eyes of humility, eyes of faith, to detect that power. It required an outlook which itself had been moulded by the cross—a cross-shaped faith which focused on the unseen, not the seen."[19]

Paul's faith was "a cross-shaped faith." Like Paul, God's sent servants need a like faith—a faith shaped by a commitment to the cross of Christ.

---

19. Savage, *Power Through Weakness*, 185.

Missionaries must place the cross before them in their every endeavor of the gospel. The cross must be moved into the center of every ministry opportunity that God opens for them.

Jesus accepted his cross, marching to Calvary to save a lost world through the weakness of humility and shame. Missionaries must daily take up their own cross to participate in salvation's plan. As ministers of reconciliation, they must boast only in the cross of our Lord Jesus Christ (2 Cor 10:17), pointing men to the Messiah who bled and died in order that the world might be delivered from death.

In their weak dependence, God's messengers will find that God's grace is indeed more than sufficient (2 Cor 12:9) for every task and every hardship. In accepting a life of weakness, they become channels of resurrection grace that can save, heal, deliver, and sanctify.

The lost world awaits such men and women—those empowered with resurrection power who will turn the world upside down (see Acts 17:6 NKJV). It is such weak servants that God will endue with power (see Acts 1:8) in bringing the message of life eternal to those still living in sin's death.

The book of Acts testifies to the fact that only a handful of fully committed missionaries were able to bring the gospel to the entire then known world (see Deut 32:20). It is men and women of the same commitment today who will see the church planted in every nation and every community of the world. As they go in "weakness" they will raise up a "weak" church that will itself become an instrument of resurrection grace to those yet in darkness.

LETTER WRITTEN BY THE SPIRIT

"Are we beginning to commend ourselves again? Or do we need, like some people, letters of recommendation to you or from you? You yourselves are our letter, written on our hearts, known and read by everyone. You show that you are a letter from Christ, the result of our ministry, written not with ink but with the Spirit of the living God, not on tablets of stone but on tablets of human hearts" (2 Cor 3:1–3).

Keener points out that letters of recommendation were common among Jewish and Greco-Roman society. It was a way to assure others that the person who sought lodging on their journey could be trusted. It was also used to give authority to a messenger.[20] Paul says that he does not need such a letter since the Corinthians are well aware of his life and had experienced the benefit of his gospel ministry. Their Spirit-transformed lives were a letter that is known and read by many.

There is bond formed between the missionaries who bring the gospel to a people and the people themselves. There is a recognition of honor for the sacrifice and sufferings of the missionaries who first brought the gospel to a community. There is a thankfulness for the coming of the missionaries who left their homeland and traveled many miles to carry the gospel to those yet in darkness who never heard the message of life. A bond of love is built as the missionaries, for the sake of imparting gospel truth, dedicate themselves to learn the native language and culture of the land where they now reside.

In Burkina Faso many "letters" were written through the labor of many missionaries. They were written over many decades through committed ambassadors who were willing to suffer and sacrifice for the sake of the lost.

Often church leaders in Burkina Faso will bring church representatives who are visiting their country to the old graveyard in the center of the capital, Ouagadougou, and show them the graves of the early missionary pioneers and their children that were buried there. These are the for them the trophies of those who gave the ultimate sacrifice to bring the gospel to them.

The churches in Burkina Faso continue to love to sing many of the hymns, that were brought to them by the early missionaries and translated into their own language. Through wise planting and nurturing of the missionaries the church in Burkina Faso had become a glorious testimony (many "letters") to Jesus' promise to build his church (see Matt 16:18).

The church has so developed that they themselves have sent out missionaries to many neighboring nations and into Europe. The church in Burkina Faso is a "letter," written not on stone but on the human heart, written by the Spirit of the living God. It is a living, powerful, letter that is read by all men, testifying to the faithfulness of almighty God.

---

20. Keener, *IVP Bible Background*, 503.

PLEASING GOD

"So we make it our goal to please him, whether we are at home in the body or away from it" (2 Cor 5:9). "The over-riding concern in 5:6–9 to 'please the Lord' renders 'indifferent' whether one is alive (in the earthly body) or beyond life in the earthly body."[21]

God's sent servants must have the same "over-riding" desire as Paul. The driving force behind every task, and every interaction—every ministry endeavor—must be to "please the Lord."

Pleasing God is not a task that will be accomplished through human strength. The sinful flesh always seeks what glorifies self and will intrinsically fail to please God (Gal 5:17). To gladden the heart of God his servants must surrender to the life of the Spirit within them for daily empowerment (see Acts 1:8) and transformation (2 Cor 3:18).

Missionaries must daily lay hold of the grace of the cross and surrender to that grace, allowing the Spirit to daily empower them for a life of service that pleases their Lord and Savior. Pleasing God our master and redeemer must be the consuming passion of the lives of his sent ones.

Every attitude, desire, and all thoughts and actions must be surrendered to the one for whom his servants live to honor. The idol of people-pleasing must be crucified (Col 3:23). Living for his pleasure must be what gives them pleasure.

LOVE'S COMPULSION

"For Christ's love compels us, because we are convinced that one died for all, and therefore all died. And he died for all, that those who live should no longer live for themselves but for him who died for them and was raised again" (2 Cor 5:14, 15).

The compelling love of the Savior is the constraining force in Paul's life and ministry. In like manner, God's sent ones live and minister out of love's constraint. His sent servants, being compelled by Christ's compassion, given by the Spirit (Rom 5:5), are enabled to embody the love of the cross.

Missionaries give up divided hearts (see Matt 6:24) and double-mindedness (see Jas 1:8), no longer living for themselves but for him who poured out his life's blood for them. Being controlled (ESV) by the love of

---

21. Sampley, "Second Epistle to the Corinthians," 86.

Christ, they are thereby prepared to go and make disciples of all nations (see Matt 28:19).

"Are they servants of Christ? (I am out of my mind to talk like this.) I am more. I have worked much harder, been in prison more frequently, been flogged more severely, and been exposed to death again and again" (2 Cor 11:23). For Paul, love led to sacrificial labor. Under the compulsion of the love of the Savior, Paul brought the gospel to the lost "with far greater labors" (NRSV). Daily he expended his God-given energy as he traveled to the cities that had not yet heard the gospel, bring them the words of life.

In following the example of the apostle, missionaries through the love given by the Spirit expend their physical and mental energies in bringing the gospel to those who have not heard.

NEW WORLD VIEW

"So from now on we regard no one from a worldly point of view. Though we once regarded Christ in this way, we do so no longer" (2 Cor 5:16). "Christ's death is the transformative event for all of life. Nothing is the same after experiencing the power of the cross and resurrection. It radically changes the way his servants live. It causes his sent ones to adopt completely new priorities of life. First among the radical changes brought about by Christ's death is the way people should live: no longer for themselves but for the one who died and was raised for them (5:15)."[22]

Christ's death and resurrection revolutionized the world. Nothing could be perceived and understood as things were perceived and understood before Christ's redemptive act. All of life, to be properly understood must now be filtered through the fact of Christ's saving act.

Christ's death and resurrection completely changed Paul's worldview—his perception of the meaning of life—what was right and what was wrong—what was of ultimate importance. God's ministers of reconciliation must have the same revolution of perception. Life for God's sent ones must be understood in relationship to the pouring out of the life of the Lamb of God (see John 1:29) and the Spirit resurrecting him to glorious life (Rom 8:11).

Like Paul, this new understanding must affect the manner of living of God's messengers. Missionaries must model this "first among the

---

22. Sampley, "Second Epistle to the Corinthians," 92.

radical changes" within a new worldview. The lives of God's sent servants must be a proclamation that they are people who have a new knowledge of life that calls for the total surrender to the lordship of Christ. They are to demonstrate that they are committed to live their entire lives for the one who gave his all for them.

God's ambassadors must have a singleness of purpose, having entered into a "new creation" (2 Cor 5:17)—a purpose that is clearly shown by a life fixed on bringing the gospel message to those that have yet not heard. With this kind of total commitment to the Savior, missionaries call others to the same revolution of understanding and to a whole-hearted commitment in following the Savior as one of his servants.

ONLY FOR THE TRUTH

The ministry of the missionary must be one of service to others. "Paul never despairs even in the worst of situations . . . because whatever the cause of the despair it may be transformed into a motive for encouragement . . . for the community's welfare."[23]

For God's messengers the priority must always be the advancement of the gospel; an advancement that comes through the forgiveness of human sin, seeing men and women ushered into the kingdom of God. Every God-honoring means must be used, every hardship endured, every sacrifice made to see lives set free and transformed by the gospel, making disciples in every nation of the earth.

Gospel proclamation is the missionary calling and is to be the missionary's passion—the driving force of life. Nothing must ever be allowed to dampen this passion. A fire must burn in the heart of every missionary wherever they find themselves in the world's ripened fields (see John 4:35).

Like Paul, the ambassadors of Christ must be able to say, "We cannot do anything against the truth, but only for the truth" (2 Cor 13:8). So many have not yet heard the truth and remain in the darkness of sin and deception (2 Cor 4:3,4). Therefore, God's sent servants must not be distracted. They must bring the world the truth (see John 14:6). Communities of Spirit-filled, discipled believers must be established, teaching them all the truth of the word of God to see them go on to maturity in Christ.

---

23. Martin, *2 Corinthians*, 220.

SUFFICIENT GRACE

"But he said to me, 'My grace is sufficient for you, for My power is made perfect in weakness'" (2 Cor 12:9a). Black explains the importance of the Savior's grace in the life of the apostle Paul as he lived in the weakness (Gk: *astheneia*) of the cross:

> This verse is the "summit of the epistle" and the crowning point of Paul's view of weakness. From this vantage point the abject weakness of God's servant is seen in its proper perspective and fundamental significance of *astheneia* for the Christian is most clearly revealed. The very *raison d'etre* of Paul's existence as an apostle and as a Christian appears to have been grounded in these words of the resurrected Lord, "My grace is sufficient for you." This is why all boasting is excluded: for Paul all strength is a gift of God, the result of the free bestowment of the grace of God. This grace suffices. . . . It suffices for all Paul's labors, all his trials, all his conquests, and especially it suffices for his thorn. This grace is mightier than any "angel of Satan," greater than weakness, and more meaningful than any vision or revelation. By it Paul does not merely endure the hinderance of his *astheneia*, but overcomes it so as to carry out his ministry fully to its divinely appointed *telos*. This grace will never abandon Paul, but will support him in every circumstance of life so that the divine power, working through human weakness, accomplishes its purpose.[24]

Many people gain importance through the association with other important people or organizations. They look at the outward rather than what is in the heart (2 Cor 5:12; see 1 Sam 16:7). They feel important because they see themselves attached to something or someone seen by others as important. Paul had no such desire. He had no such attachments. He found his identity in the humble messiah who himself was despised and attacked by the ruling religious leaders of his day, not being received by his own (see John 1:11). Paul wanted the Savior's grace more than the accolades of men.

Paul found his identity as a person who received grace. He learned to glory in his weakness because it was in the many weaknesses he suffered that an abundance of the grace of God became available to him. Heavenly grace that was brought to earth in the suffering and death of God's own son was sufficient for Paul.

24. Black, *Paul*, 98.

He clung to grace as the source of his strength in the times of his suffering, insults, and rejection that he experienced because of the life he lived and message he proclaimed. It was in the mist of his trials that he found that abundant empowering grace rested upon him, giving him strength to endure and power to overcome.

Like Paul, missionaries must live and minister through the sufficiency of God's grace. Grace must be the center of their lives—a heavenly reality that permeates their hearts and minds. It must be the guiding and empowering force that surrounds and undergirds their lives and ministry. Heavenly grace must be the atmosphere where they live and the air that they breathe. God's grace must be their enduring strength and their source of eternal joy, sufficient in every hardship of gospel ministry.

HARDSHIP DELIGHT

"That is why, for Christ's sake, I delight in weaknesses, in insults, in hardships, in persecutions, in difficulties. For when I am weak, then I am strong" (2 Cor 12:10). Black explains Paul's delight in suffering: "These situations are Paul's pleasure and delight, not in and of themselves, but because they maintain and extend the cause of Christ."[25]

Paul delighted in his suffering, seeing every difficulty as a privilege bestowed upon his life as Christ's servant. He chose the path of hardship so that his life would be a vessel of resurrection power for the saving of the lost.

To accept the call to go and make disciples of all nations (Matt 28:19,20) is to also accept the call to suffer as God's means of redemption for a hurting and lost world. It is weakness that makes his sent servants available to be a channel of resurrection power and grace that sets the prisoner free.

Taking pleasure (NKJV) in hardship is the commitment of God's messengers to the setting aside of their own will and the surrender to his will in order to be used for his purpose. Like Paul, missionaries learn to delight in the trials they bear for the gospel, knowing that the hardships and distresses of the gospel is the manner God has chosen to save the world.

---

25. Black, *Paul*, 103.

The death of the Son demands the "delighting death" of his servants. His sent witnesses must give up their lives in taking up their cross so that delivering power might be released in the dark places of the earth.

God has ordained that a price must be paid by every missionary as they carry out the call of God upon their lives. They therefore take pleasure in their participation in the suffering of the gospel since they know that their suffering will effectuate an awakening out of sin's slumber and the opening of blind eyes. Redemption cost Jesus everything; in like manner, his servants' part in redemption's plan will be costly. It is a price paid that God's sent ones accept as an eternal delight.

THE WEAKNESS OF OBEDIENCE

> Now we pray to God that you will not do anything wrong—not so that people will see that we have stood the test but so that you will do what is right even though we may seem to have failed. (2 Cor 13:7)

Speaking of Christ's obedience Black writes,

> He had no intrinsic weakness of his own, although he lived as man in the flesh. Christ's weakness was the weakness of obedience to God, an obedience that led him to assume human nature in all its poverty and to become obedient even to the point of dying on a cross. From a mere human point of view the crucifixion exposed the helplessness of Christ, but his death was completely voluntary and in complete accordance with the will of God.[26]

God chose to save the world not through a conquering warrior, but through a weak, submissive messiah. Jesus lived out his weakness in submission and obedience to God. There is no "weakness" without obedience. There is no humility and self-giving sacrifice without obedience.

Therefore, as Christ's ambassadors follow the call of God and go to the ends of the earth, they must bow their heads and humble their hearts, living with the purpose of obeying their Lord in everything. His sent ones must embrace the words of our Lord when he said, "Not my will but thine be done" (Luke 22:42). Their lives must be marked by submission and obedience. They must live and minister the gospel in humility—not

---

26. Black, *Paul*, 105.

building their own kingdom, rather in everything seeking in obedience to build the kingdom of heaven on earth.

Obedience goes to the very heart of Christlike weakness. Jesus obeyed and took on the poverty of human flesh, spoke and acted only as his heavenly Father commanded (see John 6:38). He obeyed to the point of becoming completely weak in pouring out his life on the cruel Calvary cross (Phil 2:8).

In like manner missionaries are called to a life of obedience as servants of the master. They are to live to obey. Obeying, as a submissive child to their heavenly Father, is their way of life, the foundation of their calling and ministry.

The messengers of God in weakness are to set aside their own will and aspirations and daily bow the knee before their Lord and Savior and live a life of humble obedience. They are daily to seek heavenly strength to more fully obey, knowing that it is in obedience that their Lord and Savior is honored.

The use of charismatic giftings and the longing for ministerial results cannot be allowed to supersede the necessity of obedience (see Matt 7:21–23). God's sent servants must make it their absolute priority to live in humble obedience to their Lord in everything. They must "do what is right" before the one who sees all; to whom they will one day give a full account (2 Cor 5:10).

9

Spiritual Warfare

"Satan would gladly kill me if he could. Every moment he is pressing me, is treading on my heels. Yet what he wishes will not be done, but what God wills."

MARTIN LUTHER

"Prosperity knits a man to the world. He feels he is finding his place in it, while really it is finding its place in him."

C. S. LEWIS, "THE SCREWTAPE LETTERS"

"Our Lord's determined purpose and design was to overcome the devil, not by the exercise of his power, but by means of his own self-abasement."

JEROME

"Stay alert! Watch out for your great enemy, the devil. He prowls around like a roaring lion, looking for someone to devour." (1 Peter 5:8 NLT)

THE APOSTLE PETER

WARFARE ENGAGED

"We were troubled on every side" (2 Cor 7:5 NKJV). "'On all sides' or 'in every way' (6:4; 9:8; 11:6, 9) is a way of saying that much of Paul's activity has encountered great opposition."[1] Paul's description of opposition is the experience of every God-given missionary endeavor.

Resistance (pushback) comes from many directions and from many sources, finding its ultimate source in the spirits of darkness sent by the

---

1. Martin, *2 Corinthians*, 224.

evil one. Opposition comes from expected sources (frontal attack) but also often from unexpected sources (blindside attacks). Satan continually searches for willing participants in his obstructive plans.

Opposition intensifies as his servants present the gospel of the Lord Jesus Christ. There are demonic fortifications that have operated in blinding the minds of millions for centuries. These demonic hoards have no intention of easily letting go of their spiritual slaves. Therefore, Satan seeks to thwart every gospel effort, wanting darkness to prevail.

It is in these times of opposition that the missionary must take courage in knowing that the resistance they are experiencing indicates that the proclamation of the gospel is having an effect. Advancement is being made through the word of God, which is a powerful living force that sets captives free (see Heb 4:12). God servants must stand firm in faith, believing that God will confirm his word with signs of the Holy Spirit (2 Cor 12:12) ushering lost souls into God's eternal kingdom (see Acts 2:47).

When spiritual pressures become overwhelming (2 Cor 1:8), his comfort sustains his messengers (2 Cor 1:4). Sufficient grace keeps them steadfast in faith until the present assault is vanquished, seeing the deliverance of God (2 Cor 1:10).

INTENSE SPIRITUAL WARFARE

Church history records that revival came to Singapore through the ministry of Ralf Byrd of Atlanta, Georgia. The revival came with intense spiritual warfare. Byrd entered the battle for the souls of men through prayer. Steve and Mary Nolin write, "Seeing beyond the surface beauty he sensed the deep spiritual battle to be fought, and was willing to fight the forces of darkness in prevailing prayer."[2]

Months before Byrd arrived, the churches in Malaya and Singapore made prayerful preparations: "Regular classes were held to train the personal workers, and the churches united in days of prayer. A complete follow-up system was devised to conserve the results of the meetings. Thousands of colorful handbills and attractive posters were distributed throughout the city. Most important of all, the Christians of Malaya and

---

2. Nolin and Nolin, "Revival in Singapore," para. 2.

Singapore earnestly sought God for revival. 'Praying through' proved to be the key to victory."[3]

The spiritual struggle intensified: "The intensity of Satan's attacks from the start made us know that revival was on the way. On opening day of the Singapore meetings, Brother Byrd was stricken with severe food poisoning, but God marvelously undertook for him and the meeting began with a mighty touch of God's power."[4]

God confirmed his word: "From the very first prayer for the sick, God confirmed his word 'with signs following.' One old Chinese man who had not walked in eleven years stood to his feet after prayer and has been walking ever since! People to whom the gospel was completely new were convinced of the power of the true God as they saw such miracles. Blindness, deafness, paralysis, and all manner of diseases left in obedience to the all-conquering name of Jesus."[5]

The Nolins write of one extended family that was delivered from idols after coming to know the Lord through a miracle of healing, also receiving the baptism in the Holy Spirit: "No longer did their incense-covered altar with its many idols hold them in fear, Brother Byrd and the missionaries held a consecration service in their home the day they took the idols to be burned. Numbers of times during the meetings we were called to destroy idols and dedicate the home of the new convert to the Lord. Discarded idols make a beautiful bonfire."[6]

Speaking of the outpouring of the Spirit the authors write, "As in truly Pentecostal revival, many were baptized in the Holy Spirit. Morning after morning we rejoiced to see new converts stand with hands raised, speaking in other tongues."[7]

THE GOD OF THIS AGE

Paul refers to Satan as the god of this age who has blinded those living in unbelief (2 Cor 4:4). Keener explains, "Other Jewish teachers did not explicitly speak of Satan as the 'god of this age' (NIV), but most of them

---

3. Nolin and Nolin, "Revival in Singapore," para. 2.
4. Nolin and Nolin, "Revival in Singapore," para. 4.
5. Nolin and Nolin, "Revival in Singapore," para. 5.
6. Nolin and Nolin, "Revival in Singapore," para. 6.
7. Nolin and Nolin, "Revival in Singapore," para. 7.

recognized that the nations (everyone but themselves) were ruled by spiritual powers under Satan's command."[8]

Sampley clarifies,

> Paul divided all humans beings into two categories, "those who are being saved" and "those who are perishing." Paul refines his description of those "who are perishing": "the god of this aeon has blinded the minds of unbelievers so that they do not see the light" (4:4; cf. the "hardened minds" of 3:14) . . . their reasoning capacities are blinded by their deity, the "god of this age" . . . an expression that neither he nor any other NT writer uses elsewhere (cf. John 14:30; 1 Cor 2:6–8; 8:5; Eph 2:2).[9]

Paul often reminds his converts of the spiritual realm of darkness where there are evil rulers who have power to blind and deceive (Eph 6:10–17). Paul uses the term "veiled" (2 Cor 3:14–16; 4:3) to clarify that spiritual blindness is not simply misunderstanding or mental resistance (though both are included). The blindness is much more sinister and pervasive. This fallen world has fallen into the hands of the evil one. He veils minds in darkness, inflicting spiritual blindness by obscuring the light, ever seeking to keep humanity from the light of the truth.

"It is freely conceded that the Gospel *is* veiled—but only to those who insist on having it so by clinging to an understanding of the veil that keeps it in place, and failing to appreciate that the covering is done away with in Christ. They are, alas, 'those who are on the way to perdition.'"[10]

The veiling of the mind through unbelief is the grim reality that every missionary faces. There are many—way too many—who cling to their traditions—their religious and cultural heritages—refusing to separate themselves from those things that have them bound and that are keeping them on a path to a Christless eternity.

The gospel was preached in a village in Burkina Faso and by the grace of God there were those who converted. One older man was truly touched, and his life was transformed finding peace with God and man. He began to live a new life as a new creation in Christ (2 Cor 5:17). But unbeknownst to the pastor, this man, according to the village traditions, was next in line to be the person to take over the responsibilities of the village fetish and offer the required sacrifices to demons.

---

8. Keener, *IVP Bible Background*, 505.
9. Sampley, "Second Epistle to the Corinthians," 74.
10. Martin, *2 Corinthians*, 78.

The man who had been the person for many years with the devilish responsibilities of sacrificing to the village fetish died and the grim obligation fell upon the new convert. Because of the long history of ancient tribal traditions, the new convert felt an inescapable obligation to the community and accepted the duty of what he felt was impossible to refuse.

He took his inherited assignment and made the required sacrifices, plunging his mind and soul back into deep darkness. His countenance and total demeanor changed for the worst. Joy and peace were drained out of his soul and demonic presence entered his life.

The souls of God's servants are grieved to see so many hold on to that which is destroying them. Missionaries find themselves often praying, "God have mercy on their souls. Awaken them out of the darkness. Free them from the evil one. Lift the veil from their hearts and minds. Lord, allow the gospel to set them free."

The presentation of the gospel must never be seen as simply an attempt to win an intellectual argument (though we do present arguments, 2 Cor 5:11; see Acts 17:16–31), attempting to prove that the Christian message is better than another. Cleverly planned arguments will never break through the darkness. A clear presentation of the truth of the gospel ("by setting forth the truth plainly," 2 Cor 4b)[11] must be joined with the power of the awakening Spirit (1 Thess 1:5).

Like the apostle, missionaries face the manifestations of the powers of darkness when they actively share the truth—preaching the eternal gospel. Satan and his cohorts work, day and night, to keep the world in darkness, working to suppress the truth (Rom 1:18).

Satan knows that it is the truth that sets the souls of men free (see John 8:32), so he does everything to discourage and hinder those who are Christ's faithful witnesses. He attacks God's servants physically, mentally, and emotionally, bringing oppressive pressure upon their lives, trying to wear them down, using personal attacks and persecution (see Acts 13:6–11; 16:16–24).

Missionaries must resist him in the name of Jesus (see, Matt 8:29), putting him under their feet (Rom 16:20). Missionaries must recognize that such resistance is an indication that they are doing the will of God, and that the gospel is having an effect in piercing the darkness.

---

11. It is expedient for every missionary to have theological training as a firm foundation of ministry (2 Cor 11:6).

THE IMPORTANCE OF PRAYER

The importance of prayer in the missionary task cannot be overstated. The "Great Commission" is "dead in the water" without a devotion to prayer. God works in answer to prayer. God's kingdom is advanced when the people of God pray. Central to the task of reaching the lost and making disciples is a praying church.

Missionaries themselves must be people devoted to prayer (Col 4:2). His sent servants must remain on their knees, humbly seeking the face of God. They must develop a sensitivity to the voice of the Good Shepherd by communing with God in prayer. Missionaries must daily encounter God, drawing ever close to him (see Jas 4:8) in the hidden place of prayer (see Matt 5:6).

Only God can open the sinful, rebellious human heart. Only the Spirit can draw men to repentance. Prayer is the means God uses to push back sinister darkness, humble the human heart, bringing lives to repentance and faith in the Lord Jesus Christ.

Fervent prayer tears down spiritual hindrances, removing veils of darkness, and opening blind eyes. The prayers of the messengers of God create an atmosphere of spiritual liberty so that gospel truth can have free course to save, heal, and deliver.

Paul's description of those who live in spiritual blindness is a call to urgent prayer to every ambassador of Christ. Only God can push back the darkness; only God can lift the veil off the minds and hearts of the blind. A deliverance is needed that is beyond of human capabilities. Therefore, the sender churches and his sent ones must commit themselves to uninterrupted prayer to a God of mercy.

Intercessory Prayer

" . . . as you help us by your prayers. Then many will give thanks on our behalf for the gracious favor granted us in answer to the prayers of many" (2 Cor 1:11).

Paul expresses his dependance on intercessory prayer. Paul sees a direct link between his deliverance and the prayers of the Corinthian saints. For Paul their prayers were essential for the "success" of his ministry. They prayed and God heard their payers and intervened in Paul's behalf. Paul proclaims that the answer to the prayers of the saints in Corinth will lead to prayers of thanksgiving to almighty God by many others.

The saints give thanks for God's gracious favor—gifts freely given. For Paul, grace flows when prayers are poured forth. God gives us what we do not deserve in answer to faithful intercessory praying. In Paul's mind the proper heartfelt response to God's "gracious favor granted" is thanksgiving to the almighty.

A woman in a missionary sending church is awoken in the middle of the night with an overwhelming burden for a missionary who is serving far off in Asia. She senses from the Holy Spirit that the missionary for whom she often prays is in grave danger. She continues for some time in intercessory prayer for him until the burden lifts, knowing that God has heard and answered her prayers. She then returns to her bed to sleep. Later the woman learns that indeed the missionary was in mortal danger at the moment that she was awakened to pray. God's intervention in answer to prayer becomes a testimony of thanksgiving to a faithful God.

Our Weakness in Prayer

> "Now in the same way the Spirit also helps our weakness; for we do not know what to pray for as we should, but the Spirit Himself intercedes for *us* with groanings too deep for words; and He who searches the hearts knows what the mind of the Spirit is, because He intercedes for the saints according to *the will of* God" (Rom 8:26,27 NASB).

Missionaries in their weakness yield to the Spirit in prayer and allow him to intercede through them—the one who knows perfectly the mind and will of God. His servants pray in the Spirit with wordless groans, interceding for a lost world.

Black writes concerning these verses,

> According to Paul, nothing lays bare the helplessness of believers like their "prayer-weakness." This consists in the fact that we do not know what to pray for as we ought, that is, as is suited to the occasion and as our necessities require. It is at this point that the Holy Spirit comes to our aid, praying for us in words that transcend articulation formulation, yet which ascend, understood by God, to the very throne of grace. This is one example among many passages in Paul where weakness is made parallel to the antithetical concept of power. . . . The impotence and incapability that characterize the whole range of earthly existence require divine intervention. In turn, our infirmity of understanding and

of prayer become the place in which the help and power of God come to expression.[12]

Missionaries intercede under the Spirit's inspiration and direction, asking for the lifting of darkness off the minds and souls of men. His servants pray Spirit-empowered prayers for the light of God to pierce the darkness and penetrate the human heart. His servants in prayer renew their burden for a lost and dying world. They pray that God will again show his mercy to the perishing.

Ambassadors of God "never stop praying" (1 Thess 5:17 NLT). As they continually pray, they are led by the Spirit into a "weak" life (2 Cor 4:10–11). The more his servants humbly pray, drawing near to the crucified one, the more they take on the weakness of the cross. The closer they draw near to the "suffering servant" the more willing they are to suffer for him.

Humble, open-hearted prayer leads to dependance on his grace, knowing that his sent ones are but jars of clay (2 Cor 4:7). Prayer is a wounded soldier reaching out to the only healer, seeking restoration and renewing to continue in the fight.

Prayer is laying hold of the cross, becoming one with the Savior in his shame and pain for the sake of a lost and broken world. Prayer is drawing close to the eternal one so that the crucified one can lay his nail printed hands upon his messengers, and they thereby learn to die so that resurrection power might flow through them.

Missionaries ask the Spirit to teach them how to pray. In weakness, they want to pray like Jesus prayed in the garden of Gethsemane, "Not my will, but thine, be done" (Luke 22:42 KJV).

It is prayer that brings a vision for ministry. It is prayer that never ceases (1 Thess 5:17) that brings the vision God has given to fruition. His servants hold on in prayer until that which God has spoken and promised comes into existence (see Heb 11:1).

In waiting in prayer God's purposes are created in his messengers' hearts, and persistent prayer brings their fulfillment (see Luke 11:9). Prayer opens our hearts to the grace of God to receive every necessary spiritual gift of God for the enablement of his eternal purposes.

"Thanks be to God, who put into the heart of Titus . . ." (2 Cor 8:16). Missionaries need to act out of the things God places in their hearts in prayer. Through prayer, God wants to place in his servants' hearts his

---

12. Black, *Paul*, 152.

desires and plans so that his desires and plans become theirs. In this manner Christ's ambassadors live out his purposes under his lordship for the glory of his name.

In humble prayer the will of missionaries are crucified with Christ (Gal 2:20) so that as dying servants they long to do his will. In humble waiting before God, the desire and the enablement to do his will is received as an inexpressible gift from the hand of their gracious heavenly Father.

It is only in daily, life-surrendering prayer that his messengers obtain and maintain crucified weakness—a weakness which is at the heart of missionary life and ministry. If his servants arise off their knees "strong" they kneel again asking for forgiveness, knowing that only when they are weak are they strong (2 Cor 12:10). They pray again until they realize their weakness, and thereby know the means of releasing resurrection grace.

In prayer his sent ones come to realize that the very weakness that the fallenness within them resists, perceived by the flesh as a hindrance to fruitful ministry, is the very weakness that produces Christ-honoring fruitfulness. God doesn't need our strength; he needs our weakness. God does not use the strong; he uses the weak. His sent ones find weakness as they close the door and pray to the Father, who sees in secret and rewards openly (see Matt 6:6).

Paul daily entered the battle—expending a great amount of energy in the work of God (2 Cor 11:27). But he learned in prayer to labor and toil as a man hidden in the crucified Christ.

It is only the missionary whose life is immersed in prayer that can act in resurrection power through weakness. Weakness comes from intimacy. His ambassadors take on the character of the crucified one by communing with him, where his humble gentle heart becomes their heart (2 Cor 10:1). In prayer they learn how to yield mind, soul, and body to the suffering Savior, so that leaving the place of prayer he lives his resurrected life through them.

The Prayer of Faith

Missionaries pray in faith for those who are enslaved by the power of sin. They believe for the bound to be loosed from grip of the god of this world. Prayers continually go up to the throne of grace (see Heb 4:16), asking God to reveal his mighty hand of deliverance.

Messengers of God must believe and continue to believe—holding on to God and his promises—refusing to let go. They pray for lost and bound souls until there comes a breakthrough of infinite grace. They pray for the softening of hardened hearts and a receptivity to the truth. They pray for those who are in the greatest darkness; those the farthest away from God—that God would do a liberating miracle that saves and transforms.

Missionaries in faith pray for the planting of seed—that the seed will find fertile ground (see Matt 13:8). They pray that others will come and water the seed planted. The continue to pray that the seed will germinate and then grow and produce God-honoring fruit.

His ministers of reconciliation faithfully pray for a harvest of lost souls. They pray that God will give a "people movement"—the salvation of many related lives (families, communities) as they move toward Christ, stepping out of sin and rebellion into the kingdom of God.

They pray, believing that by the mercy and grace of God, people who hear the message will be translated from the kingdom of darkness into the kingdom of God's dear Son (Col 1:13). Missionaries pray for lives to be transformed as the truth sets them free (see John 10:10).

The people of God pray the prayer of faith (see Jas 5:15), believing that the Lord of the harvest (see Matt 9:38) will continue to call out of every nation of the earth a people to be his very own. They pray that signs and wonders will follow the preaching of the gospel—confirming the word and convincing the lost (see Matt 16:20).

His sent servants pray that God will through his prevenient grace draw men unto the cross of Christ. They pray that the drawing power of Calvary (see John 12:32) will be fulfilled in the present moment of history ushering many thousands of lost souls into his kingdom.

Missionaries pray that the souls of men will know a second birth (see John 3:3), being made alive unto God (Rom 6:11) and experience the gift of eternal life (Rom 6:23). They pray that the rebellious, the helpless, the homeless, the addicted, and the enslaved, will become new creations in Christ Jesus (2 Cor 5:17 NKJV), starting a new life in following the Lord Jesus Christ.

The Weapon of Praise

> Grace to you and peace from God our Father and the Lord Jesus Christ. Blessed *be* the God and Father of our Lord Jesus Christ, the Father of mercies and God of all comfort. (2 Cor 1:2, 3 ESV)

> "Blessed be God" is taken from Paul's Jewish heritage. In Jewish literature it is only used of God (1 Kgs 1:48; 2 Chr 2:12; 6:4; Pss 34, 72:18; Mark 14:61; Luke 1:68; cf. Eph 1:3; 1 Pet 1:3).[13]

God is blessed for God's provision, faithfulness, and for God fulfilling his promises.

Paul begins his letter to the church in Corinth with a prayer of blessing upon the Corinthians and a prayer of praise to God for his merciful blessings. Every endeavor of the work of God's kingdom must begin with prayer. God's servants must pause before moving forward with gospel witness, bowing the head and heart before God in expression of dependence upon heavenly grace. Missionaries must first pray and thereby surrender to the anointing and direction of the Holy Spirit.

Martin comments on Paul's use of "Blessed be God." He tells us that "Blessed be God" was common in Jewish prayers as an expression of praise to Israel's God. Paul is full of praise as he remembers God's faithfulness in delivering him from a severe trial in Asia.[14] Like the apostle, missionaries proclaim the gospel with hearts filled with praise.

Praise is a weapon of spiritual warfare, knowing that the devil despises the praises of God's people. Sampley explains the meaning of blessing the name of our God: "It is a way of remembering, a way of reminding ourselves, and one another, that God has delivered us in the past—indeed, that God's nature is to deliver. The God of exodus is our God."[15] His servants praise the God who is faithful. They proclaim that he is the deliverer of his own people—the same God who split the Red Sea for the children of Israel to cross on dry ground, overthrowing all of their enemies (see Exod 15:1,2). "God's faithfulness and trustworthiness are bedrock Pauline convictions. . . . God's fidelity becomes a cloak with which Paul eagerly shrouds himself."[16]

---

13. Sampley, "Second Epistle to the Corinthians," 40.
14. Martin, *2 Corinthians*, 7–8.
15. Sampley, "Second Epistle to the Corinthians," 43.
16. Sampley, "Second Epistle to the Corinthians," 49.

It is a praise-filled heart that raises up a shield of faith (Eph 6:16) to resist and repulse attacks of the enemy (see Jas 4:7) and carries his servants through all the daily trails they face for his name's sake. Our prayers must be filled with many expressions of "Blessed be God . . ."

Sampley points out that the psalmist in Ps 34 is blessing God for his faithfulness, "where God is blessed explicitly for deliverance from trouble and difficulty. . . . The writer of that psalm, like Paul, recognizes that the faithful are beset by distress and affliction, but the Blessed One (God) delivers the righteous 'out of them all' (see Ps 34:19)."[17]

LIVING BY FAITH

"For we live by faith, not by sight" (2 Cor 5:7). Living by faith is the manner of life for the "weak" in Christ. Missionaries accept the call that God has placed on every believer to walk by faith not by human senses.

His messengers contact the eternal by faith. In this present time, it is faith that touches what is not tangible, embracing the invisible, that which is the greater reality. His sent servants live by faith—daily exercising faith and thereby grow in faith. They put no trust in what can be seen, knowing that it is temporal—decaying—soon to pass away (see 1 Pet 1:24–25).

Missionaries must be "faith walkers." When all seems to be collapsing around them, their hope is in an eternal home—that which is built by the hands of God—things more real and more lasting than that which is perceived by the human eye (2 Cor 5:1).

Seeing with spiritual eyes—walking—living—by faith is the manner of life of those whose hearts are fixed on the cross and live in its shadow. By faith God's ambassadors learn to daily depend on him—the one who will never fail them—the one who has repeatedly proved himself to be faithful. Jesus is invisible to his servants, but he is never absent.

Martin explains the vital nature of faith:

> Faith can be real, for Christ is real. Faith believes in things unseen (cf. 4:18) and is the basis for the Christian's walk while 'at home in the body' . . . 'walking' as our experience in this lifetime. . . . The hope of God, given in the Holy Spirit as a pledge, is unseen by the human eye. But the demand of God is that those who want to please him must believe in him (Heb 11:6). The

---

17. Sampley, "Second Epistle to the Corinthians," 40.

> Christian has hope, even though he is away from the Lord, because as a believer he walks in confidence that Christ is real, but unseen (see 1 Pet 1:8, 9).[18]

God's sent ones walk by faith, knowing that God goes before them and prepares the way; knowing he moves out with them on every journey, giving them divine appointments and giving confidence that he will continue to lead them as they hold on to the cross of the crucified one. God removes trusted, tangible things from his servants to teach them how to walk by faith rather than by sight.

As missionaries walk by faith the floor "falls out" from under them; they stand solely on his eternal promises; they know he is leading and providing; they believe that he will accomplish his own purposes; trusting, they seek to please him in all things. In their weakness they take steps of faith; they grow in dependency on him; they learn to more clearly know the Good Shepherd's voice; they learn to respond and obey the gentle voice of the beloved of God (see Mark 9:7).

Faith sees potential. Jesus saw potential in the twelve apostles at a time when they still needed to learn so much. A missionary's faith must see not only his converts' present spiritual level of maturity, but with eyes of faith, see the ever-present potential for growth unto maturity. They know that the seed of the word of God sown has power to strengthen, empower, and transform.

By faith, they see into the future—envisioning a fruitful, multiplying church growing in understanding of the word of God and experiencing the fullness of the Spirit. They must by faith lay spiritual foundations for a future, self-propagating community, which will learn to carry the full responsibility of church life to see the advancement of the work of God in their own communities.

> "But God, who comforts the downcast, comforted us by the coming of Titus, and not only by his coming but also by the comfort you had given him. He told us about your longing for me, your deep sorrow, your ardent concern for me, so that my joy was greater than ever" (2 Cor 7:6,7). The good report of Titus was evidently a personal blessing for Paul in every way.[19]

The refreshing of good news from a friendly source is needed in the midst of the struggles of ministry. Mission field testimonies of lives changed,

---

18. Martin, *2 Corinthians*, 110.
19. Martin, *2 Corinthians*, 216.

and the healing interventions of God bring much needed uplifting and encouragement in knowing the same God who worked wonders in the early church is in the same manner working to save and deliver in the same powerful name of Jesus.

Missionaries, through the eyes of faith, see the faithful hand of God at work in everything that transpires. They believe that God's good purposes are being revealed and carried out according to his own timing and plan. Throughout the day his sent ones perceive the mercies of God being revealed and know that what he has begun he is more than able to bring to completion (Phil 1:6). Both in the times of blessing and in times of great trial and sacrifice the missionary must know and confess that God is faithful to his promises (see Job 1:21, 2:10).

The faith of Abraham (Rom 4:18–21) is often needed on the missionary field; a faith to hope when there is no reason to hope. A faith to risk much, believing for an abundant reward. A faith that daily labors in the harvest field, believing that what has been sown will be reaped (Gal 6:9). A faith that stands simply upon the unchangeable promises of God (2 Cor 1:20).

Missionaries must have a God-given vision. God must speak to their hearts, awaking faith: to instill a gospel passion; to lay hold of God's promises; to hope for a better future for many; to have faith that light will break into the darkness; to believe that truth will be found more powerful than the lie; to trust that veils of darkness will be lifted; to believe that deliverances will come; to trust that renewing grace will be released to transform lives.

Often what is required is a miracle because only divine intervention will bring the help that is needed. Missionaries pray and believe that God will do what only he can do. His servants wait on him in faith—waiting for heavenly help, knowing that it will come in the precise manner and moment of his choosing—never late, always on time.

> It is written: "I believed; therefore I have spoken." Since we have that same spirit of faith, we also believe and therefore speak, because we know that the one who raised the Lord Jesus from the dead will also raise us with Jesus and present us with you to himself. All this is for your benefit, so that the grace that is reaching more and more people may cause thanksgiving to overflow to the glory of God. (2 Cor 4:13–15)

It is because of their faith that missionaries speak out. They fearlessly speak the truth. They speak words of life. They speak of a Savior who died for the sins of humanity. They speak of a redeemer who three days later rose from the dead, bringing the hope of everlasting life.

In their proclamation, God's servants spread the grace of God that is reaching more and more people. They speak boldly, knowing that they speak in the name of their Savior and Lord. His sent ones speak because they know that it is in hearing the message faith comes alive in the human heart, leading to saving confessions—affecting thanksgiving on earth and joy in heaven (see Luke 15:10).

ANOINTING FOR SERVICE

> He anointed us . . . (2 Cor 1:21b)

> The anointing will refer to the bestowal of charismatic gifts intended to equip men and women for God's work by the coming of the Spirit.[20]

Ambassadors of Christ must labor under the anointing of the Holy Spirit. Missionaries must be sent who have received the enduement of power like the early disciples received on the day of Pentecost (see Acts 1:8; 2:1–4). Praying in the Spirit, they build themselves up in faith (1 Cor 14:4) to proclaim the gospel message boldly (see Acts 4:23–31). It is Spirit-anointing that equips them to carry out the "Great Commission."

Witherington emphasizes that when Paul addresses the working of the Spirit he is not speaking in the abstract: "The Spirit that Paul is talking about is the Holy Spirit, who is palpably present in the community as an experienced reality, manifest in spiritual gifts such as tongues and prophecy . . . transforming lives and empowering the work of ministry. *Spirit* is not an essence or an abstract theological concept. It is the daily experience mode of God's powerful presence in the community of faith."[21]

> And who is equal to such a task? (2 Cor 2:16b) "

> Not that we are competent in ourselves to claim anything for ourselves, but our competence comes from God. (2 Cor 3:5)

---

20. Martin, *2 Corinthians*, 28.
21. Witherington, *Conflict and Community*, 384.

Missionaries are called to a task that is humanly impossible. Gospel ministry is never simply a matter of argument or persuasion (though Paul did both). Christ's ambassadors must yield their lives to the charismatic empowerment and manifestation of the Holy Spirit.

At times his sent ones are awakened in the middle of the night with the Spirit's promptings; there is a dream or a vision; an unexpected permission is granted; a gift of the Spirit is manifested (1 Cor 12:4–10); an unusual receptivity to the gospel is evident; a gift of healing is granted. Other times everything seems normal—uneventful—and only afterwards his messengers look back and marvel at the gracious provision of God.

Anointed by the Spirit to live in the Spirit is the description of a Spirit-filled life and ministry. It is ministry empowered by the Spirit that leads to the proclamation of the gospel message in boldness (Eph 6:19). It is as his messengers wait on the Spirit in prayer that they are clothed with a heavenly anointing to proclaim the gospel with power and great conviction.

OPEN DOORS

> Now when I went to Troas to preach the gospel of Christ and found that the Lord had opened a door for me . . . (2 Cor 2:12)

> The "opened door" means freedom to minister.[22]

The "opened door" that the Lord had placed before Paul indicates that he had the direction, empowerment, and freedom of the Spirit to preach the gospel to the lost in Troas. Paul's words may also indicate that there was at least a measure of receptivity among his hearers.

Spirit-empowered ministry (Acts 1:8) depends on the Lord opening doors of opportunity for gospel proclamation. For gospel ministry to be effective, God must go before his servants preparing the way. It is as his sent ones pray in the Spirit (1 Cor 14;15), believing that the Lord will give them "divine appointments," that God opens and closes doors to fulfill his purpose in bringing souls unto repentance and faith in the Lord Jesus Christ.

While Jesus was still with his disciples during his earthly ministry, he prepared them for "open door" ministry. When Jesus sent the disciples to obtain a donkey for him to ride in his triumphal entry into Jerusalem

---

22. Keener, *IVP Bible Background*, 502.

the disciples left with specific instructions. As the disciples obeyed and went it became clear that God went before them to prepare every encounter and arrange every provision (see Luke 19:28–35). Jesus was teaching them the importance of having "divine arrangements" in their future Spirit-directed ministry.

In the book of Acts, we see the followers of Christ dependent upon the Spirit's direction. God gives them divine appointments, opening and closing doors according to his own timing and purposes (see Acts 2:1–4; 3:1–11; 4:23–41; 5:17–28; 8:5–25; 9:1–9; 10:9–22, etc.).

In Acts 16 we have a profound example of "open door" ministry. Paul received what is now called the "Macedonian Call."

As Paul and his companions traveled through Phrygia and Galatia God closed a door, having forbidden Paul to preach in Asia. God then prevents their entrance into Bithynia, "the Spirit of Jesus would not allow them to" (v. 7). Going on to Troas, in the night Paul receives a vision of a man of Macedonia standing and pleading for Paul and his companions to come and help them. They act on the "open door" placed before them, being convinced that God was calling them to preach the gospel in Macedonia.

They travel in Macedonia to Philippi where God opens the heart of a woman named Lydia in response to the preaching of the gospel by Paul. God opened the door, and God opened the woman's heart (v. 14). Paul and his companions were carried along by the direction and empowering of the Spirit—all for the advancement of his kingdom. Like the apostle, doors of ministry that seemed to be shut tight are suddenly opened and missionaries by faith walk through each open door, believing God to bring to fruition his redemptive purposes.

God directs in opening doors of effective ministry—God reveals his eternal grace—the gospel goes forth—disciples are made—the kingdom of God advances. God closes one door to open another (see Rev 3:7, 8). His Spirit-filled messengers must pray with expectation for God to open effective doors of Spirit-empowered ministry (1 Cor 16:9).

Divine arrangements in Spirit-empowered ministry supersede the understanding of his sent ones. Though his servants cannot comprehend the mercies and wonders of God's divine arrangements, they know that they are essential in bringing the gospel to the four corners of the earth.

THE SPIRIT AND THE CROSS

The enablement of the Holy Spirit was foundational in the life and ministry of the apostle Paul. Immediately after his conversion Ananias is sent by the Lord to lay his hands upon Paul to recover his sight and to receive the Holy Spirit (see Acts 9:17). He carried out his gospel ministry as an apostle who was filled with the Holy Spirit (see Acts 13:9). He often spoke Spirit-inspired tongues (1 Cor 14:18) for personal edification (1 Cor 14:4). He was dependent on the leadership of the Holy Spirit as he went from city to city on his missionary journeys. He yielded his life to the Spirit to be used in the charismatic manifestation of the Spirit (2 Cor 12:12). Paul was thoroughly convinced of the necessity of the Spirit's empowerment (see Acts 1:8) to carry out his apostolic ministry.

Paul lived and ministered in the shadow of the cross. He was "in Christ" and therefore joined to the crucified one. Paul was a person who found his total identity in the Christ of Golgotha. He lived to participate in the sufferings and death of Jesus so that resurrection grace and power might flow through his life for the salvation of many.

In all his sufferings he found the sufficient grace (2 Cor 12:9) and sufficient comfort (2 Cor 1:4) of God his heavenly Father. His passion was that men would be reconciled to God through the forgiveness of their sins (2 Cor 5:20).

In his life and ministry, Paul joined the necessity of a Spirit-empowered life (Eph 5:18) with a life that was crucified with Christ (Gal 2:20). Paul believed that God's purpose for his servants is to make them weak (through suffering) and keep them weak (through "thorns" in the flesh) so that they might receive sufficient grace to be strong in him (2 Cor 12:9–10). In weakness Jesus' sent ones become powerful instruments of redemption as resurrection power is released through their lives.

Paul's prescription of ministry that is fruitful and pleasing to God is a life surrendered to the Spirit empowering joined with a daily participation in the suffering and death of Christ. These two joined together become "the Enablement" to carry out the ministry of reconciliation that has been given to his servants. Paul continually lived with these two realities (the Spirit and the cross) in carrying out his God-given apostolic ministry.

For Paul, both realities were a daily apostolic necessity because both were God's means of saving a lost world bound in sin and darkness. He yielded to the Spirit's leading and charismatic empowering as he clung to the cross, joining the suffering of his Savior to Spirit empowerment as God's way of saving a world enslaved in sin. In Paul's mind, it is a "dead man"—nailed to the cross—that receives the anointing of the Spirit that will be used to see the spreading of grace that reaches more and more people (2 Cor 4:15).

In like manner, missionaries must be committed to living out this joint redemptive enablement. God's servants find God-honoring effectiveness in the work of gospel proclamation as they daily take up their cross and follow after the suffering Messiah, and by daily yielding their bodies, minds, and souls to the Spirit's empowerment.

PERSECUTION AND MARTYRDOM

Missionaries need the protecting, delivering hand of God to be upon their lives. Persecution is on the arise around the world. His servants need God's angels to camp around them in their travels and in times of unrest in the lands where God has sent them.

There is no simple answer for the difficulties and uncertainties missionaries face on the mission field. They need divine intervention and wisdom from heaven for discernment on how they should react to persecution and violence.

His servants must daily walk in the Spirit. In prayer they must cultivate a sensitivity to the voice of God. In every situation they must trust the Almighty, knowing that their lives are in his hands. They must see every hardship as another opportunity to admit their weakness and their need for the Savior's sufficient grace.

In every fiery trial they learn their inability to deliver themselves, learning to lean on his everlasting arms. In the difficulties faced they surrender to his sovereign will, knowing that he always does what is best for his children.

His servants' deepest desire must be to see God's name honored in the earth and that many will be drawn to the Savior through the testimony of their lives. Missionaries know that there is no greater honor than to die as a martyr for Christ (see Acts 22:20; Rev 2:13). The length of their lives and the sufferings they must face are all in the hands of their sovereign and all-compassionate God.

Speaking concerning the "ultimate sacrifice" Collin Garbarino writes,

> The martyrs both past and present counted Christ and his resurrection more valuable than clinging to life in this tattered body. Both their lives and their deaths witnessed to their trust in Christ's sufficiency. When honoring the martyrs, the early Church said that the martyrs received a crown for witnessing to the point of death. This crown was not a crown of ruling. It was the *stephanos*, the wreath of leaves awarded to someone who had triumphed at an athletic competition. God gave them this prize because of the extraordinary steadfastness exhibited in testifying through death.[23]

"'In truthful speech and in the power of God; with weapons of righteousness in the right hand and in the left' (2 Cor 6:7). Paul speaks of the tools or equipment of ministry that he has used: word of truth, the power of God, and the weapons of righteousness on both the right hand and the left. He is a warrior of God."[24]

Like Paul, missionaries must be warriors of God. The battle is great and the struggle unending. Missionary service is not for the fainthearted. It is not a ministry for the double-minded or the half-committed. Missionaries must have the weapons of righteousness both in the right hand as well as the left. They need both hands "weaponized" so that one hand becomes weary the other can continue the fight. They must fight with the word of truth joined with the power of the resurrection (2 Cor 12:9–10). They must fight to the very end, no matter how the end may come.

THE WARFARE OF DISCIPLINE

> For though we live in the world, we do not wage war as the world does. The weapons we fight with are not the weapons of the world. On the contrary, they have divine power to demolish strongholds. We demolish arguments and every pretension that sets itself up against the knowledge of God, and we take captive every thought to make it obedient to Christ. And we will be ready to punish every act of disobedience, once your obedience is complete. (2 Cor 10:3–6)

Sampley helps us understand what Paul means by waging war:

> Paul contrasts his walking or behaving *en sarki*, "in the flesh," and therefore appearing just as every other believer, with not

---

23. Garbarino, "Martyrdom and the Resurrection," para. 6.
24. Witherington, *Conflict and Community*, 400.

making battle *kata sarka*—that is, like everybody else. A warning is implied, as suggested in this paraphrase: "Sure, we look just like everybody else who is a believer in that we carry our responsibilities in the fleshiness of life; but do not be deceived, when we (are forced to) engage in battle, we are not like anyone else, but operate with the full panoply of God's power at our beck and call."[25]

Sampley further explains,

> Worldly power, no matter how great, arrayed against Paul as God's agent avails nothing. . . . Rather, his weapons are from God and are of such power as to destroy strongholds, fortresses (10:4). Analogizing from "destroying strongholds," Paul describes his own work as a most effective and thorough military action.
>
> Every aspect of an awesomely efficient military siege is depicted, but now transferred over onto Paul's advocacy of the gospel; not by his own efforts, but by the "knowledge of God," (counter-) arguments are demolished, as is every "rampart offering resistance" (10:5). Every mind is taken captive to obey Christ, and Paul promises to be ready to punish every disobedience whenever their obedience is complete (1:5–6). Paul's picture is of military action is modeled from Roman peacekeeping and enforcing operations, which, with vast superior power, sweep away obstacles, crush resistance, and establish complete compliance.[26]

Paul is saying that "he personifies the totality of God's force . . . and no disobedience will be left unchallenged."[27] Paul is again warning against "judging by externals and not internals (4:6), by face, and not by heart."[28]

Paul refuses falsehood that distracts from the truth of the gospel. He is totally committed to the proclamation of the truth. "For we cannot do anything against the truth, but only for the truth" (2 Cor 13:8). He knows the authority that Christ had given him as an apostle, and he was determined to use it to keep the church in Corinth from being led astray by the false apostles.

---

25. Sampley, "Second Epistle to the Corinthians," 137.
26. Sampley, "Second Epistle to the Corinthians," 138.
27. Sampley, "Second Epistle to the Corinthians," 138.
28. Sampley, "Second Epistle to the Corinthians," 138.

"... since you are demanding proof that Christ is speaking through me. He is not weak in dealing with you, but is powerful among you" (2 Cor 13:3). Doubters are always a part of spiritual warfare. Through their unbelief they purpose to weigh God's sent servants down and put up spiritual roadblocks, attempting to hinder the vision God has given for the advancement of his kingdom. Being used by the devil they will try to sway others into unbelief to gain influence.

Missionaries must stand their ground and refuse to let the dark shadow of unbelief affect them. They must hold strong, knowing that their God-given faith is greater than diabolic unbelief. They must continue to believe, knowing that a powerful Christ is in their midst to protect his church (see Rev 1:13–17). "Likewise, we are weak in him, yet by God's power we will live with him in our dealing with you" (2 Cor 13:4b). In addressing this verse Black explains,

> Paul writes, "but we live with him toward you by the power of God" ... refers to Paul's impending activity in Corinth when the power of which he speaks will become manifest in a concrete place and in concrete situations. ... The death and resurrection of Christ is on Paul's thought no mere speculative doctrine for which there is no corresponding reality in life. The resurrection power of God will shortly make an unmistakable impact upon the Corinthians.[29]

The Corinthians must understand that they are not dealing with an ordinary person. Even though he lives in the world like others, he has been commissioned and empowered by the risen Lord and he will, if necessary, use his authority to discipline the unruly to preserve the church in Corinth. Paul will not be coming unprepared. He will be coming under the authority of Christ with the accompanying power of Christ's resurrection.

Missionaries must live and minister the gospel with the same confident authority. They must labor under the full assurance that, as they walk in humble obedience in fulfilling the "Great Commission," the authority of the risen Christ will accompany them. When correction is needed, they will not be acting alone, the resurrection Savior will be with them.

---

29. Black, *Paul*, 107.

THE SPIRITUAL BATTLE WITHIN.

> Now the Lord is the Spirit, and where the Spirit of the Lord is, there is freedom. And we all, who with unveiled faces contemplate the Lord's glory, are being transformed into his image with ever-increasing glory, which comes from the Lord, who is the Spirit. (2 Cor 3:17–18)

> Here is my advice. Live your whole life in the Spirit and you will not satisfy the desires of your lower nature. For the whole energy of the lower nature is set against the Spirit, while the whole power of the Spirit is contrary to the lower nature. Here is the conflict, and that is why you are not free to do what you want to do. But if you follow the leading of the Spirit, you stand clear of the Law. (Gal 5:16–18 J. B. Phillips)

Paul was aware of not only the spiritual battle without but also the spiritual battle within. Though his converts had been freed from the power of sin (Rom 3:9; 1 Cor 15:56–57) and therefore no longer a slave of sin (Rom 6:16–17; 20–22), there still remained within them a "lower nature" (Phillips) that desires what is contrary to the Spirit (Gal 5:16–18).

Because of these conflicting forces within the believer Paul calls for radical transformation. The believer must daily engage in this inward battle, by putting to death the "lower nature" through the Spirit's enablement (Rom 8:13) in order to be transformed "with ever-increasing glory" by the Lord, "who is the Spirit" (2 Cor 3:18).

In like manner, it is expedient for missionaries to daily engage in this internal battle of putting to death the "lower nature" in their members and be transformed by the life of the Spirit within them. Paul warns that this can never be accomplished through "self-effort, law-keeping," "that is why you are not free to do what you want to do." It is in following the leading of the Spirit that his servants experience liberty and transformation.

Those sent with the gospel are either bringing freedom or enslavement (see Matt 23:15). God's servants are either imparting the letter that kills (2 Cor 3:6, like the "super-apostles"), or they are transmitting the Spirit which brings an abundance of life.

Missionaries must themselves be free if they are to bring the freedom of the gospel to others. Law-keeping that leads to death gives birth to more law-keeping that leads to further death. Grace received and lived out in the power of the Spirit puts to death the "lower nature," bearing spiritual fruit that brings life to many.

10

Perseverance

"Patience and perseverance have a magical effect before which difficulties disappear and obstacles vanish."

John Quincy Adams

"Perseverance, secret of all triumphs."

Victor Hugo

"Fall seven times and stand up eight."

Japanese Proverb

"Blessed is the one who perseveres under trial because, having stood the test, that person will receive the crown of life that the Lord has promised to those who love him."

James the Less

A LIFE OF PERSEVERANCE

David Brainerd (1718–47) was a missionary to the American Indians. His life is an example of perseverance through his many trials in missionary service. At age twenty, David was converted describing the experience as "an "unspeakable glory" within his soul.[1]

In early September 1739, only two months after his conversion, Brainerd entered Yale College in New Haven, Connecticut. During his first year of studies, he contracted measles, which sent him home for

---

1. Benge, "Who Was David Brainerd?," para. 5.

several weeks. In his second year, falling ill again, he began to spit up blood, which was an early indication of tuberculosis—the disease would in the end take his life.[2] He suffered "with recurring illness, loneliness and depression."[3]

In 1741, under the ministry of evangelist George Whitefield and Pastor Gilbert Tennent, David experienced the "fire" of the Great Awakening—though the fervor of the revival was resisted by the faculty at Yale. Brainerd himself was expelled from Yale for a remark he made about a tutor at the college. "The State of Connecticut required all ministers to graduate from Yale, Harvard, or a European university and Brainerd was thus denied ordination. He answered the call to become a missionary to American Indians under the auspices of the Scottish Society for Propagating Christian Knowledge."[4]

Brainerd found grace and strength for his missionary work among the American Indians by spending many hours a day in prayer. He interceded for the salvation of lost souls. Bounds wrote concerning Brainerd's prayer life,

> Prayers never die. Brainerd's whole life was a life of prayer. By day and by night he prayed. Before preaching and after preaching he prayed. Riding through the interminable solitudes of the forests he prayed. On his bed of straw, he prayed. Retiring to the dense and lonely forests, he prayed. Hour by hour, day after day, early morn and late at night, he was praying and fasting, pouring out his soul, interceding, communing with God. He was with God mightily in prayer, and God was with him mightily.[5]

Concerning Brainerd's perseverance in missionary life and ministry, Dustin Benge writes,

> Unable to complete his formal education, Brainerd sought other opportunities to fulfill his ministerial calling. After receiving a license to preach, he was approved for missionary work on November 25, 1742. He was sent to a small church on Long Island, which served as a doorway to the vast New England wilderness the following spring. From 1743 to 1747, he served American Indian tribes near Stockbridge, Massachusetts, and at the Forks

---

2. Benge, "Who Was David Brainerd?," para. 6.
3. Banner of Truth, "David Brainerd," para. 1.
4. Banner of Truth, "David Brainerd," para. 2.
5. Bounds, "David Brainerd," para. 7.

of the Delaware River. In 1745, he began preaching to the American Indians at Crossweeksung, New Jersey.

It was here that God brought awakening to the American Indians, adding more than one hundred to Brainerd's growing congregation. While experiencing sickness, extreme hardship, and loneliness, Brainerd often took up his pen to write of his increased love for the American Indians under his ministerial care. His heart longed to show them the glory of Christ through the preaching and teaching of Scripture. He spent hours in prayer, asking God to bring about their salvation and growth in Christ.

However, his time among the American Indian tribes of New England was mingled with periods of severe depression and sickness. His diary is filled with entries chronicling these spiritual and physical battles. Finally, having no choice but to leave his missionary endeavors because of his unforgiving battles with sickness, Brainerd made a final visit to his American Indian friends in early 1747 and then rode to the house of Jonathan Edwards in Northampton, arriving on May 28. Under the care of Edwards' daughter, Brainerd died in the Edwards' home from tuberculosis on October 9, 1747, at twenty-nine years old.[6]

PATIENT ENDURANCE

"If we are distressed, it is for your comfort and salvation; if we are comforted, it is for your comfort, which produces in you patient endurance of the same sufferings we suffer" (2 Cor 1:6). "Patient endurance" is a vital character trait of every person seeking missionary service.

Missionaries are to be an example of suffering endured for the cause of Christ to the church and to the world. They are to be a living testimony of "patient endurance." Always receiving heavenly comfort in their sufferings, they are witnesses to their converts that heavenly comfort is available to them in their suffering for the gospel (2 Cor 1:3–7).

As I previously noted in my introduction, the call of God is essential. But the call of God to missionary service must be joined with a tested maturity in Christ that will enable the person to patiently endure the rigors of missionary service.

This enduring character is built into the hearts and minds of God's called servants as they, like their Savior, are led by the Spirit into the

---

6. Benge, "Who Was David Brainerd?," paras. 8–9.

"harsh environment of the wilderness" (see Mark 1:12–13). It is there in the "wilderness," as one spiritual battle is added upon the another, that spiritual backbone is formed—a resolute life that will refuse to be moved. Missionaries must be prepared to patiently endure severe trials and fierce attacks that will come from the god that rules this present age (2 Cor 4:4).

As Paul so often found, trials do not pass quickly. The pressure often mounts—one distress added upon another—even to the point of despair (2 Cor 1:9). When all human help fails, missionaries must in patience hold on to God and to his promises.

The moment when the floor falls out from under them, they find that they are sustained by his sufficient grace (2 Cor 12:9). By faith his messengers hold on, believing that in God's time deliverance will come (2 Cor 1:10) and that God will not test them beyond what they can endure but will give them a means of escape (1 Cor 10:13).

The faith that God has freely given his ambassadors will not fail because the God in whom they trust will not and cannot fail (Matt 19:26). The dark skies will surely clear, the torrential river will be crossed, and his sent ones will by his grace patiently endure to the very end (see Heb 11:32–35). Such great endurance produces a fortified faith as his sent ones know more fully the faithfulness of their God and Savior.

Patient endurance requires the dispensing of heavenly grace and power (2 Cor 1:811). When all human strength ends, divine power becomes available. Missionaries endure in patience because God enables them to endure—God intervenes, and his servants see the salvation of God (see Exod 14:13).

RESILIENCE TO PERSEVERE

> We are hard pressed on every side, but not crushed; perplexed, but not in despair; persecuted, but not abandoned; struck down, but not destroyed. We always carry around in our body the death of Jesus, so that the life of Jesus may also be revealed in our body. For we who are alive are always being given over to death for Jesus' sake, so that his life may also be revealed in our mortal body. So then, death is at work in us, but life is at work in you. (2 Cor 4:8–12)

Witherington writes, "Paul then gives a catalog of trials that he has gone through that demonstrate both his frailty and his resilience and composure (vv. 8f.). . . . One could be distressed without being totally desperate.

He has been hard pressed but not at his wits' end; at a loss but not completely lost, persecuted, abandoned, and knocked down, but not knocked out. Taken as a whole this catalog suggests . . . miraculous preservation."[7]

Paul ministers in the weakness of the cross. Having been nailed to the cross with his Savior, his life is in another's hands. His weakness is an opportunity for God to reveal his power and deliverance, accomplishing his will through an "earthen vessel." In his resilience in the hardships that befell him, he experienced God's "miraculous preservation," allowing him to continue in his apostolic ministry.

He is able to persevere because the Lord Jesus is at his side strengthening him (2 Tim 4:17; see Acts 18:9–10) giving him an inner strength in the midst of every storm of life. He is pushed to the limit of his human resources but never gives up.

He is never overcome by the hardship he suffers because it is in those moments when the difficulties are beyond his human strength that God becomes his strength (Phil 4:12–13; see Prov 18:10). God intervenes with miracles of deliverance, showing himself mighty to save (2 Cor 1:10).

GREAT ENDURANCE

> Rather, as servants of God we commend ourselves in every way: in great endurance; in troubles, hardships and distresses; in beatings, imprisonments and riots; in hard work, sleepless nights and hunger; in purity, understanding, patience and kindness; in the Holy Spirit and in sincere love; in truthful speech and in the power of God; with weapons of righteousness in the right hand and in the left; through glory and dishonor, bad report and good report; genuine, yet regarded as impostors; known, yet regarded as unknown; dying, and yet we live on; beaten, and yet not killed; sorrowful, yet always rejoicing; poor, yet making many rich; having nothing, and yet possessing everything. (2 Cor 6:4–10)

In 2 Cor 6:4, 5 there is a description of the "situations and circumstances in which Paul has found himself." In 6:6 Paul tells us about "his modus operandi in those circumstances." And in 6:8–10 Paul lays out the "extremes" of environment in which he carried out his ministry.[8]

---

7. Witherington, *Conflict and Community*, 387.
8. Sampley, "Second Epistle to the Corinthians," 97.

This is Paul's description of his life of perseverance in his battle for the souls of men. Paul's life was a life of daily challenges lived often in erratic and resistant cultures where men lived in spiritual darkness. To see the gospel advance called for "great endurance."

The world where missionaries live and minister is a fallen world filled with demonic activity that causes spiritual blindness (2 Cor 4:3–4). God's sent servants daily face resistance to the truth. Missionaries therefore must commit themselves to "great endurance" in obeying the "Great Commission." To remain faithful and continue in the work of God, God's sent servants must endure many difficulties. As Paul labored "in the Holy Spirit" (2 Cor 6:6) so God's sent servants must be clothed by his powerful Spirit (Acts 1:8), to remain faithful, enduring to the very end (see Matt 10:22).

Jesus warned, "No one who puts a hand to the plow and looks back is fit for service in the kingdom of God" (Luke 9:62). Missionaries must hold firm, not looking back, never taking their hands off the "plow" that God has given them. They must persevere in sowing the eternal seed of the gospel, watering that seed, believing for a harvest.

For Paul, the most important way for him to authenticate his missionary calling and ministry was endurance in hardship. His enduring "in tribulations, in needs, in distresses" (2 Cor 6:4 NKJV) over many years was proof of his apostolate.

As missionaries continue in lifelong ministry the need for "great endurance" only increases. They must not grow weary in doing good, for in God's own timing they will reap a harvest if they faint not (Gal 6:9).

When a missionary is engaged in the struggle for the souls of men the battle against the powers of darkness goes on unabated. Only "great endurance" will insure the realization of God-given victories.

"Great endurance" is a bedrock of missionary life and ministry. Without endurance missionary labor is feeble and short lived. It is perseverance in the struggle over many years that plants the church of God on a foreign field in a manner that will bring lasting results.

Proclamation of the truth brings resistance from the enemy. Knowing that the battle will rage, his messengers must purpose to endure in the calling that God has given them. Without an unwavering commitment to remain on the field of their calling they will weaken and falter, losing their determination and never see the fruition of all that God purposed to do in them and through them for advancement of his kingdom. To bear eternal lasting fruit (see John 15:1–8), missionaries must endure hardship as good soldiers of Jesus Christ (2 Tim 2:3).

THE TESTIMONY OF ENDURANCE

> In everything we do, we show that we are true ministers of God. We patiently endure troubles and hardships and calamities of every kind. (2 Cor 6:4 NLT)

> The hardship list (6:1–10) . . . is fitting; it serves to demonstrate that Paul is tried and true (. . . see 10:18, 31:7), that he has been and is for the Corinthians through thick and thin, and that he is worthy of their affirmation and affection.[9]

The missionary must be a person who stands with his converts through thick and thin. They must be a testimony to those they are reaching with the gospel of endurance in the trials and difficulties of life.

The lack of endurance of missionaries puts a stumbling block in the path of others. Endurance is proof of his sent ones' commitment to the cause of the gospel—to the truth they proclaim. It is in enduring troubles and difficulties that accompany the making of disciples that God's messengers can truly say, "Follow my example, as I follow the example of Christ" (1 Cor 11:1).

Hardship fortifies missionaries' testimony. Suffering difficulties demonstrates that God's sent servants are committed to and engaged in the sanctification process of Christlike transformation (2 Cor 3:18). Difficulty reinforces Christ's ambassadors' commitment and keeps their focus squarely on Christ and his kingdom (see Matt 6:33). God's global witnesses fail much less when they suffer (see 1 Pet 4:1).

Missionaries must plant churches that will not be surprised and overwhelmed when persecution arises for the name of Christ. They must plant churches that become a testimony of endurance as the followers of Christ are willing to sacrifice and zealously labor, proclaiming the saving grace of our Lord Jesus Christ.

---

9. Sampley, "Second Epistle to the Corinthians," 97.

PARADOXICAL PERSEVERANCE

Martin in addressing 2 Cor 6:8b–10 writes, "Paul launches into a catalogue of the 'vicissitudes of the apostolic life' . . . by composing a mosaic that contrasts the worldly and divine. In this strophe we find seven specimens of paradox: impostors/true; unknown/well-known; dying/living; punished/preserved from death; sorrowful/always rejoicing; poor/making many rich; having nothing/having everything."[10]

God's messengers, like Paul the apostle, are called upon to live as "specimens of paradox" with their own vicissitudes of missionary life. Examples of this paradox life include: dwelling in a far off land/but learning to feel at home; speaking different languages than one's mother tongue/but still enjoying conversations in one's own; eating different foods/some good, some not so good; becoming more familiar with another culture than one's own/though having times of nostalgia; often understood/but sometimes misunderstood; being climate afflicted/finding bodily adaptation to the weather; living on the edge where health concerns take on a whole different meaning/learning to self-medicate; being subject to danger in circumstances of revolt and upheaval/finding tranquility in simplicity of life and trust in God; ongoing suffering from previously unknown illnesses/gaining new spiritual strength and vitality; living with less/rejoicing in a full soul satisfaction; often insulted/at times given honor; undermined by unbelievers and by false brethren/supported by those with sincere faith and love; afflicted by demonic oppression/rejoicing in the Holy Spirit; some unprovoked enemies/great friendships and trust; many trials, hardships, persecutions and sorrows/a peace that passes understanding; despised by some/brotherly loved by many; difficulty, resistance, and disappointment/eternal victories of the Messiah's eternal grace.

Paul's heart had been joined to the very heart of God for a lost and dying world. He endured distress in the "vicissitudes of the apostolic life," daily taking up his cross in order to present the crucified one to a world that so desperately needed him. His driving unmovable desire was that others would know the same saving power that had transformed his life from a persecutor to a proclaimer of the truth (Gal 1:13).

Paul could persevere in gospel ministry, living in paradox, because he knew in whom he had believed (2 Tim 1:12) and that in knowing God, his heavenly Father, he possessed all things (2 Cor 6:10). All the riches

---

10. Martin, *2 Corinthians*, 163.

of heaven were his because God in his mercy had redeemed him and brought him into the family of God (2 Cor 4:17). He was now an heir of God and a joint heir with the Lord Jesus Christ (Rom 8:17).

Missionaries persevere in paradox because of their eternal hope (2 Cor 4:6–5:5). Their suffering in weakness leads to groaning for glorification (2 Cor 5:2). The longing for our eternal home makes their sufferings for the gospel seem insignificant (2 Cor 4:17). It is in the sharing in the sufferings of the cross that God's messengers maintain their eternal perspective, not being distracted by the affairs of this life. They live for the eternal unseen and lay up a sure indestructible treasure in heaven (see Matt 6:19–21).

PERSEVERANCE THOUGH DYING

> Known, yet regarded as unknown; dying, and yet we live on; beaten, and yet not killed. (2 Cor 6:9)

> Paul was constantly aware of death (noted by the present participle) but God's power for triumph over death was also known to the apostle.... Paul was constantly both dying and living.... His ministry called him to die both "physically" and "spiritually," yet the power of God enabled Paul to "live" in triumph, both now and in what the future might bring him.[11]

Missionaries often live with the danger of death. They minister in unstable countries where haphazard violent uprisings and revolts can occur on any given day. They face diseases in the air and those transmitted through insect bites. They live with the reality that the water they drink and the food they eat is often contaminated.

They face the dangers of wild animals and of violent men. They are confronted by dangers from those who practice their demonic inspired traditional religions—those who despise the gospel and the gospel's servants.

God's messengers count it a privilege to live their lives in danger of death for the cause of the gospel—whether it is disease or the sword—the ultimate sacrifice for an eternal cause. They willingly give their lives in some foreign land for precious souls for whom Christ died; messengers "of whom the world was not worthy" (Heb 11:38 a); living the "weak" life of the crucified one unto the very end, knowing that the world could not

---

11. Martin, *2 Corinthians*, 181–82.

be redeemed without the participation of his sent servants in the suffering and death of the Savior.

Like Paul they live not only with dangers of death but with the reality that God is able to deliver them in every life-threatening adversity. The desire to persevere grows in their hearts as God intervenes and makes a way of escape, surrounding them with his angels of protection, intervening at just the right moment, showing his loving hand of care and deliverance. Some do not escape, giving their lives for the Savior they love (see Heb 11:36–40).

In writing about the life and ministry of Alexander Mackay, Ruth A. Tucker writes:

> As a leader of this team of missionaries, Mackay felt an awesome responsibility, but his farewell message reflected the courageous determination such a venture required: "I want to remind the committee that within six months they will probably hear that some one of us is dead. Yes, is it at all likely that eight Englishmen should start for Central Africa and all be alive six months after? One of us at least—it may be I—will surely fall before that. When the news comes, do not be cast down, but send someone else immediately to take the vacant place." Mackay's words were still ringing in the director's ears when the news came that one of the eight had died. Five of them succumbed to the African graveyard in the first year, and by the end of the second year, Mackay was the only one left. Though at times Mackay was at the point of death, he refused to give up.[12]

ENDURING REJECTION

> I do not think I am in the least inferior to those "super-apostles." I may indeed be untrained as a speaker, but I do have knowledge. We have made this perfectly clear to you in every way. (2 Cor 11:5–6)

Martin explains how Paul's life of "weakness" brought doubt and rejection: "Instead, because he exemplified God's power through weakness, his credentials as a minister of the Gospel are in doubt. Desiring a 'powerful' leader and preacher, some of the church at Corinth have attacked

---

12. Tucker, *From Jerusalem to Irian Jaya*, 168.

Paul as being inferior. The underlying premise is that a strong preacher would not have his life characterized by weakness and tribulation."[13]

Missionaries often must endure rejection. People in the sending churches want to hear of miracles and conversions, but they don't want to hear about the sacrifice and suffering experienced in bringing the gospel to the lost. A message of suffering is too unsettling. They want a "painless gospel."

Many think that the free gift of God is free, when in reality it is very costly. "Why would you ever want to go to such a God-forsaken place?" "You are not going to take your family there, are you?" "There is much gospel work to be done here, why are you leaving us?" Redemption of a lost world cost Jesus everything and it costs deeply (misunderstanding and rejection) those who choose to leave friends and family to participate in God's redemptive plan.

The church wants a painless means of bringing the gospel to a demon-infested world. The history of missions tells us something very different. Wherever the gospel has been taken to the dark places of the earth an enormous sacrifice has been made requiring great perseverance to see the souls of men delivered from the power of sin and darkness.

Trials and rejections befall his servants as they bear witness to the resurrection by experiencing the same suffering as their Lord and Savior. "Thorns in the flesh"—demonic oppression and attacks—befall them as they preach the crucified one, but never beyond their ability to withstand—God makes a way of escape (1 Cor 10:13). As they experience hardship and rejection, they persevere, finding an outpouring of God-given grace to sustain them, finding his grace more than sufficient for their souls (2 Cor 12:9).

PERSEVERANCE IN THE LIFE-GIVING SPIRIT

> He has made us competent as ministers of a new covenant—not of the letter but of the Spirit; for the letter kills, but the Spirit gives life. Now if the ministry that brought death, which was engraved in letters on stone, came with glory, so that the Israelites could not look steadily at the face of Moses because of its glory, transitory though it was, will not the ministry of the Spirit be even more glorious? If the ministry that brought condemnation was glorious, how much more glorious is the ministry

---

13. Martin, *2 Corinthians*, 133.

that brings righteousness! For what was glorious has no glory now in comparison with the surpassing glory. And if what was transitory came with glory, how much greater is the glory of that which lasts! (2 Cor 3:6–11)

Paul in these verses contrasts the life given under the new covenant imparted by the Holy Spirit through the message of the gospel with the death given under the old covenant, brought about by the weakness of fallen men. Paul writes that the letter kills but the Spirit gives life.

Martin explains the reasons why the law could not impart life:

> First, the law set the standard, but offered no power to reach it. For that reason Paul does not mince his words: the law "kills" (v 6); it is "the ministry that leads to death" (v 7) which, in turn, produces "condemnation" (v 9). These strong terms can only mean that the law set the target of a perfect standard; but men and women, who are sinfully weak, are unable to attain it. . . .
>
> Second, Paul goes on to teach that the law had an honorable purpose, but it was only temporary . . . is seen in the way in which the glory of both law (vv 7, 11) and the lawgiver, Moses (v 7), was only a passing one. . . . The glory of God is to be sought now, not in the law or the Temple or the priesthood, but in the face of Jesus Christ (2 Cor 4:6; Titus 2:13). John's prologue says the same thing exactly (John 1:17), as does the main argument of the letter to the Hebrews (chap. 8 in particular) . . . a third element. . . . The law betokened a barrier between God and the people of Israel, both in Moses' day and in Paul's. Why did the lawgiver place a veil over his radiant face (v 13; Exod 34:33)? Part of the reason was to prevent the people's disappointment when they saw the glory fading; but Exod 34:30 reports that "they were afraid to come near him," partly because of the radiation of his face. . . . Paul finds in this circumstance a profound explanation, for the veil which Moses wore is no mere historical detail. It speaks of a barrier which still hides the truth from the Jewish reader of the OT. . . . They fail to perceive its true significance.[14]

Paul's explanation of the failure of law to give life reminds us of the veil of darkness over the minds of millions of religious people all around the world. Satan uses the lies of the religious traditions practiced to keep the masses in darkness, in bondage to spiritual deception (see Mark 7:1–23). Only through perseverance in the life-giving Spirit—believing

---

14. Martin, *2 Corinthians*, 72–73.

in what often seems impossible—will God's messengers see such bound souls be free from such enslavement.

Often it is those devoted to their religion, those who have invested so much in their self-righteous practices, who find it the hardest to believe the gospel message. They find it difficult to accept that the sacrifices and investments they have made in their religion are all in vain.

Often the more religious a person is, being zealously devoted to their faith, the more resistant they are to any thought of change. In many societies there is great family and community pressure to remain in the established religious traditions that have been passed down from generation to generation.

Escaping the darkness of lies of religious darkness often seems like an insurmountable barrier. Those who are seen listening to gospel preaching are warned to not join the fellowship of Christians, to never be baptized—threatening to take their lives if they ever choose to convert.

The practicing Jews of today as well as every practitioner of any of the major faiths in this world need a miracle of prevenient grace. Missionaries in unwavering faith must pray and believe that God will do the miracle of "turning on the light" in their minds and souls. Miraculous interventions of revelation and deliverance are needed to see men bound in religious traditions of darkness set free unto a new life in Christ (2 Cor 5:17). Victories only are achieved through Spirit-given faith, believing for mountains to be removed (see Mark 11:23).

It is Paul's message of grace that brings life through a glorious new covenant that must be comprehended and accepted. Missionaries hold on in faith knowing the hopelessness of the codes of religious practice. Such practices will always fail because they do not have the power to change the human heart and free from the grasp of the power of sin.

This calls for a daily yielding to the Spirit on the part of God's sent messengers. This demands a perseverance in prayer. This requires times of fasting and prayer, believing that God will do what is totally impossible from a human perspective. The Holy Spirit must reveal the truth, convicting of sin, righteousness and of the final judgment (see John 16:8).

God's sent servants must be faithful to be salt and light to those whom God brings into their lives. They need God-given wisdom to be shrewd as serpents and innocent as doves (see Matt 10:16). They must yield to the Holy Spirit and let him speak through them (see Matt 10:20).

Ministers of reconciliation must surrender to the Holy Spirit, allowing him to produce his fruit in their lives (Gal 5:22,23), taking every opportunity to give acts of kindness as Jesus lives his life through them (Gal 2:20). His servants must labor in proclaiming the gospel (2 Cor 11:27), being steadfast in faith at times when ministry appears to be bearing little fruit. In faith they must stand on the promise that one plants, another waters, but is God who makes the seed grow and gives the harvest (1 Cor 3:6–9).

There are many testimonies around the world of religious people who heard the gospel in many forms (radio, internet, personal testimony) and in many different situations over many years, who finally had a conversion experience as the Holy Spirit mercifully penetrated their souls, turning on the light of the truth within them. The truth was faithfully imparted to them by many sent servants over many years—in the end imparting the hope of everlasting life.

Many face persecution when they decide to leave their religious traditions and begin to follow Jesus. They are threatened with the loss of employment and at times the loss of life.

In a remote African village, the government set up a training school for young ladies. Young women came from all the surrounding villages to stay for one year to learn practical skills (sewing, cooking, health) that would help them in supporting themselves back in their own villages.

The government allowed a Spirit-filled pastor to come every Sunday to preach the gospel to the young girls—those who were willing to come to the services. A young Muslim girl named Fatima came to the services and after attending many services over several months decided to surrender her life to the Savior.

This young lady, on the completion of her studies returned to her home village. When Fatima's father learned of his daughter's conversion, he grabbed her and proceeded to attempt to break her arm. Fatima fled for her life to the village of the pastor who had brought her the gospel at the school.

STEADFAST FAITH

"Because of this, having this ministration, according as we did receive kindness, we do not faint" (2 Cor 4:1 YLT). "Because of this" refers back to chapter 4 where Paul explains the surpassing glory of the new covenant.

> We faint not—This is one of the effects of being entrusted with such a ministry. The word used here (. . . ekkakoumen) means,

properly, to turn out a coward; to lose one's courage; then to be fainthearted, to faint, to despond, in view of trial, difficulty, etc.—Robinson. Here it means, that by the mercy of God, he was not disheartened by the difficulties which he met; his faith and zeal did not flag; he was enabled to be faithful, and laborious, and his courage always kept up, and his mind was filled with cheerfulness.... He was deterred by no difficulties; embarrassed by no opposition; driven from his purpose by no persecution; and his strength did not fail under any trials. The consciousness of being entrusted with "such" a ministry animated him; and the mercy and grace of God sustained him.[15]

God's sent messengers do not faint because they have been given something most precious—a much greater, more glorious, enduring new covenant. Missionaries experience this glorious covenant by gazing into the face of Jesus and seeing his glory (2 Cor 4:6). It is the gazing into the face of Jesus in contemplation that transforms them to be more and more like the one who is perfect in all his ways (2 Cor 3:18).

Missionaries labor on the precipice of losing heart (4:1, 16). But in steadfast faith (2 Cor 5:7) they refuse to be moved, knowing that their sacrifices and sufferings are accomplishing the will of God on earth in bringing the gospel to a lost world.

Distresses of gospel ministry build faith as his servants are "forced" to trust. As God's servants face hardship, they obtain a new level of fortitude to honor God in their daily life.

God's messengers must not allow themselves to become weary in doing good, always believing that they will reap a harvest if they do not give up (Gal 6:9). They must have the faith of Abraham (Rom 4:18–21) that believes even though everything in the natural points in the opposite direction ("contrary to hope, believed in hope" [Rom 4:18 NKJV]). Like Abraham, they must believe the promises of God, knowing that God is not willing that any should perish but that all would come to repentance (see 2 Pet 3:9).

Ambassadors of Christ must believe what Jesus promised. He told his disciples that when was lifted up on the cross, he would draw all men unto himself (see John 12:32). With unwavering faith, missionaries must believe that Calvary's power is still drawing men—even the most resistant—unto the truth that sets free.

---

15. Godtube, "Barnes's 2-Corinthians 4:1," para. 4.

God's sent ones must in perseverant faith share the truth in wisdom and love through whatever venues are available in the cultural context of where they minister. They must believe the words of Isaiah the prophet who wrote that God's word never returns void but that it will accomplish what God intends for it to accomplish (see Isa 55:11).

Missionaries must labor with all the energy God has given them, in steadfast faith sowing seed and watering that seed. They must wait like the farmer with eyes of faith, believing that what has been sown will bring forth a harvest (see John 4:35).

His messengers do not lose heart because they walk by faith, seeing the unseen—the eternal being more real than the temporal (2 Cor 4:18). They remain resolute, choosing to hold on in faith until God's hand of deliverance is revealed (2 Cor 1:10).

Missionaries stand unmovable in faith knowing that all that they have received has been given freely out of God's mercy. They have been given a most precious calling to be one of God's sent servants, in bringing the words of life to the ends of the earth. They refuse to give up, seeing God's grace reach more and more people, resulting in thanksgiving to the glory of God (2 Cor 4:15; 9:11–12).

There is absolutely nothing within his servants that merits such a precious gift—the calling to stand between God and man (see Ezek 22:30) and offer the forgiveness of sins by eternal redemption found in Christ. Paul says that knowing the gift of mercy his servants have received, they find strength during the ongoing battle to persevere in faith and by God's mercy be found faithful.

God's sent servants must stand in faith, fighting the good fight of faith (1 Tim 6:12) in resisting the enemy. In the battle they must surrender to the loving sovereign will of the almighty. His servants must be unmovable in faith, knowing that he will not test them beyond what they are able to withstand, but will make a way of escape (1 Cor 3:18).

God allows pressures and difficulties—at times severe temptations—to bring about his sanctifying purposes in transforming his messengers' lives in conformity to his only Son. He will give wisdom and strength and lead his messengers to joyous victory as they entrust their souls to the "God and Father of our Lord Jesus Christ, the Father of compassion and the God of all comfort" (2 Cor 1:3).

As his children, his sent ones must put their unwavering trust in his goodness and faithfulness, believing that God will fight at their side in every battle (see 2 Chr 20:15). God will use every fiery trial to fortify their faith and to sanctify their minds and souls.

His global witnesses must rest in the knowledge that their lives are not controlled by men, nor Satan, rather by almighty God, the maker of heaven and earth who is working out his own purposes for his own glory and honor. Such steadfast faith crushes the devil's head (Rom 16:20) and leads his ambassadors on to victory in the Victorious one (see Rev 17:14).

PERSEVERANCE IN ACCUSATIONS

"We are hard pressed on every side, but not crushed; perplexed, but not in despair; persecuted, but not abandoned; struck down, but not destroyed" (2 Cor 4:8–9). This is Paul's description of the struggles he daily faced as he persevered as an apostle sent to the nations. "Paul seems to be claiming here that while his opponents are powerful—they can knock him down—they are not able to subvert his apostleship or destroy his work."[16]

On every mission field of the world, the battle is uninterrupted—a continuous struggle against sin and its enslavement and the powers of darkness that work to keep men enslaved. The kingdom of God only progresses through perseverance in the face of daily resistance.

Missionaries must remember that their lives are in the hands of God and not in the hands of men. Opposition comes from many quarters. Like Paul's experience, opposition often comes from within the church (false brethren, 2 Cor 11:26); those who in their jealousy and self-ambition (Phil 1:17) seek to undermine what the Holy Spirit is doing through the ministry of God's servants. These are people who themselves are carnal—devoid of the Spirit (see Jude 19 NASB)—who like the "super-apostles" (2 Cor 11:5; 12:11) seek influence and position within the church for their own benefit.

Paul was accused of not being a true apostle. They accused him of being "a dishonest schemer" unlike his accusers in Corinth who claimed to be true apostles. Paul feels it necessary, for the preservation of the church, to refute these "true apostles."[17]

The false teachers wanted to discredit Paul so they could gain control of the church. Paul refused to let them have their way. Paul used the

---

16. Martin, *2 Corinthians*, 87.
17. Witherington, *Conflict and Community*, 371.

present-day persuasion methods to refute his accusers and to bring back the new converts in Corinth to the gospel by accepting his God-given authority as an apostle sent to them by God.

"The goal of all these allegations was to prove that he was not an apostle and that his ministry had no proper basis, there being no tangible evidence to support his apostolic claims. . . . Paul must completely undercut the basis of the essential charge against him, in order to disprove the argument that he was no true *apostolos*."[18]

Black summarizes, "In short, the charge was that Paul was inconsistent, superficial, even 'two-faced.'"[19] The "super-apostles" accused Paul of things that they themselves exemplify. The false teachers were themselves "inconsistent, superficial, and two-faced." They pointed their finger at God's servant wanting to destroy him, claiming that their self-chosen enemy was the one demonstrating deceitful behavior, while all along it was blatantly apparent in their own lives. "These considerations show that Paul's adversaries in Corinth were looking for some pretext to undermine Paul's credibility so that they could eventually enhance their own authority."[20]

Missionaries must persevere in faith as they face the same sort of accusations. Missionaries need wisdom and discernment as they encounter those who seek to undercut their ministries. False teachers must be exposed as those having evil intentions; those wanting to sow dissent in the body of Christ.

Missionaries often face messengers of evil (false believers: 2 Cor 11:29) that have joined together their minds and actions with the devil and plan to bring harm through division (see Acts 20:29,30). They come to discredit God's servants so that they can exalt themselves.

These workers of evil demonstrate that their souls are diseased with unrepented sin motivated by their fleshly desires (see Jude 16). Their minds have wandered into darkness, having forgotten the cross of the crucified one. They have set a trap that in the end they themselves fall into (see Ps 35:7, 8).

Those with sinful ruling desires for position and dominance maneuver their way to far off mission fields. Carnally minded missionaries come to the mission fields of the world seeking to "enhance their own authority" at the expense of anyone who dares stand in their way.

18. Witherington, *Conflict and Community*, 372.
19. Black, *Paul*, 88.
20. Black, *Paul*, 88.

Often in word they are with you, but in their hearts, they store other devilish desires, seeking to exalt themselves above all others. They are men void of spiritual understanding, who should never have been given a plane ticket to travel to a foreign land.

They brag about their "accomplishments," but all their labor is wood, hay, and stubble—works that will be consumed on the day of judgment (1 Cor 3:12). They discourage and divide and end up gathering around themselves others of the same spirit so that they can together spread their venom. They make promises that they never plan on keeping. They are driven by jealousy and self-importance. Their lives and tactics become a "thorn in the flesh" of sincere missionaries who only want to do the will of God.

"Paul wishes to show that, in spite of the negative accusations brought against his ministry, God has brought him safely through."[21] As missionaries put their unwavering faith in God their rock, he will bring them through every false accusation and place their feet on high solid ground (see Hab 3:19).

In unwavering faith, missionaries must step aside and let God step in to fight their battles (see 2 Chr 20:15 ESV). Missionaries must know that during these unprovoked attacks God will be their strength and shield (see Ps 28:7). They must believe that God will use every false accusation for their good, becoming a means for their own sanctification as they commit their souls to God their ever-present help (see Ps 46:1 KJV).

Whether the accusative attacks come from outside the church or within the church missionaries must prayerfully bow their heads in submission to the almighty, rejoicing, knowing that in the moment when they are weak, they are strong (2 Cor 12:10). His grace will not fail them (2 Cor 12:9).

Like Paul, missionaries must remain steadfast in faith when falsely accused by those who want to bring their ministry into question. "Rather, in light of his opponents' attacks, Paul has survived as the true apostle of God."[22] Often a defense of one's life and ministry is required for the good of the church—not allowing the devil an opportunity to tear down what the Holy Spirit through the gospel has built.

Martin warns of the temptation of being well spoken of:

---

21. Martin, *2 Corinthians*, 163.
22. Martin, *2 Corinthians*, 163.

> While the minister of God is to be faithful and loving in the face of "whispers behind the back," there is the other side of the temptation, namely, to be well spoken of. One must resist this temptation, which can lead to pride and complacency. Thus Hughes is adroit (232) when he summarizes Paul's idea that he was demonstrating his steadfastness to his ministry for "no evil report, however false, can harm him and no good report, however true, can distract him."[23]

Missionaries must not base their lives and ministry on the voices of men. God's sent servants must pray for humility and a pure heart, living like men who are crucified with Christ (Gal 2:20).

Critical attacks of others expose what is ruling the hearts of God's sent ones. When pride rules the heart, words spoken against them will cause deep discouragement (or anger) and thoughts of abandoning their God-given ministry (not feeling appreciated).

Words of praise also expose the heart. Praise will be taken by the prideful heart too seriously, feeding an inflated self-perception, opening one's life to destructive influences. To remain steadfast in faith, praise and fault-finding must be evaluated with humility and wisdom. Both must be put in their proper place, understanding them to be mere voices of men. His sent ones must make it their priority to please their Lord and Savior before whom they will give an account of their lives (2 Cor 5:10).

Accusations become particularly disconcerting when they come from the missionaries' leaders who should be affirming rather than accusing. At such painful moments, messengers of God must understand the origin of the attacks, not giving "the devil an opportunity" (Eph 4:27 NASB). They must rest in their faithful God and remain unmoved in faith. They must continue faithfully in the labor God has given them, doing everything for the honor of Christ.

Martin addresses how Paul found his security in God: "Regardless of others' evaluation of him, Paul knows his standing before God is secure. It is true standing, held with good conscience (4:2; 5:11). He had been faithful to God's call; he was open and sincere to the Corinthians. . . . Paul rebuts this accusation in a mild manner. He offers no criticisms or sarcasm, but simply reports that he is also known as true. For Paul the truth will vindicate his ministry."[24]

---

23. Martin, *2 Corinthians*, 180, citing Hughes, *Second Epistle*.
24. Martin, *2 Corinthians*, 180.

For God's ambassadors, there is a great advantage of working for God with a clear conscience. A clear conscience does not mean missionaries are living in sinless perfection. It simply means that to the best of their knowledge, by the grace of God and the help of the Holy Spirit, they are living with a humble, pure heart before God and man. In such a state of mind and assurance in their hearts missionaries will not be swayed by the critical attacks of others (even though they are vexing to the soul).

Messengers of God must live with hearts surrendered to the one who is always near, allowing him to fight their battles. God's ambassadors must stand in the assurance that their heavenly Father has not abandoned them. God in his love is always at work in disciplining his children for their good (see Heb 12:6–11).

COURAGEOUS PERSEVERANCE

> Therefore, being always of good courage, and knowing that while we are at home in the body, we are absent from the Lord. (2 Cor 5:6 NASB)

> The contents of this earthen vessel (4:7–11) are priceless. And though the vessel, the tent, is fragile and temporary, there is no room for despondency.... There is no reason for Paul to despair since the Spirit is with him.... Thus Paul expresses confidence in God's work, not in his environment. The latter argument is even more obvious, for Paul has the ability, with the help from God, not to allow circumstance to dull his peace of mind (Phil 4:10–13).[25]

Missionaries often labor in very difficult circumstances. They labor among people who are often resistant to the gospel. Therefore they must always be of good courage, keeping themselves from despondency and despair.

People become instruments of the devil, bringing his sent servants times of heartache and confusion. Missionaries face the disappointments of working with people who fail to live up to their confession of faith—while others abandon the faith all together.

In those moments of trial missionaries must rest in the hope of everlasting life, knowing that though they walk by faith while "at home in the body," one day their faith will be turned into sight no longer being

---

25. Martin, *2 Corinthians*, 109.

absent from the Lord they love. This hope must be their daily bulwark, sustaining them in the most difficult of trials.

There is no advancement of the kingdom of God on earth without a courageous, crucified faith. All other apparent "growth" is simply human strivings that honor men more than God. It is when missionaries courageously hold on in faith, knowing that all the promises of God find their "amen" in Christ (2 Cor 1:20) that light breaks into the darkness and imparts the hope of life to the hopeless. The messengers of God must hold on in faith until the church is firmly established for the glory of God.

PERSEVERE UNTIL THE END

> Therefore we do not lose heart. Though outwardly we are wasting away, yet inwardly we are being renewed day by day. For our light and momentary troubles are achieving for us an eternal glory that far outweighs them all. So we fix our eyes not on what is seen, but on what is unseen, since what is seen is temporary, but what is unseen is eternal. (2 Cor 4:16–18)

Martin writes of the assurance of a eternal destiny, "Paul is attempting ... to set side by side the totality of the human person seen from opposite angles in order to draw the conclusion that this life is running down, and the eternal destiny set for the person is already in making. That hope is not a shedding of the existing 'body,' but its being taken up into God's purpose in the eschatological body that awaits the resurrection."[26]

Paul's eternal perspective is vital for the life of missionaries. To remain unwavering in the difficulties of missionary life there must be a grasping of the reality of the unseen world as being the much greater reality. God's servants must live for what is the unseen and eternal (2 Cor 4:18). Grasping at and holding on to that which this fallen, perishing world offers will divide the heart of the missionary and set his mind on what is of no lasting value (Col 3:2).

Missionaries must live with the certainty of outward decay. "While the outward part is being destroyed, the inner person is being renewed day by day.... It is the new person or the new creation, the spiritual part, which is constantly being renewed in the life of the Christian."[27]

---

26. Martin, *2 Corinthians*, 92.
27. Witherington, *Conflict and Community*, 389.

Many missionaries must face the reality of the "dying" of the outer man while living in a faraway land in difficult and harsh environments. Daily physical and mental stresses carry with them an affliction on the body that can shorten life—the outer body "wasting away."

Since Paul was living for the eternal and since his hope is in the resurrection and of the life to come, he is not discouraged by the degeneration of the body since he is experiencing a daily spiritual, inner renewal. This inner renewal is a foretaste of the life he will know for eternity in God's presence. This constant spiritual renewing enables him to persevere in suffering and persecution for Christ, being fortified by a surge of resurrection power within his soul.

Paul saw the outward man perishing as an opportunity for the renewal of the inner man. God gave Paul spiritual renewing grace in his bodily afflictions to make him inwardly strong.

In bodily affliction, God's messengers learn to trust God in new ways, strengthening their faith. As his servants yield to the Spirit of God in their difficulties, there comes within them an inner renewing, leading to a steadfast hope.

The hope of the resurrection and of an unending life in the presence of our Lord and King in God's eternal kingdom must rule God's messengers' hearts and direct their personal lives and ministries. There must be a touch of the longing for heaven that rests upon their lives that points to their love and devotion to Christ. Their "first-choice" desire (Phil 1:21–24) to above all else be with the one they love must be palatable in their life and ministry.

In steadfast faith his ministers of reconciliation must daily look backward and cling to the cross of Christ bearing its shame and in the same moment gaze upward and forward to the unseen but more-real world of Christ's heavenly eternal kingdom as their destination. Such a gaze produces within them a growing, unwavering, foundation of hope—hope to persevere.

His servants' eternal destination must cast its shadow backward upon their lives, influencing all their desires and all their decisions. They must live every day under the shadow of the unseen world, wanting above all else to look by faith upon his glorious face and through that sight find glorification (see 1 John 3:2).

Paul purposes to persevere until the end in unwavering faith in all of his hardships for the gospel, living with the tension of the present weakness with the reality of the future hope. For Paul the hope of the resurrection places all of life in a proper perspective, enabling perseverance until the very end.

Missionaries faithfully persevere until the end because of their proper spiritual fixation. Seeing the unseen fortifies their lives and makes them unwavering during the uncertainties of the missionary journey.

Missionaries endure, knowing that they are just pilgrims passing through a world that will soon pass away (see Heb 11:13). Through a "forever gaze" they build their lives on the promise of an eternal inheritance that is being prepared for them in God's eternal kingdom (2 Cor 4:17; 5:1–8).

The "seen" is always pressing all around Paul's life but by faith he sees the unseen, which is for Paul a much surer reality on which to base his life and ministry. Therefore, he accepts the suffering of this present time, the "light affliction," because he knows that the present weakness will be one day swallowed up in an eternal glory.

The strength of God will overcome all the weakness of this present world, and his sent ones will enter into a glorious eternity. Like Paul, missionaries persevere in weakness—awaiting the restoration of all things.

Appendix A
Missionary Vow of Simplicity[1]

MATTHEW 6:19-34 (NKJV)

"Do not lay up for yourselves treasures on earth, where moth and rust destroy and where thieves break in and steal; but lay up for yourselves treasures in heaven, where neither moth nor rust destroys and where thieves do not break in and steal. For where your treasure is, there your heart will be also.

"The lamp of the body is the eye. If therefore your eye is good, your whole body will be full of light. But if your eye is bad, your whole body will be full of darkness. If therefore the light that is in you is darkness, how great *is* that darkness!

"No one can serve two masters; for either he will hate the one and love the other, or else he will be loyal to the one and despise the other. You cannot serve God and mammon.

"Therefore I say to you, do not worry about your life, what you will eat or what you will drink; nor about your body, what you will put on. Is not life more than food and the body more than clothing? Look at the birds of the air, for they neither sow nor reap nor gather into barns; yet your heavenly Father feeds them. Are you not of more value than they? Which of you by worrying can add one cubit to his stature?

"So why do you worry about clothing? Consider the lilies of the field, how they grow: they neither toil nor spin; and yet I say to you that even Solomon in all his glory was not arrayed like one of these. Now if God so

---

1. This vow can be freely duplicated and used by whoever so wills.

clothes the grass of the field, which today is, and tomorrow is thrown into the oven, *will He* not much more *clothe* you, O you of little faith?

"Therefore do not worry, saying, 'What shall we eat?' or 'What shall we drink?' or 'What shall we wear?' For after all these things the Gentiles seek. For your heavenly Father knows that you need all these things. But seek first the kingdom of God and His righteousness, and all these things shall be added to you. Therefore do not worry about tomorrow, for tomorrow will worry about its own things. Sufficient for the day is its own trouble."

MY PLEDGE:

Knowing my remaining sinful inner brokenness and utter helplessness in accomplishing anything of eternal value in my own strength and my total dependency on his grace I surrender to his eternal grace and love vowing:

To live in the simplicity of the gospel—the place of God's total provision and peace.

To live in simplicity as an act of received grace which leads to freedom— freedom to enjoy God and all his spiritual blessings.

To live in the simplicity that leads to the freedom of trust that God will meet my every need.

To live in the simplicity of living in the liberty of the faithfulness of God.

To live in the simplicity of life, experiencing the daily truth that God is my provider.

To surrender to an atmosphere of grace where I can walk at liberty in the Spirit where all my desires are satisfied in him.

To live in the place where I need nothing else because he is more than enough.

To enter, by the grace and help of God, into the place of living for the eternal rather than the temporal; of wanting a treasure in heaven rather than any treasure on earth.

To live with a pure heart where material possessions have no control over my soul and do not hinder my walk with God or the ministry God has given.

With heavenly help, to cling to God with all my strength, not letting anything else distract me from knowing and serving him.

To daily ask God to teach me how to know how to have a simple, humble heart in the times of the abundance of his provision, and how to live satisfied in the times of need because he enables me to do all things through Christ who strengthens me.

To allow God to give me a simplicity of heart and life so that through the love he gives me I can give and serve freely, knowing that it is more blessed to give than to receive.

To ask God in prayer to give me grace to order my life according to his priorities concerning the advancement of his kingdom in reaching a lost world for which Jesus gave his all.

To live in such a way that by his grace I can demonstrate a simple life to those observing my manner of living, by the eternal priorities that demonstrate that I love God with my whole being.

To live in the simplicity of casting all my cares upon him, knowing the daily provision of my heavenly Father.

In making this vow I understand that this vow of simplicity is personal that I make before God, to whom alone I will give an account of my life. I understand that my vow is not given in comparison with someone else but in comparing myself with the purity and simplicity of heart that the word of God demands. Therefore, I pledge myself, by his infinite mercy and love, in humbly committing my own soul, through the help of the Holy Spirit, unto a merciful God to live in heartfelt simplicity according to the above stated principles.

_____

Date

_____

Print Name

_____

Signature

Bibliography

Banner of Truth. "David Brainerd." https://banneroftruth.org/us/about/banner-authors/david-brainerd/.
Bauer, Walter, et al. *A Greek-English Lexicon of the New Testament and Other Early Christian Literature*. 2nd ed. Chicago: University of Chicago Press, 1979.
Benge, Dustin. "Who Was David Brainerd?" Ligonier Ministries: Missionary Biographies, Oct. 4, 2022. https://learn.ligonier.org/articles/missionary-david-brainerd/.
Black, David Alan. *Paul, Apostle of Weakness*. Eugene, OR: Pickwick, 2012.
Bounds, E. M. "David Brainerd, an Example of Prayerful Devotion." Deeper Christian. https://deeperchristian.com/david-brainerd-an-example-of-prayerful-devotion/.
Bruce, F. F. *1 and 2 Corinthians*. New Century Bible Commentary. Grand Rapids: Eerdmans, 1980.
Bultmann, Rudolf. *Der Zweite Brief an die Korinther*. Göttingen: Vandenhoeck und Ruprecht, 1976.
Chisholm, Thomas O. "O to Be Like Thee." https://www.hymnal.net/en/hymn/h/398.
Dionysius of Halicarnassus. *Roman Antiquities*. Lacus Curtius: Latin and Greek Texts. http://penelope.uchicago.edu/Thayer/e/roman/texts/dionysius_of_halicarnassus/home.html.
Egorov, Boris. "How German Soldiers Marched Through Moscow During WII." *Russia Beyond*, July 17, 2019. https://www.rbth.com/history/330588-how-german-soldiers-marched-moscow.
Family Finder. "Rev James Philip Hogan." Find a Grave, May 6, 2011. https://www.findagrave.com/memorial/70399433/james-philip-hogan/.
Finn, Nathan A. "Missionaries You Should Know: Adoniram Judson." International Mission Board, Mar. 27, 2018. https://www.imb.org/2018/03/27/missionaries-you-should-know-adoniram-judson/.
Garbarino, Collin. "Martyrdom and the Resurrection." Houston Christian University, Oct. 12, 2016. https://hc.edu/news-and-events/2016/10/12/martyrdom-and-the-resurrection/.
Godtube. "Barnes's 2-Corinthians 4:1 Bible Commentary." https://www.godtube.com/bible/2-corinthians/4-1.
Grounds, Vernon. "People Who Care." Our Daily Bread, Aug. 2, 1994. https://odb.org/1994/08/02/people-who-care.
Groves, J. Alison, and Winston T. Smith. *Untangled Emotions*. Wheaton, IL: Crossway, 2019.

Hughes, Philip Edgcumbe. *The Second Epistle to the Corinthians*. International Commentary on the New Testament. Grand Rapids: Eerdmans, 1962.

Innes, Richard. "Beautiful Music." ACTS International, July 26, 2006. https://www.actsweb.org/articles/article.php?i=1426&d=2&c=2.

Jones, Robert D. *Uprooting Anger: Biblical Help for a Common Problem*. Philipsburg, NJ: P & R, 2005.

Keener, Craig S. *The IVP Bible Background Commentary: New Testament*. Downers Grove, IL: IVP Academic, 2014.

Kimmel, Tim. *Little House on the Freeway*. Colorado Springs: Multnomah,1987.

Klaus, Byron D., and Douglas P. Peterson, eds. *The Essential J. Philip Hogan*. Springfield, MO: Assemblies of God Theological Seminary, 2006.

Macchia, Frank D. *Tongues of Fire: A Systematic Theology of Christian Faith*. Eugene, OR: Cascade, 2023.

Martin, Ralph P. *2 Corinthians*. Word Biblical Commentary 40. Waco, TX: Word,1986.

Nolin, Steve, and Mary Nolin. "Revival in Singapore." *Pentecostal Evangel*, Aug. 20, 1961, 5–6. https://archives.ifphc.org/DigitalPublications/USA/Assemblies%20of%20God%20USA/Pentecostal%20Evangel/Unregistered/1961/FPHC/1961_08_20.pdf.

Oberg, Ruthie Edgerly. "J. Philip Hogan: From Rural Colorado to Assemblies of God World Missions Leader." Flower Pentecostal Heritage Center, Nov. 30, 2023. https://ifphc.wordpress.com/2023/11/30/j-philip-hogan-from-rural-colorado-to-assemblies-of-god-world-missions-leader/.

Rissi, Mattias. *Studien zum Zweiten Korintherbrief: Der alte Bund, der Prediger, der Tod*. Zurich: Zwingli Verlag, 1969.

Sampley, Paul J. "The Second Letter to the Corinthians: Introduction, Commentary and Reflections." In *The New Interpreter's Bible: A Commentary in Twelve Volumes*, edited by Leander E. Keck, 11:1–180. Nashville: Abingdon, 2000.

Savage, Timothy B. *Power Through Weakness*. Cambridge: Cambridge University Press, 2004.

Steer, Roger. *J. Hudson Taylor: A Man in Christ*. Bletchley: OMF, 2019.

Tucker, Ruth A. *From Jerusalem to Irian Jaya: A Biographical History of Christian Missions*. Grand Rapids: Zondervan, 2004.

White, R. E. O. "Reconciliation." In *Evangelical Dictionary of Theology*, edited by Daniel J. Treier and Walter A. Elwell, 726-27. Grand Rapids: Backer Academic, 2017.

Wilson, Everett. *Strategy of the Spirit: J. Philip Hogan and the Growth of the Assemblies of God Worldwide, 1960-1990*. Carlisle: Paternoster, 1997.

Witherington, Ben, III. *Conflict Community in Corinth: A Socio-Rhetorical Commentary on 1 and 2 Corinthians*. Grand Rapids: Eerdmans, 1995.

www.ingramcontent.com/pod-product-compliance
Lightning Source LLC
Chambersburg PA
CBHW052340230426
43664CB00041B/2503